INFLATION: ARE WE NEXT?

*This book was made possible through
the generous contributions of*

*Columbia University's
School of International and Public Affairs*

The Pew Charitable Trusts

Mr. Herbert M. Singer

INFLATION: ARE WE NEXT?

Hyperinflation and Solutions in Argentina, Brazil, and Israel

edited by
Pamela S. Falk

Lynne Rienner Publishers · Boulder & London

Published in the United States of America in 1990 by
Lynne Rienner Publishers, Inc.
1800 30th Street, Boulder, Colorado 80301

and in the United Kingdom by
Lynne Rienner Publishers, Inc.
3 Henrietta Street, Covent Garden, London WC2E 8LU

Library of Congress Cataloging-in-Publication Data
Inflation—are we next? : hyperinflation and solutions in Argentina,
 Brazil, and Israel / edited by Pamela S. Falk.
  Includes bibliographical references.
  ISBN 1-55587-150-X (alk. paper)
  1. Inflation (Finance)—Argentina. 2. Inflation (Finance)
—Brazil. 3. Inflation (Finance)—Israel. 4. Economic
stabilization—Argentina. 5. Economic stabilization—Brazil.
6. Economic stabilization—Israel. I. Falk, Pamela S.
HG815.I55 1990
332.4'1—dc20   89078263
                                                        CIP

British Cataloguing in Publication Data
A Cataloguing in Publication record for this book
is available from the British Library.

Printed and bound in the United States of America

The paper used in this publication meets the requirements
of the American National Standard for Permanence of
Paper for Printed Library Materials Z39.48-1984.

Contents

Foreword

Herbert M. Singer

Inflation has had a powerful effect on the course of history. The decline of great empires has been triggered by this economic disfunction. Some historians argue that inflation is the *effect* of factors underlying the fall of a world power. Others argue with great effectiveness that it is the *cause*.

It is generally agreed however, that it is part of a syndrome of economic disease. This study examines three cases of inflation where the nations involved have taken dramatic steps to counteract rampant inflation. Certain aspects of the anti-inflation efforts of these nations have been successful, some have failed. Some have been tolerable to the public, some have been subject to dangerous discontent. Let us hope that these three case histories may give guidance in coping with rampant inflation should it occur on a more global level. It is my hope that this project can throw some important light on the problem of inflation, which not only confronts Third World countries but threatens to engulf the total global economy of the world, including the major industrial powers.

It is important to know what can be done to curb this destructive trend in a nation's economy and its cost to government, to social institutions, and to the people. It is essential to know whether such curbing of inflation is merely a palliative or a cure, and whether, in curing inflation, it is necessary to pay the heavy price of economic chaos, loss of personal freedom, and the establishment of autocratic control to deal with this difficult economic disease.

We need to know the limits to which the affected public can sustain the pain and sacrifice of programs seeking to curb inflation and what happens when the public ignores or rebels against anti-inflation curbs and how vital the resolve of governments and the public is in the fight against inflation.

We know that overwhelming debt and unbalanced budgets contribute to runaway inflation. We must learn how to deal with debt, which today engulfs the economy of most nations of the world; and how budgets, both in the public and private sectors, can be brought under control so that credit can be restored and so that trade, vital to buyer and seller, can be restored.

This book brings together the planners, the architects, the implementers, and the interpreters of comprehensive anti-inflation. Their planning, their experience, their successes, and their failures are profoundly enlightening in diagnosing and seeking to establish relief and, possibly, a cure for the economic disease we call inflation.

Acknowledgments

Inflation is a moving target, and writing and editing a study on the subject requires patience, careful monitoring, and a keen eye for the subtleties of economic theories in each of the different prescriptions for change. All this was done with meticulousness and aplomb by Lynne Rienner Publishers. I want to thank Lynne Rienner for her devotion to and care with the project and Steve Barr, the project editor, for his hard work in coordinating the production of the volume.

All of the contributors to this book are distinguished in their field—several are the policymakers who formulated the programs the book discusses. But even with their busy schedules, all of the authors were a delight to work with. They read and reread the manuscript. I particularly thank David Hale for his synthesis of the different analyses as well as his careful attention to his own research on the applicability to the U.S. economy.

In addition, several sponsors of the project helped make sure that the quality of the research was unparalleled and I thank the Herbert and Nell Singer Foundation—Mr. Herbert Singer in particular—and the Pew Charitable Trusts for their contributions to the work. Generous support was also provided by the Consuls General of Argentina, Brazil, and Israel, particularly Liliana Iribarne of the Argentine Consulate.

Several Columbia University students and staff assisted in the preparation of the project. The school's dean, Alfred C. Stepan, participated in the initial conference. The project would not have taken place without the skill and management of Laura Rich. Gabrielle Brussel sheparded it through its early development, and background research was skillfully completed by Norberto Terrazas, Fernando Sanchez, Lisa Bhansali, Lisa Markowitz, Stephen Gaull, Harry Jeffcoat, and Efrot Weiss.

Inflation has taken a devastating toll on dozens of countries, not only the nations we featured in this project. We hope that this study contributes to the control of this often-misunderstood economic phenomena and that future research continues the analysis.

Pamela S. Falk

Introduction

Pamela S. Falk

Inflation is the scourge of modern economies. The massive U.S. federal and trade deficits that exist today give rise to the fear that Washington will promote inflation in order to ease the repayment of our national debt. The consequence will be that our purchasing power and, ultimately, our standard of living will be eroded.

Controlling inflation once the spiral upward has begun, however, is enigmatic. A Brazilian finance minister, Mailson Ferreira da Nobrega, once likened it to a tiger running wild in a populated town. The dilemma was how to capture the tiger. You must kill it, he said, for to wound it would only make it angrier.

How have other nations coped in recent years with triple digit inflation, or worse, inflation that reached 1,000 percent to 21,000 percent annually? The three countries of Argentina, Brazil, and Israel present alternate models, but all three have implemented far-reaching stabilization programs and issued new currencies (seven currencies have been used in the three countries during the past decade) to respond to inflation that they could not control.

The economists, political analysts, and finance ministers that have contributed to this book analyze the phenomena of inflation and its economic and political consequences. In all three countries, inflation was considered endemic. In Israel, a dramatic program was introduced in 1985—the Economic Stabilization program—which sought to curb inflation by reducing government intervention in the economy. That program included tax reform, cutbacks of government workers, privatization of state-owned corporations, and a reduction of government participation in capital markets. The author of the program, Foreign Minister Emanuel Sharon, describes in this book its conceptual and practical formulation. And, while the initial effects of the 1985 program were two years of steady economic growth and controlled inflation, the subsequent years were not as kind. By mid-1987, growth began to slow in Israel, and by 1988 economic growth had slowed to

1

1982 levels. Political consequences increased with the unemployment level, which in 1989 rose to the highest point since 1967.[1]

In Brazil, 1990 witnessed a new "radical" effort by the economic team of President Fernando Collor de Mello to curb hyperinflation by reducing the government direction of the economy and by privatizing large segments of Brazilian industry previously run by the state. The "New Brazil" program took some steps similar to previous programs, but Collor de Mello's plan, announced the day after the new president took office in March 1990, was far more comprehensive. It included a program of frozen wages and a block on withdrawals from all bank accounts of over $1,000 (amounting to almost $80 billion, 25 percent of Brazil's gross domestic product) in an effort to repay Brazil's massive $62 billion debt. The plan included a variety of anti-inflationary measures tailored to Brazil's debt service dilemma. Unlike previous economic programs, this one hit Brazil's middle and upper classes hard, and over a short period of time the popularity of the program dropped precipitously. One poll showed a drop in popular support for the program from 81 percent a few weeks after the program was announced to 54 percent support only two months later.

With the latest program came the costs as well as the benefits. The hasty schedule proposed for the privatization of industry encouraged bankers to swap Brazil's loans at a discounted rate for shares in the new companies. The short-term economic hardship to the economy was devastating: small businesses went bankrupt, the stock market dropped, and almost 400,000 state employees lost their jobs—additionally difficult because the 1988 Brazilian Constitution bars the dismissal of certain categories of civil service positions. Yet, for the lower classes, the price freeze finally allowed families to resume the purchase of basic necessities, after consumer prices had jumped 5,000 percent in the year before Collor de Mello initiated the plan. For the government, the bank swap programs allowed for the reduction of state subsidies and a significant decrease in debt service, since a large segment of the government debt could be retired. The effect was that, in the month immediately following the introduction of the new plan, Brazil's rate of inflation dropped from the previous month's 80 percent to 10 percent. But the long-term prognosis for Brazil's hyperinflation remains unsettled.

In an effort to answer the weightier questions about hyperinflation and its causes, this book does not attempt to monitor daily changes in inflation or evaluate the latest round of inflation-fighting programs in each of the three countries. New programs are introduced quarterly. Rather, the analyses in the book seek to evaluate the twists and turns of inflation in each of the three countries and what has contributed to the upward spiral, as well as to examine the initial "inflation-buster" packages in the three cases and describe the successes and failures of the programs from the points of view of those who drafted them. Explaining the spiral of inflation, one economics correspondent comments, "from small price acorns do mighty hyperinflation oaks grow."[3] The added uncertainty, he said, "wreaks havoc on the daily lives of ordinary people," explaining in part why the remedy for hyperinflation, particularly in Latin America, combines a change in the names and looks of currencies along with more substantive changes in economic programs.[4]

Inflation in the United States is more difficult to assess, and economists do not agree on the solutions. James K. Galbraith's recent contribution on the subject suggests that Americans learn to live with inflation—as long as it is not excessive. Some inflation, along with low interest rates and dollar devaluation, might accomplish the principal objective of the U.S. economy: preeminence as a manufacturer and exporter of capital goods. Others caution that, in the United States, the shocks of inflation take far longer than they do elsewhere to be felt after the programs that feed them are put into place. And, there are the optimists who argue that inertial forces are more likely to keep down inflation today than they were during the oil-price shock days of 1974 and 1979: they point to the Federal Reserve Board's and the financial markets' ability to keep interest rates above the inflation rate, thus dampening the economy as needed; also, due to foreign competition, U.S. businesses are less likely than before to be able to pass on rising costs, and they consequently pressure suppliers to keep costs down.[5]

Looking at the overall relationship between inflation and large government deficits, David D. Hale, in Chapter 1, distinguishes the three models of Argentina, Brazil, and Israel and describes their lessons for the United States. The budget deficit and trade account no longer are the major contributors to inflation and the exchange rate, Hale argues. Rather, international capital transfers, which enable both developing nations and large industrial countries to have fiscal deficits while controlling inflation, is the major factor. Thus, the question, "Inflation: Are We Next?" is answered by U.S. domestic and foreign economic policy, including the ability to adjust to changes in international financial markets in Asia and Eastern Europe, as much as the ability to control savings imbalances and fiscal excesses at home.

Notes

1. U.S. Department of Commerce, "Foreign Economic Trends and Their Implications for the United States." International Trade Administration: Washington, D.C., September 1989.

2. Data Folha poll, in James Brooke, "Belt-Tightening in Brazil Brings Anguished Gasps," *The New York Times*, 23 May 1990, p. 1.

3. Peter Passell, "Translation of Inflation," *New York Times*, July 6, 1989, p. 6.

4. Ibid.

5. James K. Galbraith, *Balancing Acts*. New York: Basic Books, 1989.

6. Barry Bosworth cited in Paul Blustein, "The Inflationary Inflation Talk," *The Washington Post* Weekly Edition, September 26–October 2, 1988, p. 23.

1

Why Large Government Deficits Cause Inflation in Latin America But Not the United States

David D. Hale

One of the most interesting features of the world economy during the 1980s was a sharp rise in the inflation rates of most Latin American nations coincident with a decline in the inflation rates of the major industrial nations to their lowest level in nearly two decades (see Table 1.1). In the period 1975–1981, inflation rates averaged 9.2 percent in the United States, 7.1 percent in Japan, 11.2 percent in OECD Europe, and 58.4 percent in Latin America. During the years 1981–1988, inflation rates fell to 4.7 percent in the United States, 1.9 percent in Japan, and 7.8 percent in Europe, but rose to 132 percent in Latin America. Four Latin nations (Brazil, Argentina, Peru, and Nicaragua) had inflation rates of several hundred percent or more, but in the rest of the world there was not a single case of triple-digit inflation. Four other Latin nations also had inflation rates in 1988 between 50 percent and 125 percent—Mexico, Uruguay, Ecuador, and the Dominican Republic.

The remarkable divergence in the inflation performances of the Northern Hemisphere industrial nations and Latin America during the 1980s was not accidental. The disinflation in the industrial countries resulted in part from global economic shocks, which helped set the stage for Latin America's hyperinflation. In 1981/82, a sharp rise in dollar real interest rates and break in commodity prices caused a suspension in bank lending to Latin America, which forced governments in the region to choose between severe fiscal austerity or financing public spending by creating domestic money. The high real interest rates and commodity price depression of the early 1980s also inflicted great damage on other commodity-producing nations, such as Australia, New Zealand, Indonesia, and South Africa; but the Latin nations suffered the greatest adjustment shocks, for two reasons. First, their 1970s borrowing upsurge had not been used to finance productive investment; much of it was instead consumed by a large rise in public consumption or private capital flight. Second, as the economic crisis struck, many Latin nations were embarking upon experiments in democracy after several years of

5

6   David D. Hale

Table 1.1 World Inflation Rates[a]

	1975–1981	1981–1988	1982	1983	1984	1985	1986	1987	1988
Industrialized countries									
United States	9.2	4.7	6.2	3.2	4.4	3.6	1.9	3.7	4.1
Japan	7.1	1.9	2.7	1.9	2.3	2.0	0.6	0.1	0.7
Germany	4.6	2.6	5.3	3.3	2.4	2.2	–0.2	0.3	1.2
France	11.0	7.1	12.0	9.4	7.7	5.8	2.6	3.3	2.7
United Kingdom	15.4	6.1	8.6	4.6	4.9	6.1	3.4	4.2	5.1
OECD-Europe	11.2	6.8	10.1	7.8	6.9	6.1	3.5	3.5	4.2
OECD-Total	9.9	5.4	7.8	5.3	5.3	4.6	2.7	3.2	3.7
Latin America									
Mexico	21.4	82.0	58.9	101.9	66.5	57.6	86.2	131.8	125.4
Brazil	56.3	212.7	98.0	142.0	196.7	227.0	132.7	217.9	582.0
Argentina	191.6	307.8	165.2	344.2	626.7	672.2	90.1	131.3	328.9
Chile	114.9	20.2	9.9	27.3	19.8	30.7	19.5	19.9	14.7
Colombia	24.7	22.8	24.6	19.8	16.1	24.0	18.9	23.3	28.1
Latin Composite	58.4	132.3	79.1	129.2	157.6	168.3	84.5	129.4	246.7
Other commodity producing nations									
Australia	11.1	8.3	11.1	10.1	4.0	6.8	9.0	8.5	7.2
New Zealand	14.9	12.0	16.2	7.4	6.2	15.4	13.2	15.8	6.4
Philippines	11.7	15.0	10.3	10.0	50.3	23.1	0.8	3.8	8.8
Malaysia	5.2	3.4	5.8	3.7	3.9	0.3	0.7	0.9	2.0
Indonesia	15.6	9.0	9.5	11.8	10.5	4.7	5.9	9.3	8.0
Nigeria	41.6	18.5	7.7	23.2	39.6	5.5	5.4	10.2	35.9

Sources: International Financial Corp. and Data Resources.
[a]Global inflation rates diverged greatly in the 1980s because of falling inflation in the Northern Hemisphere and rising inflation in the Southern Hemisphere.

military rule. The transition to democracy made it difficult for them to control public spending, because outgoing governments had often used their final months in office to give favors to their supporters, while the incoming leaders had campaigned on platforms promising to boost the real incomes of urban voters. In most cases, such promises could be satisfied only through increased public expenditure.

Paradoxically, at the start of the 1980s, many economic commentators had been optimistic about Latin America's prospects because of the expectation that commodity prices would continue to rise, and pessimistic about the U.S. economic outlook as a consequence of the Reagan administration's commitment to a fiscal program that threatened to produce large multiyear government deficits. Although it will be several years before economists concur about the all theoretical implications of 1980s economic history for future textbooks, one conclusion clearly stands out. The contrasting inflation performance of the United States and its southern neighbors during the 1980s demonstrates that the size of budget deficits is a less critical determinant of a country's inflation performance than the size of its domestic debt markets or its government's access to foreign capital.

Although the U.S. federal debt expanded from $1 trillion in 1980 to $2.7 trillion at the end of the Reagan era, the inflation rate averaged only 4–5 percent during most of the decade because several factors combined to lessen pressure on the Federal Reserve (the Fed) to monetize the large growth in public borrowing. First, much of the initial upsurge in the federal deficit resulted from an anti-inflationary monetary policy that increased the size of the deficit by pushing up interest rates and depressing the growth of tax receipts. Second, the growth in U.S. public borrowing during the early 1980s coincided with a movement towards global financial integration and restrictive fiscal policies in other countries, which made it possible for the United States to reemerge as a large-scale capital-importing nation for the first time since the nineteenth century. Finally, when private capital flows to the United States ceased during the dollar crises of 1987 and 1988, the Japanese Ministry of Finance came to the rescue of the Reagan administration through a series of policy actions designed to stabilize the U.S. dollar and interest rates. If the United States had been a small or medium-size country, the balance of payments crises of the late 1980s might well have forced it to go to the International Monetary Fund (IMF), but other countries provided support for the dollar because they recognized its role as "a key currency" and wanted to avoid the potentially nasty economic and political consequences of U.S. election year recession. As a result, the second great policy lesson of the 1980s is that the large size of the U.S. economy and its strategic importance to Western security permits the United States to operate under different fiscal and monetary rules than other industrial countries.

Inflation Theory

In 1981, the Federal Reserve Bank of Minneapolis published an article by T. J. Sargent and N. Wallace that argued that large deficits would ultimately force governments to pursue inflationary monetary policies. According to Sargent and Wallace, large deficits would set in motion a chain of events that would make debt monetization difficult to resist. First, large deficits would push real interest rates to levels well above the growth rate of real output. Second, this upsurge of real interest rates would cause the stock of public debt to rise sharply in relation to real income. Third, the growth in the debt stock and its servicing costs would ultimately overwhelm the absorption capacity of both investors and taxpayers, forcing central banks to buy the government's paper to prevent it from defaulting. Because of the potential linkages between government debt creation and political constraints on central bank autonomy, Sargent and Wallace argued that countries could achieve price stability only if governments pursued fiscal policies that were compatible with noninflationary monetary growth.

Although the Sargent and Wallace thesis was regarded as heretical by many monetarists, it enjoyed considerable historical support from the experience of Europe after the First World War. The war had a devastating impact on the economies of all the European participants. In eastern Europe, new nations emerged with large public debts and no tradition of public respect for the tax system. Since they could not collect revenue, the new governments extinguished the real value of their debt through Central Bank purchases of government paper and through hyperinflation. In western Europe there was no hyperinflation after the war, but there was a debate about how to finance the resulting debts, which demonstrated an awareness among policymakers of the tradeoffs posed by the Sargent and Wallace model. In Britain, a few commentators advocated a rise in the inflation rate to lower the real costs of debt servicing, but there was strong opposition on the grounds that Britain's long-standing tradition of honoring war debts had played an important role in helping her defeat Germany. The British people had been prepared to buy war bonds on a scale that could not be duplicated in countries with less responsible traditions of public finance. In fact, John Maynard Keynes had written in 1916, "If we can go on giving the army what they want longer than the Germans can do this to theirs, we may appear to win by military prowess. But we shall really have won by financial prowess" (Grossman 1988, p. 8). Hence, instead of proposing currency depreciation to lessen the cost of satisfying bondholder claims on taxpayers and workers, British socialists proposed the imposition of a special capital tax on bondholders. Although the idea was not accepted, the very fact that such taxes were discussed indicates how strong Britains' commitment to price stability was before the Second World War. France had an even more divisive debate than Britain about how to pay for the war, because France had a much weaker tradition of public respect for the tax system; but the French also rejected the inflation option. In fact, France remained on the gold standard for several years longer than Britain during the 1930s and thus experienced a period of deflation, which increased the real cost of France's debt servicing. This large interest-payment burden was one of the factors that produced recurring crises in French politics during the 1930s and crippled the country's response to the rise of German military power.

When the Sargent and Wallace paper appeared, it was considered to be a major challenge to the economic policies of the Reagan administration because its principal monetary advisers, such as Beryl Sprinkel, had argued that there was no automatic inflation link between fiscal and monetary policy. According to Sprinkel, the country would be able to enjoy prosperity with low inflation if the Fed merely adhered to a low monetary growth target and let the Treasury worry about financing the fiscal deficit.

Meanwhile, UCLA Professor Michael Darby (later assistant secretary of the treasury for economic policy) wrote a rebuttal to the Sargent and Wallace paper contending that its assumptions about real interest rates exceeding real growth rates for a sustained period and thus setting the stage for inflationary monetary policy were not supported by U.S. historical experience. Darby wrote in the Minneapolis Fed *Quarterly Review* during the spring of 1984,

> As anyone who has ever looked at before-tax real yields on government securities is aware, it is a simple matter to show that long-term before-tax real yields have not approached corresponding growth rates of real output. It flows directly that after-tax real yields must be even less. This is not to suggest that the real return to capital in the economy is less than the growth rate of real output; but the real rate of return on government bonds and bills is clearly far below this average social return. Presumably, the difference between government and private returns reflects both nonpecuniary services and a very low correlation with the market return, but that really is not at issue in understanding the implications of the government budget constraint.
>
> Ibbotson and Sinquefield (1982) have complied before-tax real rates of return for U.S. government bonds and Treasury bills from 1926 to 1981. The arithmetic means of the yields for long-term government bonds and Treasury bills are 0.3 and 0.1 (geometric means: −0.1 and 0.0) percent per annum, respectively. So even if all holdings were tax exempt, the experience of the last 55 years suggests that the after-tax real yield on government securities has been nowhere near the 3.0 percent per annum average growth rate of real income over the same years.
>
> It would be possible to increase the estimated real yield somewhat, but I have been unable to find any study that indicates an average real yield on government securities as high as 3 percent, even without any allowance for income taxes. Taking account of income taxes would lower these estimates; so there seems to be no doubt empirically that for the United States, the growth rate of real income exceeds the after-tax real yield on government securities.

Sargent and Wallace, as well as other economists, rebutted Darby's assertions by pointing to the high level of real interest rates prevailing in the United States during the early 1980s. In the first half of the decade, the level of real interest rates on Treasury bonds with ten-year maturities had averaged nearly 5 percent compared to negative numbers during most of the 1960s and 1970s. The real yield on Treasury bills also rose to levels never before experienced in the modern history of the United States. As a result, the U.S. financial markets appeared to be concurring with the Sargent and Wallace argument that large government deficits would ultimately set the stage for a sharp rise in the domestic inflation rate.

Fortunately, though, two factors prevented the U.S. economy from serving as a test case for the Sargent and Wallace thesis. First, the Congress and the White House took the threat of inflation seriously enough to start curtailing the deficit. They enacted a series of business tax hikes and spending cuts after 1981, which gradually reduced the deficit to a level equal to only federal interest payments. The ratio of federal debt to GNP therefore peaked at 43 percent of GNP in 1986 and moved sideways for the next three years. Second, during Reagan's first term, the United States did not adhere to an exchange rate target. As a result, the high level of real interest rates produced by the interaction of a restrictive monetary policy and loose fiscal policy triggered a sharp rise in the dollar exchange rate, which encouraged an influx of cheap imports. The financial counterpart to the resulting trade deficit was a large capital inflow, which lessened pressure on the Fed to monetize the budget deficit. The import boom also produced a sharp slowing in U.S. manufacturing output and investment during 1985 and 1986, which permitted interest rates to fall despite the persistence of large government deficits.

Instead of being tested in the United States, the Sargent and Wallace hyperinflation thesis was acted out in classic fashion by several Latin American nations during the first half of the 1980s. The Latin hyperinflations had different historical causes than the eastern European hyperinflations of the 1920s, but the economic processes at work were broadly similar: rapid growth of government borrowing in countries without domestic debt markets or a tradition of public respect for the tax system followed by a funding crisis resolved through central bank monetization of the government's paper. The big difference between the European and Latin hyperinflation was the role played by foreign capital.

In the 1970s, the Latin American nations had run large government deficits financed by external borrowing. Between 1973 and 1982, Latin America's external debt had grown from $48 billion to $331 billion. The debt of the public sector had grown tenfold while the debt of the private sector grew fourfold. Much of the public sector borrowing went to finance the losses of government-owned enterprises, which expanded from one quarter of Latin America's public sector deficits in the early 1970s to about one half by the early 1980s. Meanwhile, a large share of the private borrowing financed capital flight, as Latin investors took advantage of the real exchange rate appreciation resulting from the influx of bank loans to purchase foreign assets. Such heavy external borrowing to finance low-return public investment and private capital flight would have led to a debt-servicing crisis in Latin America at some point during the 1980s. It set the stage for hyperinflation as well, because Latin governments had no domestic financial market alternatives to foreign borrowing when the banks abruptly ceased lending to them in 1982. As Latin governments were unable to switch their lending to domestic debt markets, they faced a choice between severe fiscal austerity or central bank monetization of public borrowing. As Tim Congdon (1987, pp. 82–83) explained in an article on the debt trap created by government deficits, the hyperinflations of the 1980s resulted from the inability of Latin governments to replace external borrowing with domestic bond sales.:

> The ratios of domestically held public sector debt to national income are uniformly low in Latin America, because of the profound skepticism with which government is regarded. In Brazil, which is fortunate compared to neighboring countries because it has never suffered extreme political turmoil, there is a market in government debt. But it is small scale and short-term, and is dominated by two instruments, national treasury indexed bonds (ORTNs) and national treasury bills (LTNs). In 1978 their total value was 357.5 billion cruzeiros, equal to about 10 percent of national income, with 52.5 billion held by the central bank and publicly-owned Banco de Brasil, and most of the remainder with the banking system. The situation in Brazil was typical and it would be reasonable to take 10 percent as the debt to income ratio in Latin American countries before the debt crisis.

In its 1989 World Development Report, the World Bank devoted considerable attention to the role backward financial systems played in retarding the economic performance of many developing countries during the 1980s. The report found a strong correlation between the size of countries' capital markets and pressure on central banks to monetize budget deficits. The study examined how a sample of twenty-four developing and eleven high-income countries financed their central government deficits in 1975–1985. It found:

> The contrast between the two groups is striking. In the developing countries 47% of the deficit was financed by borrowing from central banks, 15% by borrowing from domestic financial institutions and markets, and 38% by borrowing from abroad (although foreign financing declined from 44% in 1975–82 to 26% in 1983–84). High income countries, in contrast, relied mainly on non-bank financial institutions and markets to finance their deficits, borrowing less than 12% of the total from central banks (Crook 1989, p. 61).

The contrast in how government deficits were financed had a major impact on inflation performance. As the study noted,

> The governments of developing countries turned to their central

banks because domestic financial markets were too shallow to meet their needs. To the extent that central banks financed such borrowing by issuing money, the result was higher inflation. The average inflation rate in developing countries increased from 10 percent a year in 1965–73 to 26 percent in 1974–82 and 51 percent in 1983–87. Inflation rates in high-income countries also rose in the 1970s but have been held to less than 5 percent a year in the 1980s. Half of all developing countries continue to enjoy single-digit inflation, but the number of countries with double and triple-digit inflation has risen in recent years. During 1983–87, seven countries (Argentina, Bolivia, Brazil, Nicaragua, Peru, Sierra Leone, and Uganda) had average inflation rates of more than 100 percent, whereas in 1965–73 none did, and between 1974 and 1982 only Argentina did. Four of the seventeen highly indebted middle-income counties had triple-digit and eleven had double digit inflation during 1983–87, which underscores the interrelation of external debt, fiscal deficits, and inflation. Other factors, such as repeated devaluation have added to inflationary pressures, but deficit financing has provided the primary impetus (Crook 1989, p. 62).

The study computed an inflation tax for a variety of developing countries based on the ratio of their inflation rates to their stocks of reserve money (currency and bank reserves). The outcomes ranged from over 4.0 percent of GNP in Argentina and Zaire to 0.5 percent of GNP in the Ivory Coast. Inflation is a tax on reserve assets, because currency pays no interest and the yield on bank reserves is typically very low. The relationship between inflation and the money stock in countries dependent upon inflation taxes illustrates how hyperinflations can evolve. Because a legacy of high inflation usually encourages the private sector to maintain a low ratio of reserve assets to GNP, central banks have to permit increasingly rapid monetary growth and accelerating rates of price change in order to achieve a particular revenue target.

The absence of domestic debt markets in Latin America is not an accident. It reflects a history of economic mismanagement and social conflict, which has made Latin Americans deeply distrustful of both their political institutions and long-term contracts denominated in local currencies. As the contrasting economic performance of Asia and Latin America demonstrates, there is a strong relationship between a country's record of price stability and the depth of its financial markets. In Malaysia, for example, several years of low inflation encouraged the ratio of M2 to GNP to rise to 80 percent recently from 31 percent in 1970 (Miller 1983, pp. 9–10). In Argentina, by contrast, the ratio of money supply to GNP fell to under 20 percent from 30 percent in 1970 and over 50 percent before the Second World War. Latin American governments also have used coercive financial regulatory policies to fund their deficits. Bank reserve requirements are as high as 70 percent in

Argentina and 40 percent in Brazil. Reserve requirements constitute a form of loan to the government, usually at below market interest rates. In Mexico, the government's financial position got so bad during the early 1980s that it also forcibly converted the dollar deposits within Mexico's banking system into pesos. Because of such policies, Latin America's private savings are low, domestic debt markets are practically nonexistent, and governments impose nominally high tax rates, which encourage tax evasion and capital flight rather than sound public finance.

In retrospect, the borrowing boom of the late 1970s was one of those unique moments in history when Latin America had an opportunity to embark upon a dash for growth without curtailing consumption. But because of the price distortions resulting from interventionist microeconomic policies, most of the Latin nations were unable to use the sudden influx of foreign loans effectively. Instead of funding private capital investment, much of the foreign borrowing financed an upsurge of consumption through a mixture of real exchange rate appreciation and government spending that did not have to be financed through taxation. Moreover, many of the microeconomic distortions that impeded Latin America's ability to sue its foreign loans productively stemmed from government attempts to control interest rates and prices. As the World Development Report (Crook 1989, pp. 63–64) stressed,

> Interest rate controls and inflation have set back financial development in many countries. Governments kept interest rates low partly to encourage investment, partly to redistribute income, and partly because they themselves wished to borrow cheaply. Many governments also believed that low deposit rates (the corollary of low lending rates) would not discourage financial saving.
>
> Experience has shown that some of these ideas were wrong. There is strong evidence that real interest rates and inflation have a significant effect on financial savings, and various studies have found that financial savings and the rate at which these are lent are positively related to economic growth.

The study examined the relationship between real interest rates and economic performance in thirty-five countries. It found that economic performance was best in countries with positive real interest rates and poorest in those with negative real yields. Positive real interest rates helped to generate more savings and to allocate capital efficiently. Negative real yields discouraged savings and provided a poor screen for allocating resources.

While the Latin American hyperinflations of the 1980s can be explained by simple economic relationships, such as government deficit/GNP ratios the origins of this destructive economic behavior lie in the region's scarred social and political history. Because of deeply entrenched income inequalities, the

Latin nations have been unable to reach any form of political consensus about the economic reforms needed to achieve sound public finance and a healthy level of private investment financed by domestic savings. Latin America's poor people regularly demand large increases in public spending to raise their income levels, whereas the wealthy export their savings or use the political process to block tax increases that might redistribute income. Latin America's economic performance also has suffered from the fact that the struggle for income shares often takes the form of competition between urban electorates employed in sectors producing nontradeable goods and rural elites who control the major export industries. The tension between these divergent social and economic interest groups encourages fiscal policies that are "distributive" and inflationary rather than "redistributive" and fiscally neutral.

Because of Latin America's financial experience during the 1980s, one of the most important focal points for economic recovery in that region during the 1990s should be the creation of viable capital markets. Although such changes will have to occur within a comprehensive macro- and microeconomic adjustment program, several factors suggest that financial market reform will be an essential prerequisite for reviving investment and controlling inflation in the region.

Latin American elite have extensive funds deposited offshore that will not return home until they are able to earn internationally competitive after-tax yields on domestic financial assets. It's also doubtful that there will be any large-scale resumption of commercial bank lending to Latin America during the 1990s. U.S. money center banks have a large portfolio of loans still in the process of being written down, while regulatory authorities are now compelling them to strengthen their balance sheet. Because of the pressure to raise equity/asset ratios, bank lending will become increasingly expensive relative to securitized forms of financial intermediation, such as bonds and commercial paper. Finally all developing countries should create vehicles for securitized forms of investment, because equity and bond markets are reemerging as important intermediaries for global capital movements for the first time since the 1920s.

The potential economic benefits of stock market development in Latin America are illustrated in Table 1.2. In 1988, the newly industrializing countries of Asia had a stock market capitalization of almost $500 billion, or over 100 percent of GNP if India is excluded. In Latin America, by contrast, total stock market capitalization in 1987 was only about $40 billion, or less than 7 percent of GNP. Yet, if the Latin nations could expand their stock market capitalization to just 50 percent of GNP by 1995, while expanding nominal GNP by 7 percent per annum in dollar terms, they would have a potential menu of $500–600 billion of investible financial assets available for reviving foreign capital flows or retaining domestic savings

Despite their large size today, Asia's stock markets did not play a major

Table 1.2 Stock Market Capitalization (Billions of Dollars)

	1988 Asian Stock Market Capitalization		
	Market Cap. ($)	GNP ($)	Ratio (%)
Hong Kong	87.2	54.5	161.0
Singapore	31.3	24.8	126.0
Malaysia	29.3	32.6	90.0
Thailand	12.6	57.0	22.0
Philippines	6.2	38.7	16.0
South Korea	105.2	169.2	62.0
Taiwan	207.8	119.7	174.0
India	25.3	281.5	9.0
Total	504.9	778.0	65.0

	1987 Latin America Stock Market Capitalization[a]		
	Market Cap. ($)	GNP ($)	Ratio (%)
Brazil	16.9	314.0	5.4
Mexico	12.7	149.0	8.5
Chile	5.3	16.5	32.0
Venezuela	2.27	48.2	4.7
Argentina	1.5	75.0	20.0
Columbia	1.25	36.0	3.5
Total	39.92	638.7	6.2

[a]If Latin America could duplicate Asia's success in developing large security markets, it would have a useful vehicle for attracting new investment capital during the 1990s.

role in financing that region's economic development during the 1960s and 1970s. In that period, Asia financed its development primarily through a mixture of retained profits, high households savings, and bank lending targeted on export-oriented industries. But in the 1960s and 1970s, stock markets played only a modest economic role in most countries, and the dominant channels for international capital transfers were bank loans and government aid. In the 1990s, though, stock markets are likely to be far more important funding vehicles in both the industrial and developing countries because of the structural weaknesses of the commercial banking industry and the rapid growth now occurring in institutional savings intermediaries, such as pension funds, mutual funds, and insurance companies. The Nomura Research Institute, for example, estimates that Japanese institutional savings flows could approach a trillion dollars by the mid-1990s, or a sum equal to Latin America's probable GNP (Koo 1989). If only one-twentieth of such funds were invested in developing country equity markets, Japan would be able to provide capital on a scale large enough for Latin America to raise its investment share of GNP by 5 percent.

Stock markets would not be a totally new concept for Latin America. Before the 1930s, Buenos Aires had such a dynamic and robust stock market that many British investment trusts had a 15–20 percent portfolio weighting for Argentine equities. But Latin American equity markets faded as vehicles for global capital transfers after World War II because of political hostility to foreign equity investment, the nationalization of numerous industries, and the adverse impact of escalating inflation on the viability of Latin financial assets.

Before the 1987 stock market crash, there has been growing interest in New York, London, and Tokyo in the idea of Third World stock market diversification. It ceased for nearly a year because of the crash, but diversification into Third World equity markets is now resuming. While much of the new interest has focused on Asian developing countries, such as Indonesia, Thailand, India, and the Philippines, successful country funds have been launched for Chile and Brazil and Mexico. More will follow if the Latin nations agree to open their stock markets to foreign investors and expand their role in the economic development process. Although the creation of viable capital markets would not resolve all the structural problems retarding Latin America's economic progress, they would be a useful step towards boosting private savings, reviving foreign investment, and permitting Latin America to run moderate external deficits without high inflation, as the United States did during the Reagan years.

The Reagan Experiment in Deficit Finance

Between 1981 and 1989, the Reagan administration accumulated a larger public debt than all the previous U.S. administrations combined. When Reagan took office, the official debt of the U.S. Treasury was $970 billion. By the end of 1988, the Treasury's debt was $2.7 trillion. Because of robust economic growth, the stock of federal debt as a share of GNP remained comfortably below its peak after World War II (120 percent), but it still grew to 43 percent of national income by 1986 from 26 percent in the late 1970s. Despite the rapid growth of federal borrowing in the 1980s, monetary policy was not excessively expansionary, and the U.S. inflation rate averaged 4–5 percent during most of the decade, or half its level when Reagan took office.

The large federal deficits of the 1980s failed to produce a major inflation upsurge for several reasons. First, the growth of the deficit during 1981 and 1982 stemmed in part from a restrictive monetary policy that drove interest rates and unemployment to record high levels for the postwar period. The sharp rise in the level of interest payments increased government financing costs, while the slowdown in economic growth depressed tax receipts. As a result, the nominal budget deficit grew to levels nearly twice as large as the structural of full-employment budget deficit.

Second, concern about the potential inflationary consequences of large federal deficits caused the White House and Congress to take several remedial actions to prevent the federal debt from ballooning out of control. They raised revenue by repealing a number of business tax allowances in 1982, 1984, and 1986. They reformed social security and medicare in 1983. They slowed the defense buildup after 1985. Finally, there was a continuing squeeze on nondefense discretionary spending programs, which reduced those programs' share of GNP from nearly 6 percent in 1980 to under 4 percent in 1988. Because of these fiscal policy changes, the noninterest portion of the federal deficit fell sharply after 1986, while the federal debt to GNP ratio plateaued at 43 percent after expanding by nearly 14 percent during the previous six years.

The final reason why the fiscal deficits of the early 1980s did not produce inflation was the ability of the United States to import foreign capital. The original goal of the Reagan fiscal program had been to boost the growth rate of U.S. investment by encouraging a higher level of domestic savings. But instead of increasing the domestic savings rate, the Reagan fiscal program produced a new financial equilibrium characterized by large government deficits, declining household savings, and steady private investment funded by a large rise in external borrowing. The reemergence of the United States as a capital-importing nation on a scale equal to 3–4 percent of GNP took most economists by surprise, because the United States had not imported significant amounts of capital since the late nineteenth century, and it was conventional wisdom that only developing countries should import foreign savings. But in the early 1980s, a series of economic and regulatory upheavals in the international financial system profoundly altered the ground rules for capital mobility and inadvertently turned the United States in to the world economy's borrower and spender of last resort.

First, there was a major divergence between the fiscal policies of the United States and other OECD countries during the early 1980s. While the United States embarked upon the most expansionary fiscal policy in its history, most other industrial countries were pursuing highly restrictive economic policies in order to crush inflation. As a result of this OECD policy divergence and the collapse of bank lending to less developed countries (LDCs), Reaganomics turned the U.S. business and consumer sectors into the world economy's primary growth locomotives.

Second, the Reagan deficits coincided with a global movement toward financial liberalization, which made it possible for Japanese institutions to buy a large volume of U.S. securities. Japan had briefly emerged as a capital importer during the early 1970s, but the process had quickly stopped because of the two OPEC oil price shocks. By the early 1980s, though, Japan was once more ready to experiment with liberalization of capital outflows. Since

1981 Japanese private investors have purchased over $300 billion of dollar financial assets. Although the United States also imported capital from Europe, Latin America, and other Asian nations during the early 1980s, it was the willingness of Japanese institutional investors to recycle their excess savings into U.S. financial assets that made it possible for the Reagan administration to borrow externally on a scale twice as large as the United States had done during the late nineteenth century, when capital inflows from Britain equal to 1–2 percent of GNP had helped to finance the construction of the western railways.

Third, the ability of the United States to import capital was enhanced by the microeconomic components of the Reagan fiscal program, especially the large rise that occurred in corporate depreciation allowances between 1981 and 1986. These investment incentives increased the corporate sector's tolerance for high real interest rates and helped limit the decline in U.S. business capital expenditures during the recession produced by the Fed's monetary crunch. If the Reagan deficit had been financing only higher public expenditures, monetary policy would have produced a more severe downturn in private investment during 1981/82 than actually occurred. Instead, the resilience of private investment, coupled with the generally expansionary thrust of fiscal policy, helped set the stage for an unusual period of robust demand growth combined with high real interest rates during 1983 and 1984. But output grew more slowly than demand after 1982, because the large rise in real interest rates encouraged an appreciation of the dollar exchange rate, which boosted imports and depressed exports. Although capital inflows permitted America to sustain a high level of business investment in the face of large federal deficits and low private savings, the real economic counterpart to external borrowing was a rapidly expanding merchandise trade deficit, which slowed the growth rate of industrial production to zero by 1985.

Some analysts have argued that the Fed should have restrained the dollar's appreciation by holding down interest rates in 1983/84, but real exchange rate stability was impossible in the United States during the early 1980s because of the magnitude of the country's savings and investment gap. If the Fed had held down interest rates to stabilize the dollar's nominal value, there would have been a sharp rise in the real exchange rate through capacity shortages and higher inflation rather than the appreciation that occurred in the nominal exchange rate. Because of the savings shortfall and demand stimulus produced by Reagan's macro- and microeconomic policy mix, it was inevitable that the United States would become a capital importer during the early 1980s. (See Table 1.3.) *What policymakers had to decide was the price mechanism through which the balance of payments would adjust; would the dollar's real value rise through higher inflation or through an appreciation of the nominal exchange rate?* By permitting real interest rates to rise to levels that attracted a large capital inflow, the Federal Reserve implicitly decided

Table 1.3 Savings and Investment as a Percentage of GNP[a]

	1980	1981	1982	1983	1984	1985	1986	1987	1988	1989
Gross saving	16.2	17.1	14.1	13.6	15.1	13.2	12.3	12.3	13.2	13.1
Gross private saving	17.5	18.0	17.6	17.4	17.9	16.5	15.8	14.7	15.3	15.3
Personal saving	5.0	5.2	4.9	3.8	4.4	3.1	2.9	2.3	3.1	3.3
Retained earnings										
w/IVA & CCA adj.	1.4	1.4	0.6	1.9	2.5	2.5	2.2	1.8	1.7	1.6
Depreciation	11.1	11.4	12.1	11.6	11.0	10.9	10.8	10.6	10.5	10.4
Government surplus	−1.3	−1.0	−3.5	−3.8	−2.8	−3.3	−3.5	−2.4	−2.1	−2.2
Federal	−2.2	−2.1	−4.6	−5.2	−4.5	−4.9	−4.8	−3.3	−3.1	−3.2
State and local	1.0	1.1	1.1	1.4	1.7	1.6	1.3	1.0	1.0	1.0
Gross investment	16.5	17.2	14.1	13.8	15.2	13.1	12.3	12.3	12.9	12.9
Gross priv.										
domest. invest.	16.0	16.9	14.1	14.7	17.6	16.0	15.7	15.8	15.9	15.7
Priv. domestic invest.	16.3	16.1	14.9	15.0	15.8	15.7	15.3	14.9	14.9	15.0
Nonres. fixed invest.	11.8	12.1	11.6	10.5	11.0	11.0	10.2	9.9	10.2	10.3
Res. fixed invest.	4.5	4.0	3.3	4.5	4.8	4.7	5.1	5.0	4.7	4.7
Change in bus.										
inventories	−0.3	0.8	−0.8	−0.2	1.8	0.3	0.4	0.9	1.0	0.7
Net foreign investment	0.5	0.3	0.0	−1.0	−2.4	−2.9	−3.4	−3.5	−3.0	−2.8
Statistical discrepancy	0.2	0.1	0.0	0.2	0.1	−0.1	−0.1	−0.1	−0.3	−0.2
Addendum:										
Federal surplus	−2.2	−2.1	−4.6	−5.2	−4.5	−4.9	−4.8	−3.3	−3.1	−3.2
Exc. social security									−3.7	3.9	−4.1
Social security									0.4	0.8	0.9

[a]This table shows changes in the U.S. savings and investment accounts during the 1980s. In the savings account, there was a sharp rise in government borrowing and decline in housing savings through the mid-1980s, which was offset by a rise in corporate savings. Government borrowing peaked in 1983 and personal savings bottomed in 1987. But corporate savings are now sliding because of weaker profitability and cuts in depreciation allowances. Despite generous tax allowances, nonresidential private investment has been falling as a share of GNP since 1981, but residential investment rose until 1986. The growth in foreign investment represents the capital inflow (current account deficit), which was necessary to reconcile the sharp fall in domestic savings with relatively stable private domestic investment.

that a rise in the trade deficit stemming from nominal exchange rate appreciation was preferable to a rise in the inflation rate. Although many supply-siders attacked the Fed for letting interest rates rise so sharply, the upsurge in yields on financial assets was partly a function of the sharp rise in the after-tax profitability of new capital goods purchases resulting from the supply-siders' fiscal program, not just the Volcker monetary policy. It also was necessary for the United States to import capital, because the changes in personal taxation during the early 1980s failed to raise the household savings rate. Instead of increasing their savings rate in response to high real interest rates and buoyant asset markets, U.S. citizens behaved like target savers (Gay 1989, pp. 5–10). They responded to buoyant asset markets by curtailing their savings rate and increasing consumption. In fact, the personal savings rate fell to a postwar low of 3.2 percent during 1987 as a consequence of households realizing large asset gains from takeovers, leveraged buy-outs, and equity sales initiated during 1986 before the capital gains tax rate rose back to 28 percent from 20 percent. Although some of the drop in personal savings probably also resulted from demographic factors, such as a bulge in the number of young families with high consumption propensities, the primary cause was the populist bias of the U.S. tax system. The United States is unique among the major industrial nations in having a fiscal system that provides large tax allowances for mortgages and no dividend credits to shareholders for tax paid at the corporate level. During the 1980s, the United States was also the only major industrial nation to pursue a significant income tax reduction program that was not offset by higher consumption taxes.

The inflation performance of the United Kingdom during 1988 and 1989 illustrates how attempts to stabilize exchange rates can backfire when a country is experiencing robust domestic demand and large capital inflows. The British Treasury wanted to lay the groundwork for European Monetary System (EMS) entry by pursuing a shadow exchange rate target vis à vis the German mark during 1987 and 1988. Because the de facto exchange rate targeted prevented the Bank of England from raising interest rates in the face of rapid credit growth, there was a boom in property lending and an upward spiral of home prices, which depressed British personal savings, boosted consumption, and encouraged a surge of imports despite only a modest rise in the nominal sterling exchange rate and a large surplus in the government budget. By 1989, the U.K. monetary policy had driven the inflation rate from 4–5 percent to 8–9 percent, while the current account deficit swelled to 3–4 percent of GNP from a surplus in 1986. Although financial liberalization also contributed to the upsurge in U.K. consumer borrowing during the late 1980s, the British experience suggests that if the United States had attempted to control the dollar during the early 1980s, the Reagan fiscal stimulus would have produced higher inflation as well as a large trade deficit, not just deterioration in the trade account.

Looking at the pattern of U.S.capital inflows that emerged as a consequence of the large U.S. budget deficit and low household savings during the 1980s, in the first half of the decade, the primary channel for capital inflows was foreign buying of U.S. Treasury securities and bank liabilities. In 1986 and 1987, the private capital inflow broadened out to include much larger foreign purchases of U.S. equities. In fact, during the six months prior to the October 1987 stock market crash, foreign buying of U.S. equities ran at levels equal to $40 billion at annual rates or 1 percent of GNP, the highest level since before 1914. After the stock market crash, foreign portfolio demand for U.S. equities fell sharply, but foreign corporations significantly increased their direct investment through $55 billion of takeover bids for U.S. firms in 1988. There also was heavy foreign central bank financing of the U.S. external deficit in 1987 and early 1988 because of capital flight from U.S. debt instruments by private investors.

The ability of the Reagan administration to finance large government deficits with low private savings and modest inflation during the 1980s demonstrates how profoundly global capital mobility is now altering the parameters for economic policy in the major industrial nations. If the Reagan fiscal program had been introduced during the 1950s or 1960s, it would have led to far worse inflation or crowding out pressures in the financial markets than occurred during the 1980s, because such large-scale foreign borrowing would have been impossible. But because Reaganomics coincided with a period of global financial liberalization as well as highly divergent fiscal policies in other industrial nations, the United States was able to finance its external deficits by selling financial claims during the years of dollar appreciation and real assets during the years of dollar depreciation. As a result of the increasing mobility of capital in the international economy, the U.S. financial scene during the 1980s has had more in common with the world we knew in the 1880s than with the 1960s and 1970s.

Although the history of the 1980s demonstrates that countries with large and open asset markets can finance big budget deficits without recourse to inflation for several years, it remains to be seen whether the long-term consequences of Reaganomics will be as benign for price stability. There are four potential reasons why there could be a delayed inflation effect from the Reagan fiscal policy.

First, as Table 1.4 illustrates, the United States' external and domestic debt levels grew far more rapidly during the 1980s than its capital stock. It is true that the growth rate of real investment during the early 1980s was much more robust than the growth rate of nominal investment because of the falling price of computers. But because the United States was borrowing to make equipment purchases in nominal dollars, the falling deflator cannot be used to justify such a dramatic buildup in the debt stock. In theory, the falling price of computers should have lessened the economy's need to borrow externally. Because of the imbalance between borrowing and investment during the 1980s, the United States will have to allocate a growing share of its future output to servicing foreign debt without the benefit of a significantly larger capital stock. This will require policymakers to reduce the growth rate of domestic per capita consumption to very modest levels by historical standards in order to free up resources for generating exports. A few numbers illustrate how this growth constraint is likely to work. The nation's labor force is projected to expand by 1.0 percent per annum during the early 1990s, while the trend growth rate of productivity is about 1.2 percent. Hence, once the economy achieves full resource utilization, its optimal

Table 1.4 Growth Rates of U.S. Capital Stocks[a]

	1950–1988	1950–1960	1960–1970	1970–1980	1980–1988
CAPITAL STOCK					
Nominal gross					
Manufacturing	8.14	6.53	7.36	12.52	5.48
Nonmanufacturing	7.86	5.34	6.58	12.88	6.34
Nominal net					
Manufacturing	7.97	6.60	7.97	12.02	4.33
Nonmanufacturing	8.18	6.29	7.34	12.64	5.91
Real gross					
Manufacturing	3.49	3.49	4.17	3.74	2.15
Nonmanufacturing	3.31	2.62	3.42	3.80	3.45
Real net					
Manufacturing	3.34	3.55	4.80	3.26	1.10
Nonmanufacturing	3.64	3.62	4.10	3.65	3.04
DEBT OUTSTANDING					
Nominal					
Total federal debt	7.82	1.29	3.30	8.84	14.19
Nonfinancial nonfederal	10.00	9.77	8.87	10.96	10.35
Nonfinancial corporations	8.89	7.44	8.61	8.93	10.67
Real					
Total federal debt	3.64	–1.50	1.11	2.49	9.09
Nonfinancial nonfederal	5.59	8.35	6.56	4.49	5.42
Nonfinancial corporations	4.84	6.08	6.31	2.58	5.72

Source: U.S. Commerce Department data.

[a]The major long-term problem posed by Reaganomics was not the growth of federal debt; it was the sluggish growth rate of the capital stock relative to the size of the borrowing.

noninflationary growth rate is likely to be only about 2.2 percent per annum. Since the U.S. population is growing by just under 1.0 percent per annum, the prospective noninflationary growth rate of real per capita consumption will be 1.3 percent per annum if the export and investment shares of GNP remain static; but it will be only half that level if the United States attempts to reduce the trade deficit from 2.5 percent of GNP to zero between 1990 and 1994. In the postwar period, by contrast, the average per capita growth rate of consumption was just over 2.0 percent. There is no precise way of predicting how rapidly the United States will have to reduce its external debt and thus how restrained consumption growth will have to be. If foreign investors permit the United States to borrow at a rate equal to 2.5 percent of GNP indefinitely, there will be no need to reduce the consumption share of GNP to free up resources for closing the trade deficit. But most forecasting models suggest that the United States will have to reduce the trade deficit significantly by 1995 to stabilize its ratio of external debt to GNP. Under such circumstances, political resistance to restraining consumption through tighter fiscal or monetary policy could cause demand to grow more rapidly than output and force Washington to chose between accepting higher inflation and permitting the trade deficit to resume expanding.

Second, the U.S. investment mix during the first half of the 1980s was not optimal for an industrial nation accumulating a large external debt. Although the sharp rise in the value of the dollar did not depress total U.S. investment because of the enhanced depreciation allowances, the dollar's overvaluation did distort the sectoral composition of investment. The manufacturing investment share of GNP remained at relatively low levels during the 1980s despite the big defense buildup, while investment in the economy's nontradeable sectors boomed.

As with Latin America's experiments with populist finance and real exchange rate appreciation, the dollar's sharp rise during the early 1980s encouraged a boom in U.S. sectors catering to domestic consumption and a profit squeeze in the country's export industries. The retail share of profits skyrocketed during the early Reagan years while manufacturing profits slumped. The United States also experienced a commercial real estate boom during the early Reagan years because of the positive effects of the 1981 depreciation changes on the after-tax return from new buildings and the impact of the dollar's rise on investor preferences for projects catering to nontradeable sectors of the economy rather than manufacturing. In fact, there was so much overbuilding that the United States now has high commercial vacancy rates in several cities and a growing regional bank problem with bad real estate loans. The dollar shock did produce a healthy improvement in U.S. manufacturing productivity during the mid-1980s by forcing firms to shed labor and rationalize operations, but there was no significant addition to industrial capacity. As a result, the export boom that followed the 1985–1987 dollar devaluation quickly triggered a large rise in wholesale prices, which forced the Fed to raise interest rates by over 300 basis points after mid-1988 and to countenance a 15–20 percent rally in the dollar exchange rate against other industrial country currencies. Although the resulting slowdown in exports and domestic demand helped to lessen inflation pressures during the second half of 1989, the U.S. economy's capacity constraints suggest that policymakers will have to adhere to cautious growth targets for domestic spending well into the 1990s. As with Britain in the 1950s and 1960s, the United States may now be headed for an extended period of stop-go economic performance, as the Fed attempts to fine-tune a 2.0–2.5 percent growth rate for real output against a policy backdrop of only gradual improvement in the budget deficit and private savings.

The third Reagan economic legacy that could cause more inflation in the U.S. economy during the 1990s than during the 1980s is the increasing tendency of the United States to respond to its trade deficit with microeconomic tinkering rather than macroeconomic adjustment. During the Reagan years, the share of U.S. imports subject to some form of official restraint grew form 12 percent to 23 percent. Reagan also signed a trade bill that greatly increase the danger of future protectionism by establishing unilateral criteria for determining when other countries' trade policies are detrimental to U.S. commercial interest. Finally, the U.S. government has begun experimenting with interventionist industrial policies in high-technology sectors, such as semiconductors, supercomputers, and high-definition TV. Protectionist trade policies usually raise domestic prices. As the U.S. government has little experience in conducting industrial policies outside of the defense sector, there also is a significant risk that such intervention will misallocate resources and hurt future productivity. Meanwhile, there is growing political concern about the long-term implications of the United States selling assets to foreign investors in order to finance a high level of consumption. If the U.S. Congress decides to restrict foreign purchases of U.S. assets, the external deficit would have to be financed solely through borrowing. Such a narrowing of the window for capital inflows would tend to weaken the dollar, push up interest rates, and generate political pressure for the Fed to monetize more of the federal deficit. In fact, the 1987 stock market crash resulted in part from investor concern about the possible effects of renewed dollar weakness on foreign demand for U.S. equities. As in the bear markets of the late nineteenth century, foreign buying of U.S. equities had been so large during the summer of 1987 that many domestic institutions feared further dollar depreciation would trigger capital flight from the New York financial markets and drive up interest rates.

Although there is natural public concern about the large-scale foreign buying of U.S. real estate since the 1985–1987 dollar devaluation, the export of ownership claims on office blocks is actually a logical market adjustment to the U.S. economic policies of the early 1980s. The interaction between the 1981 tax bill and the dollar's sharp appreciation gave the United States an international comparative advantage in erecting surplus office towers. Indeed, because of the big job losses in manufacturing during that period, the commercial real estate sector evolved into a Reagan-era version of the WPA, in which full employment was maintained through private sector waste rather than public sector boondoggles. Now the sale of U.S. office towers to Tokyo insurance companies can help stretch out the balance of payments adjustment process and prevent real estate prices from plummeting in cities with high vacancy rates.

The final factor that could tilt U.S. policy more in favor of inflation during the 1990s is the large gap developing between the United States' dollar-denominated external assets and dollar-denominated foreign claims on the U.S. economy. According to official estimates, the United States now has $1.7 trillion of dollar-denominated foreign claims on its economy and only $740 million of dollar-denominated claims on other countries. By 1992, this gap is likely to be at least $500 billion larger, especially if the U.S. banks now write off a large share of their LDC loans. Because the U.S. external debt is dollar-denominated, some Washington policymakers may favor using devaluation to reduce the real value of foreign claims on the economy. The Latin American nations, by contrast, had borrowed in dollars and thus could not use currency depreciation to reduce the real value of foreign claims on their output. Since the external debt-servicing burden of the United States during the early 1990s will be equal to only 1.0–1.5 percent of GNP compared to 4–5 percent for much of Latin America, it is far from clear that policymakers in Washington will regard devaluation as an attractive policy option. But, as even members of the Reagan Council of Economic Advisers acknowledged during the mid-1980s, the fact remains that the United States is unique among the world's major debtor nations in being able to choose whether it should service its external debt in a stable currency or a depreciating currency.

Japan to the Rescue

The final factor that permitted the United States to sustain a much larger balance of payments deficit during the 1980s than would have been possible in medium-size countries was the willingness of other countries' monetary authorities to support the United States dollar and bond market during periods when private capital inflows stopped. Although several countries contributed to the dollar stabilization efforts of the late 1980s, Japan played the most decisive role for several reasons. Japan is highly dependent upon the United States for both markets and military security and has been the world's largest capital exporter during the 1980s. The Japanese government can use a mixture of orthodox and nonorthodox policy instruments to guide capital flows during periods of currency market turmoil.

There were three channels through which the Japanese Ministry of Finance (MOF) tried to protect the U.S. dollar and restrain upward pressure on U.S. interest rates during 1987 and 1988. The first was traditional central bank buying of dollars. In 1987 and 1988, the MOF instructed the Bank of Japan to purchase over $55 billion of U.S. securities and received budget authority to purchase another $60 billion worth if necessary. Second, the Ministry of Finance often used moral jawboning to prevent Japanese institutional investors from dumping dollar securities during periods of exchange rate uncertainty. Richard Koo (1988) of the Nomura Research Institute explained in testimony submitted to the Join Economic Committee of Congress on October 17, 1988, as follows:

One of the greatest mysteries in international finance during the last three years (1985–1988) must be the courage of Japanese investors to stay with the dollar when its value was falling rapidly. In the same period, most other Western investors shunned the dollar as soon as they realized that the G-5 central banks were serious about pushing the dollar down. Wet German investors, for example, stopped buying dollar securities as early as the first quarter of 1986. In contrast, and contrary to textbook recommendations to get out of falling currencies, Japanese investors persisted with the dollar for at least a year and a half longer.

Although some of these purchases were hedged, foreign securities–related losses during this period also reached astronomical levels. The top five life insurance companies alone, which account for about 23 percent of all Japanese foreign securities purchases, lost $25.3 billion by the end of March 1988. Total losses sustained by the entire Japanese investment community during the last three years are likely to have reached many times this amount.

To argue that bad judgement was everything, however, misses the important policy actions that were taken to make sure that the necessary adjustments to the dollar, the key reserve currency, could be completed without the entire international financial system coming apart. In particular, there were numerous occasions when Japanese and US authorities tried to keep these investors from bailing out of the dollar.

During 1986 and 1987, the most difficult years of exchange rate adjustment, when the dollar and financial markets around the world came precariously close to total collapse, Japanese authorities tried to keep investors in dollars by telling them how much good the US had done for Japan after the war, and how important it was for Japan to stay with the dollar to prevent the total collapse of the world financial system.

The effectiveness of this moral suasion is based on the tradition of the long-term give-and-take which characterized the relationship between Japanese authorities and the private sector. In crisis situations, therefore, some institutions are willing to put aside their private interest in favor of containing problems to keep them from developing into a major disaster.

In spite of the mounting losses, therefore, the senior management of major insurance companies and trust banks refrained from selling dollar securities as long as they could. Fortunately, many insurance companies had large unrealized capital gains on their domestic stock holdings which they had patiently accumulated over the last 40 years. By realizing some of these gains, they were able to offset the losses arising from their foreign securities holdings and still remain solvent. It was sheer luck that this cushion, a product of conservative Japanese accounting practices, was available to help the US.

Nor did the MOF merely use moral suasion to support the dollar in 1987 and 1988. When it came under massive selling pressure in the spring of 1987, the MOF reimposed de facto capital controls on Japanese investors in order to stabilize the U.S. financial markets. As Mr. Koo explained,

> The situation was so bad that in May (1987), the Ministry of Finance required banks handling foreign exchange to submit detailed reports including the daily maximum and minimum positions taken, a process which made the usual conduct of foreign exchange business difficult. This way, the authorities were able to find out quickly who was engaged in selling dollars.
>
> Many banks and other financial institutions bitterly complained about the imposition of such reporting requirements and the implicit threat behind them. Even though the imposition of such quasi-capital controls was against the spirit of the Yen/Dollar Committee sponsored jointly by the Japanese Ministry of Finance and the US treasury to deregulate Japanese financial market, no complaints were heard from the US.

The knowledge of market participants outside Japan that the MOF was taking extraordinary pressures to support the dollar also helped lessen selling pressure elsewhere. Although foreign exchange traders are reputed to be contemptuous of central banks, they make a distinction with Japan's monetary authorities because of both the scale of Japan's financial power and the country's unique capacity for collective action. Indeed, the MOF was able to stop the dollar rally of June 1989 with less direct intervention than had occurred during 1987, partly because of investor apprehension about the size of Japan's foreign exchange reserves and the knowledge that the MOF could apply effective moral suasion over private dollar holdings in the Tokyo institutional community exceeding $300 billion.

The MOF's ability to use moral suasion more effectively than other monetary authorities reflects both the unique corporatist features of the Japanese development process and the highly compact structure of the Tokyo financial community. The United States has over 14,000 commercial banks; Japan has 13 large city banks and 145 small banks; the United States has over 1,500 life insurance companies while Japan has 24; the United States has nearly 1,900 property casualty insurance companies compared to 23 in Japan. Nomura controls 30 percent of the trading volume of the largest companies listed on the Tokyo stock exchange, and the three next largest firms control another 25–30 percent of the volume. Meanwhile, more than half of Japanese equity is tied up in corporate cross-shareholdings. This highly compact financial structure coupled with the cross-shareholding system permits the brokers to collaborate with banks and companies in guiding share prices to achieve government policy objectives, including the privatization of public sector organizations, such as Nippon Telephone, and the recapitalization of industries experiencing major structural upheavals, such as steel and banking in 1987/88. As a result, Japan's top fifteen banks were capitalized at over $700 billion compared to $100 billion for the United States' top fifty. The Tokyo share of world stock market capitalization also grew from 18 percent in 1980 to 45 percent in 1989, while the U.S. share shrank from 55 percent to 30 percent.

In addition to the MOF using moral suasion over private capital outflows, the Bank of Japan (BOJ) pursued a low-interest rate policy during 1987/88 in order to boost the U.S. dollar; they then attempted to neutralize the potential inflation consequences through administrative guidance of credit growth. The BOJ ordered the banks to reduce the growth rate of total lending and sharply curtailed the supply of funds available for property speculation. As a result, the growth rate of bank lending for real estate fell from 32 percent to 8 percent, and there was a modest decline in Tokyo real estate prices during 1987 and 1988, despite monetary policy that was highly accommodative in every respect. The MOF also used restrictions on land availability to prevent the slowdown in property lending from producing a price collapse (Woodhall 1989).

It was not for altruistic reasons that Japanese policymakers took such extraordinary steps to protect the dollar. They did so because of perceptions that a recessionary hard landing in the U.S. economy during 1987 and 1988 would spawn even greater pressure for economic nationalism in the U.S. political process than is apparent today. Japan's dollar-support operations also evolved into a de facto form of defense burden sharing, which helped lessen public pressure for large military spending cuts in the run-up to the 1988 presidential election. For the fourth time in modern U.S. and Japanese history, the foreign exchange market became an instrument of foreign policy and a vehicle for mobilizing resource transfers that could not occur quickly through other channels. In 1968, the United States also had pursued a balance of payments "offset" program with Germany, in which the Bundesbank had stopped converting dollars into gold as a quid pro quo for U.S. defense forces remaining on German soil. In 1965, the United States had made a then secret loan to the British government to support the pound and lessen pressure on the Wilson government to shut down the large British military base in Singapore (Ponting 1989, pp. 41–84). In the first decade of the twentieth century, Japan had kept her foreign exchange reserves in the British banking system as a quid pro quo for London loans during the Russo-Japanese War of 1905 and British recognition of Japanese supremacy over Korea. Although the Japanese support for sterling in 1910 was far less important than U.S. loans to the Wilson government in the mid-1960s, it did bolster sterling's international reserve role at a time when France and Germany were aggressively promoting the international use of their own currencies. Indeed, the pound's share of international reserves had fallen to 36 percent by 1914 from over 70 percent in the late nineteenth century.

The internationalist orientation of Japanese policymakers during the 1980s also makes for a vivid contrast with the role played by U.S. policymakers during the 1920s, when there was previously a major upheaval in global financial power. In that period, only one important U.S. policymaker, Benjamin Strong, governor of the New York Federal Reserve, had displayed any awareness of the policy implications of the United States' new role as the world's dominant creditor power. Strong had pursued a highly expansionary policy during the late 1920s to help bolster the much-beleaguered British pound and encourage more robust world economic growth, but his efforts to stave off a breakdown of the global financial order failed for four reasons. First, the U.S. Congress enacted two highly punitive tariff laws during the 1920s, despite the fact that the United States had a trade surplus. The imposition of such severe trade restraints by the world's leading creditor power created a bottleneck in the world balance of payments adjustment process. Second, Strong died in 1928 and thus was unable to engineer a gradual deflation of the stock market boom spawned by the easy monetary policy he pursued to help the British. Third, other U.S.officials were often resentful of Strong's efforts to pursue such an internationalist monetary policy. Herbert Hoover even chastised Strong for being "a mental annex of Europe." Finally, the other great creditor power of the period, France, deliberately pursued destabilizing policies to punish Britain for supporting reductions in German war reparations.

The ability of the Japanese Ministry of Finance to protect the U.S. dollar through administrative guidance over capital flows provides a further illustration of how international policy divergence has worked in favor of the U.S. economy during the 1980s. If Japan had had a financial regulatory tradition comparable to U.S. free market ideology, it would have been far more difficult for the MOF to have supported the dollar as aggressively as it did without jeopardizing Japan's domestic financial stability. In the absence of the MOF's administrative guidance, there might have been a much larger rise in both Japanese and U.S. interest rates during 1987 and 1988.

Conclusion

The economic history of the 1980s demonstrates that the creation of a global capital market has significantly altered the parameters for national economic policies. For the first time since the 1920s, stock markets and bond markets are reemerging as important conduits for international capital transfers. It is now possible for large industrial countries, not just small developing nations, to sustain fiscal deficits and savings imbalances without recourse to inflationary monetary policies. As a result, the dominant variables in a country's inflation and exchange rate performance are no longer just its budget deficit and trade account; rather, they are a mixture of micro- and macroeconomic factors that determine its capacity for attracting foreign savings, including the size and liquidity of its capital markets, its political tolerance for foreign ownership of domestic assets, and its tax treatment of capital. In the 1980s, the United States was able to fund an unprecedented savings imbalance through capital inflows because of the large size of its financial markets, its lack of restrictions on foreign ownership, generous new tax allowances for investment, and a special relationship with the Japanese Ministry of Finance, which provided official funding for the United States' deficit when private inflows ceased. Latin America, by contrast, has weak capital markets, significant restrictions on foreign equity investment, and tax regimes that encourage capital flight by domestic savers.

Although foreign borrowing and asset sales can reduce the short-term inflation dangers posed by large government deficits, they can produce other distortions with potentially adverse long-term consequences for investment, productivity, and inflation. As U.S. history during the 1980s demonstrated, there are at least four major dangers posed by heavy reliance on external borrowing or asset sales to restore equilibrium in a country's savings and investment account after a large increase in the government's structural deficit. First, heavy dependence upon external borrowing to fund a rise in the government deficit could cause the country's debt level to increase far more rapidly than its capital stock. If such an imbalance occurs for a long period, the country eventually will have to restrict domestic consumption to free up resources for servicing the debt. Second, in a floating exchange rate system, the rise in real interest rates that typically accompanies a large increase in government borrowing could cause the real exchange rate to appreciate to levels that would cause an overconcentration of investment in nontradeable industries at the expense of the export sector. Although such distortions will not depress total output in the short term, they will erode the country's capacity to export and thus increase the danger of the trade deficit expanding to levels that might frighten investors and provoke a balance of payments crisis later. Third, a large rise in the trade deficit will tend to encourage protectionist trade policies and other microeconomic forms of intervention designed to slow import penetration and restore export competitiveness. Protectionism will usually increase the prices paid by domestic consumers.

Finally, the large rise in foreign borrowing and asset sales needed to compensate for the low U.S. domestic savings rate could provoke political hostility to foreign investors. In the late nineteenth century, there was widespread popular antipathy in the United States towards British financial power because of the perception that London favored high interest rates and low commodity prices in order to maximize the real value of its debt claims on the U.S. economy (Hale 1988). At the end of 1988, the U.S. external investment deficit (net debt and foreign investment in the United States) was only about 10 percent of GNP compared to a previous peak of 23 percent in the early 1890s. Yet, there is already widespread congressional concern about foreign buying of U.S. assets, while Treasury Secretary Nicholas Brady publicly blamed the Japanese for helping set in motion the October 1987 stock market crash by dumping U.S. bonds during the preceding week. Such complaints could grow as foreign ownership of the U.S. economy expands.

Because foreign capital flows to the United States are a function of conditions in other countries, not just the United States, there also is no way of predicting when foreign investors may be satiated with dollar assets. In the late nineteenth century, U.S. financial crises did not stem merely from domestic events that frightened away foreign investors, such as Washington's flirtation with dollar devaluation in 1893 and 1896; they also stemmed from financial shocks in Europe, such as rising interest rates (1873) or bank failures (1890), which temporarily suspended capital outflows from London to the United States. In fact, the large rise that occurred in U.S. bond yields during early 1990 demonstrated how changes in foreign financial markets can push up U.S. interest rates even when the trade deficit is falling. There was a 200-basis- point rise in German long term interest rates during the three months after the fall of the Berlin Wall because of investor concern about the potential financial costs of German reunification. The large rise in German interest rates helped to divert Japanese capital flows from New York to Frankfurt as well as to attract funds from the United States. Meanwhile, interest rates rose sharply in Japan itself because of attempts by the Bank of Japan (BOJ) to restrain the asset inflation that resulted in part from the pro-dollar policy of the late 1980s. Senior MOF officials attacked the BOJ's new preoccupation with asset prices on the grounds that Tokyo was an "anchor for global financial stability." But because Japan's high asset prices were depressing the yen by encouraging large capital outflows, the BOJ was able to prevail with a tighter monetary policy. In the 1980s, global financial integration helped the United States solve its saving problem because it was the system's de facto buyer and seller of last resort. In the 1990s, by contrast, the capital needs of Eastern Europe and a recovery of investment in other developing countries could alter the direction of global savings flows and boost U.S. interest rates unless there is an offsetting increase in domestic savings.

As a result of these uncertainties, it will not be possible to pass a conclusive judgment on Reaganomics for several more years. Many aspects of the Reagan economic record are not flattering: the debt stock grew more rapidly than the capital stock; the United States has been selling assets to finance consumption; and Reagan has bequeathed the people of the United States a legacy of populism in fiscal policy and protectionism in trade policy that could haunt the U.S. political process for a generation and encourage even worse economic demagoguery during the 1990s. But there were achievements as well: the Reagan fiscal stimulus provided a growth locomotive for the world economy at a time when fiscal policy was restrictive nearly everywhere else; the Reagan fiscal program corrected the U.S. tax system for the inflation-driven bracket creep of the 1970s and helped encourage a worldwide decline in marginal tax rates; the reemergence of the United States as a capital importer has demonstrated that in an age of global financial liberalization it is possible for countries to attract large external savings through tax regimes favorable to investment; and the Reagan deficits helped rebuild U.S. defenses after a decade of Soviet expansionism and this helped to lay the groundwork for the collapse of the Soviet empire in 1989–1990. Because it is so difficult to separate economic and political issues in evaluating the consequences of Reaganomics, the ultimate verdict on it will be highly conditional upon whether the Bush administration can manage the United States' transition to a new multipolar international order characterized by eroding East-West tensions, increasingly intense commercial and technological rivalry between the industrial nations, and a deepening sense of anxiety among U.S. citizens about their place in a world where the United States is important but no longer dominant.

References

Berg, Andrew, and Jeffrey Sachs. 1988. "The Debt Crisis: Structural Explanation of Country Performance." Working Paper No. 2607, National Bureau of Economic Research, Cambridge, Mass., June.

Congdon, Tim. 1983. "The Rise and Fall of the Chilean Economic Miracle." Based on a talk given to the Latin American Study Group, January. (Used by permission of author.)

———. 1984. "The Debt Crisis and the American Financial System." Background articles, L. Messel (London), August.

———. 1985. "Can Britain Escape the Debt Trap?" L. Messel (London), June.

———. 1987. "The Link Between Budget Deficits and Inflation." Economic Research Paper No. 3, L. Messel (London), March.

Crook, Clive, ed. 1989. *World Development 1989*. New York: Oxford University Press. (Publication of the International Bank for Reconstruction and Development/World Bank).

Cumby, Robert E., and Sweder van Wijnbergen. 1987. "Financial Policy and Speculative Runs with a Crawling Peg: Argentina 1979–1981." Working Paper No. 2376, National Bureau of Economic Research, Cambridge, Mass., September.

Darby, Michael R. 1984. "Some Pleasant Monetarist Arithmetic." *Federal Reserve Bank of Minneapolis Quarterly Review* (Spring).

———. 1987. "Accounting for the Deficit: An Analysis of Sources of Change in the Federal and Total Government Deficits." Research Paper Series, U.S. Treasury Department, Office of the Assistant Secretary for Economic Policy, October 2.

Dornbusch, Rudiger. 1988. "Credibility, Debt and Unemployment: Ireland's Failed Stabilization." Working Paper No. 2785, National Bureau of Economic Research, Cambridge, Mass., December.

Dornbusch, Rudiger, and Mario Henrique Simonsen. 1987. "Inflation

Stabilization with Incomes Policy Supports: A Review of the Experience in Argentina, Brazil and Israel." Working Paper No. 2153, National Bureau of Economic Research, Cambridge, Mass., February.

Edwards, Sebastian. 1987. "Exchange Controls, Devaluations and Real Exchange Rates: The Latin American Experience." Working Paper No. 2348, National Bureau of Economic Research, Cambridge, Mass., August.

———. 1989. "The International Monetary Fund and the Developing Countries: A Critical Evaluation." Working Paper No. 2909, National Bureau of Economic Research, Cambridge, Mass., March.

———. 1989. "Openness, Outward Orientation, Trade Liberalization and Economic Performance in Developing Countries." Working Paper No. 2908, National Bureau of Economic Research, Cambridge, Mass., March.

Edwards, Sebastian, and Peter Montiel. 1989. "Devaluation Crises and the Macroeconomic Consequences of Postponed Adjustment in Developing Countries." Working Paper No. 2866, National Bureau of Economic Research, Cambridge, Mass., February.

Entin, Stephen J. 1986. "Remarks on the Reagan Economic Program." *Treasury News*, Department of the Treasury, December 1.

Fernández, Raquel, and Jacob Glazer. 1989. "Why Haven't Debtor Countries Formed a Cartel?" Working Paper No. 2980, National Bureau of Economic Research, Cambridge, Mass., May.

Gay, Robert S. 1989. "Behind the Recovery in Personal Savings." *Economic Perspectives*, Morgan Stanley, New York, June 9.

Grossman, Herschel I. 1988. "The Political Economy of War Debts and Inflation." Working Paper No. 2743, National Bureau of Economic Research, Cambridge, Mass., October.

Hale, David. 1988. "Will We Hate Japan as We Hated Britain?" *International Economy* 1, no. 2 (January–February).

Koo, Richard C. 1988. "Japanese Investment in Dollar Securities after the Plaza Accord." Statement submitted to the Joint Economic Committee, U.S. Congress, October 17.

———. 1989. "Japan and International Capital Flows." Nomura Research Institute (Japan).

Kuczynski, Pedro-Pablo. 1988. *Latin American Debt*. Baltimore: Johns Hopkins University Press.

Leiderman, Leonardo, and Assaf Razin. 1986. "Propagation of Shocks in a High-Inflation Economy: Israel, 1980–85." Working Paper No. 2003, National Bureau of Economic Research, Cambridge, Mass., August.

Lessard, Donald R., and John Williamson. 1985. "Financial Intermediation Beyond the Debt Crisis." Institute for International Economics, Cambridge, Mass., September.

McLure, Charles E., Jr. 1988. "U.S. Tax Laws and Capital Flight from Latin America." Working Paper No. 2687, National Bureau of Economic Research, Cambridge, Mass., August.

Miller, Preston J. 1983. "Higher Deficit Policies Lead to Higher Inflation." *Federal Reserve Bank of Minneapolis Quarterly Review* 7, no. 1 (Winter).

Ponting, Clive. 1989. *Breach of Promise, Labor in Power*. London: Hamish Hamilton.

Roach, Stephen S. 1989. "Capacity Paradox: A Disturbing Update." *Economic Perspectives*, Morgan Stanley, New York, May 11.

Roubini, Nouriel, and Jeffrey Sachs. 1989. "Government Spending and Budget

Deficits in the Industrial Economies." Working Paper No. 2919, National Bureau of Economic Research, Cambridge, Mass., April.

Sachs, Jeffrey, 1988. "Conditionality, Debt Relief, and the Developing Country Debt Crisis." Working Paper No. 2644, National Bureau of Economic Research, Cambridge, Mass., July.

————. 1989. "Social Conflict and Populist Policies in Latin America." Working Paper No. 2897, National Bureau of Economic Research, Cambridge, Mass., March.

Sargent, Thomas J., and Neil Wallace. 1981. "Some Unpleasant Monetarist Arithmetic." *Federal Reserve Bank of Minneapolis Quarterly Review*, no. 5 (Fall).

Tatom, John A. 1989. "U.S. Investment in the 1980s: The Real Story." *Federal Reserve Bank of St. Louis Quarterly Review* 71, no. 2 (March–April).

Turnovsky, Stephen J., and Mark E. Wohar. 1987. "Alternative Modes of Deficit Financing and Endogenous Monetary and Fiscal Policy, 1923–1982." Working Paper No. 2123, National Bureau of Economic Research, Cambridge, Mass., January.

Woodall, Alan. 1989. *Merrill Lynch Japanese Real Estate Report*, March. Merrill Lynch, Inc. New York.

Zwick, Burton, et al., 1989. "Foreign Investors: Buying, Not Building." Kidder Peabody Equity Research, New York, June 16.

2

Inflation, Indebtedness, and Investment in Argentina, 1985-1988

Santiago O. del Puerto

This chapter addresses the challenge Argentina is facing to ensure needed investment—and therefore sustained economic growth—in the context of high and persistent inflation and high and increasing indebtedness. Since 1982, when the international debt crisis began, both debtors and creditors have made great efforts to prevent the crisis from producing the collapse of the international financial system. From this perspective, the results have been positive, since such collapse has been avoided.

Nevertheless, the crisis remains, and there is a growing feeling that the strategy that thus far has been pursued has not led to the solution of the deepest problems confronting debtor and creditors. In general, and clearly in the case of Argentina, the debtor countries have not been able to return to the path of sustained economic growth. It is evident now that, although a reduction of net transfers abroad, through periodic granting of new loans, may be necessary to deal with the problem of the balance of payments, it is not a sufficient answer to the essential element of any overall solution—restoring private investor confidence in the economies of the indebted countries.

It is also clear that there is a limit to the capacity of debtor countries to repay their debts, since a country that must make a large and sustained net remittance of financial capital also must experience a net outflow of goods and services, that is, generate a trade surplus. Despite the enormous effort of some debtor countries to implement the necessary structural adjustment of their economies, the level of debt servicing has become unsustainable in relation to those countries' potential exports, so that they are unable to fully service their international obligations.

My recollection of the numerous meetings I have had with bankers at the Commercial Bank Steering Committee at Citibank is full of lengthy discussion in which each side (the creditor banks and the Argentine delegation) competed in presenting different views about how to defeat inflation, reduce the need for new borrowings, and promote investment under the sound and traditional principle of all similar discussions: "What's mine is mine, what's yours is negotiable."

At the negotiation table, questions as to how to quickly reduce the fiscal deficit while achieving economic growth, how to implement economic adjustment to pay the debt while getting political support at home, and how to make eliminating inflation compatible with easing domestic credit, are not debated from the standpoint of macroeconomic considerations only. Negotiators have very specific interests, and the result of such negotiations is often more an accumulation of individual claims than a comprehensive and consistent program.

It is not surprising that instability has been the characteristic of major, highly indebted Latin American countries that tried to meet contradictory targets through concerted financing programs. Instability, at the same time, has concentrated the problem in the debtor countries and the creditor banks by increasing or maintaining capital flight. Lack of direct investment, together with increased borrowing needs, produced a negative result that is clearer today than at the beginning of the debt crisis. Debtor countries will not regain access to capital markets, nor will the creditor banks obtain repayment of the debt, unless investment in LDC countries is reestablished in a way that permits sustained growth.

Fortunately, markets tend to develop and accommodate themselves to changing situations by recognizing reality. Prices of LDC loans at secondary markets today reflect approximately the proportion of interest payment on the debt that a given country can maintain current without increasing forced borrowing. Prices at the secondary markets, reserves on loans made by the banks, and a progressive recognition of reality by all parties alike are elements that may be combined to reestablish needed investment.

Debt to equity and debt to debt are recently developed devices that attempt to make investment possible in LDCs still affected by high inflation and high indebtedness. As regards the Argentine experience, my recollections go back the beginning of 1987, particularly to the early government and bank committee discussions we held on possible debt/equity programs for Argentina. At that time, I was outnumbered by colleagues who favored a very restrictive and negative debt/equity program, based on the assumption that converting debt into equity essentially meant prepaying long-term debt to increase monetary expansion in an already inflationary situation and incurring the political cost of "denationalizing" the economy. So negative was our initial device that it facilitated the banks' counterattacking us by saying that what we really wanted was not to have a debt/equity program and thus not to have investment. The banks were favoring, of course, a very flexible program of conversion, as well as other monetary expansive programs, on the basis of passing along to private sector clients the "new money" that they would be lending to Argentina within the 1987 Financing Plan.

At a given time, all the members of the official team became real supporters of debt/equity as a means of getting investment back in Argentina and of negotiating better terms for the whole package with commercial banks. So we had to develop a new debt/equity program that was simpler and more flexible than our first, and in a way that reversed the general opinion formed about our previous position; and to gain momentum we had to do it quickly. Our procedure was to eliminate a mandatory clause demanding additional matching funds—on a one-to-one basis—proportional to the debt to convert. We concentrated the approval process for projects in a single office at the Ministry of Economy, which had to make decisions within forty-five days following each presentation. Furthermore, to ensure that the program would win general credibility, we inserted in it three principles—which happens to be an ancestral precondition for all believable programs. In ours, these principles were:

1. *Growth orientation.* Debt conversion has to finance new investment, not just transfers of stock.
2. *Nondiscrimination.* All Argentine external public debt is admitted to conversion on an equal basis for both Argentine and foreign investors.
3. *Durability.* Auction amounts are regulated in such a way that they are consistent with other macroeconomic variables so that debt/equity swaps can be maintained and eventually expanded.

The Argentine program got support from the banks and became effective in January 1987. Between 1987 and 1988, two auctions took place and the results have been very positive, with more than $240 million of approved projects. Foreign debt for about $200 million has been rescued by the central bank at the cost of $108 million in equivalent Argentine currency, and both foreign and domestic investors have expressed increasing interest in the program.

Discounts offered at the second auction—ranging from 52 to 57 percent—were substantially higher than the ones resulting from the first bidding. Consequently, the index that relates total cost of winning projects to debt/equity financing increased from 1.89 at the January auction to 2.59 at the second one in March. This demonstrates that the program constitutes a good incentive for investment without replacing other sources of project financing.

Although debt/equity swaps are not the solution to the debt problem, and although they produce an increase in inflationary pressures that has to be compensated for at a cost, they are worth trying, given the few alternatives available to restore a minimum level of investment in LDCs. They are, at this stage, the only debt program that is working positively with catalytic effects. They have the genuine support of debtors and creditors alike and are bringing back to the scene a long-isolated participant, the investor.

It is not yet possible to count on general support to implement more profound and general measures within long-term programs involving debtors, creditors, multilateral organizations, and creditor countries. But the market itself has presented conditions that has allowed at least one voluntary debt relief program to proceed.

3

Success and Failure of a Heterodox Shock: The Austral Plan

Miguel A. Kiguel

Inflation was and continues to be one of the most pressing macroeconomic problems in Argentina. The high rates of inflation prevalent in the last four decades have tended to increase over the years. Inflation survived the implementation of several stabilization attempts and the use of alternative anti-inflation strategies. A variety of policies have likewise been unsuccesful. Strict monetary and fiscal orthodoxy was used in Alsogaray's 1959 program; income policies were tried in Krieger Vassena's program of 1967; and more recently (in the late 1970s) the preannouncement of the exchange rate (the *tablita* experiment) was followed by Martínez de Hoz. Despite the dissimilarities in the programs, most of them were able to strike some transitory gains in the war against inflation. The ultimate outcomes, however, were very similar—and disappointing. The programs were eventually abandoned as a result of a deterioration in the fiscal situation and in the balance of payments, and inflation returned invigorated, reaching even higher levels.[1]

The inflationary developments of the early 1980s were complicated by the dramatic and continuous deterioration in internal and external economic conditions. Massive budget deficits were the primary force fueling the rampant inflation, which on an annualized basis exceeded 1,500 percent during the first half of 1985. The overall economic situation deteriorated as a result of the worsening in terms of trade, the sharp reduction in external financing resulting from the Malvinas war in 1982, and the beginning of the debt crisis. The performance of the economy during this period was by and large poor; high rates of inflation were accompanied by a continuous fall in per capita GDP, net negative investment, and persistent external imbalances.

The relentless acceleration in inflation from 100 percent in 1981 to over 1,800 percent during the second quarter of 1985 made the situation unsustainable. Budget deficits were high by any standards, ranging from 12 to 18 percent of GDP, and were primarily financed by printing money. Seigniorage levels were also very high, reaching 10 percent of GDP in 1984.

The situation was very delicate, and, in the absence of a shift in policies, the country was heading toward hyperinflation.

The Austral Plan, launched in June 1985, was a response to this crisis. Its main objective was to lower inflation very quickly. The stated purpose was more ambitious: to start a new era of price stability in the economy. The program followed a heterodox strategy in the sense that it combined orthodox components, namely tight fiscal policy and monetary restraint, with the less conventional instruments of price and wage controls. A new currency was introduced, the austral; there was a devaluation of the domestic currency followed by an exchange rate freeze; and a novel strategy for neutralizing the effects of the unexpected reduction in inflation was introduced, the *desagio*.

The program was initially very successful in controlling inflation. As shown in Figure 3.1, inflation fell from 30 percent in June 1985 to 3.1 percent in August, when measured in terms of consumer prices, while the reductions were much more impressive in wholesale prices. Unfortunately, as in many of the previous stabilization efforts in Argentina, price stability was short-lived. After one year of relatively low inflation, there was a relentless increase in inflation rates, with inflation approaching pre-austral levels in 1988.[2]

In this paper I will examine the evolution of the Austral Plan from its inception. I will discuss the basic strategy of the program and raise some policy and analytical issues regarding its initial implementation, trace the sequence of stabilization programs launched during the "Austral era," and conclude with a discussion of the lessons from the Argentine experience for the implementation of the so-called heterodox shocks.

Implementation of the Austral Plan

The basic strategy of the Austral Plan, discussed in more detail in de Pablo (1987), Canavese and Di Tella (1988), and Machinea and Fanelli (1988), among others, shares many elements with the 1985 Israeli plan.[3] It was a heterodox program in the sense that it combined orthodox elements, such as fiscal discipline and monetary restraint, with price and wage controls. The latter were introduced on the assumption that in chronic high-inflation countries, such as Argentina, inflation is driven by inertial factors that tend to maintain it at prevailing levels even when sound "fundamental" policies are followed. Orthodox measures alone are not sufficient to bring about a rapid disinflation process in chronic inflation countries. The wage/price/ exchange rate freeze was viewed as the appropriate instrument to deal with this problem.

In the following section I will analyze the central aspects of the strategy of the Austral Plan and describe the management of its various policy

Figure 3.1 **Argentina: CPI and WPI Inflation**

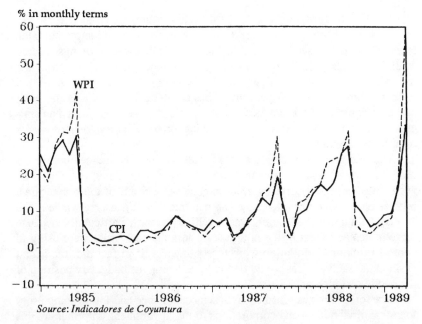

% in monthly terms

Source: *Indicadores de Coyuntura*

instruments. I will discuss the overall consistency and viability of the plan and the initial effects of the program on inflation, output, and the balance of payments.

The Strategy

Orthodox and heterodox measures were combined to increase the chances of success of the program. I will discuss in the following paragraphs the various components of the stabilization effort, the characteristics of the fiscal adjustment, the strategy for nominal variables and monetary policy, and the *desagio*.

Fiscal policy. The fiscal adjustment was seen as an important part of the program. As Table 3.1 shows, there was a drastic reduction in the budget deficit from almost 12 percent of GDP in the first two quarters of 1985, to 2.3 percent in the fourth quarter of that year. A closer analysis, however, indicates that most of this reduction was of a transitory nature and was likely to evaporate very quickly if inflation resurfaced. Government expenditure was basically unaffected by the program, although some reductions had already been started several months before the program. Reductions in real wages in the public sector and in public investment programs were made prior to the

Austral Plan, particularly during the second half of 1984 and the first months of 1985.

The fiscal adjustment was primarily effected through an increase in tax revenues. The four main elements of the adjustment were an increase in trade taxes, higher public sector prices, the introduction of a forced savings scheme (a disguised tax), and improvements in tax collections resulting from the reduction in inflation. The first one was the only tax that could be expected to increase revenues on a permanent basis, although it was also the most detrimental for an efficient allocation of resources, since it introduced an anti-export bias at a time when it was crucial for the country to improve its balance of payments.

The realignment of public sector prices was largely attained before the program began. This adjustment was reinforced on June 14, when the authorities increased them by 23.6 percent. As a result of these measures, relative public sector prices reached at that time their highest real value in the 1980s. This unusual situation was not likely to last, particularly because these prices were part of the nominal anchors the authorities were using to control inflation. If inflation were to continue, as it in fact did, the initial cushion in relative prices would be lost, weakening the budgetary position of the public sector enterprises.

The forced savings scheme was designed as a once-and-for-all compulsory loan from individuals and corporations to the government. In principle, this was not a tax, since the government had to repay that loan. Nevertheless, at that time, it was considered as genuine income for the purpose of calculating the budget deficit. In practice, however, it did work as a tax, because the government ended up borrowing at a very low nominal interest rate, which became negative with the increases in inflation in later years.

The final element contributing to the increase in tax revenues was a gain in efficiency in tax collection, which, paradoxically, resulted from the reduction in inflation. Because most taxes are paid with a lag, an increase in the rate of inflation erodes the real value of government revenues (this is the well-known Olivera-Tanzi effect). A drastic reduction in the rate of inflation works in reverse, resulting in an increase in the real value of tax revenues. Thus, the initial success of the Austral Plan on the inflation side provided an important support for the consolidation of the fiscal situation.

Nominal anchors. The reliance on income policies required careful management of nominal variables and the choice of a subset of variables to be used as anchors for the stabilization program. In the orthodox approach, money supply is the main nominal anchor. When there are inertial elements in the inflationary process, however, the short-run effectiveness of a serious and comprehensive stabilization attempt will benefit, at least temporarily, from the use of additional nominal anchors such as price and wage controls.

The designers of the Austral Plan were aware of this situation and hence targeted, in addition to the budget deficit, the behavior of prices, wages, and the exchange rate.

There was a 15 percent devaluation at the outset of the program, followed by an exchange rate freeze. The initial devaluation was important to create a cushion in the real exchange rate in case inflation showed persistence during the first months of the program. Given the limited access to external financing, the country could not afford a significant appreciation of the real exchange rate.

The exchange rate freeze was accompanied by a freeze of most prices[4] (to the level of June 13) and on wages (after a 22.6 percent increase at the end of June). The objective of these measures was to halt inertial pressures and to give time for the program to establish its credibility. The structure of relative prices at the time of the freeze was most favorable for public sector enterprises and traded goods (as a result of the depreciated exchange rate); it was less advantageous for workers, because real wages were relatively depressed.

In this strategy, the exchange rate was the main nominal anchor in the program, and its role was strongly supported by the system of price and wage controls. The adoption of a similar type of rule for most nominal variables was important to provide support and consistency to the overall program.

Monetary reform. A new currency was created at the beginning of the program, the austral. One austral was equivalent to 1,000 units of the old currency (the peso). The monetary reform in practice did not introduce new restrictions for money creation, because the austral was fiat money and was not backed by any real assets. The most important aspect of the monetary reform was that it provided a legal foundation for the introduction of the *desagio* (to be discussed later).

A more substantive measure was the announcement not to print any more money to finance the budget deficit. This promise was especially important at the time, since there was a wide (and well-founded) perception that central bank financing of the deficit was at the core of the inflationary process. Despite its importance, this measure was received with skepticism because no mechanism was created to make it enforceable. In addition, the lack of transparency in the central bank balance sheet and in its accounting practices greatly complicated any efforts to verify the truth of this statement.

Monetary policy. The management of monetary policy during the early stages of a stabilization program is very delicate. On the one hand, the authorities might want to increase the money supply in order to satisfy the greater demand for money resulting from a sharp reduction in the opportunity cost of holding it. This policy, when implemented appropriately, might help to avoid the high real interest rates usually observed in the early stages of a stabilization program. On the other hand, it is advisable for the authorities to remain on the cautious side and avoid an initial excess supply of money that could jeopardize the whole stabilization effort.

The evidence indicates that the authorities followed a prudent approach at the outset of the program. There was a large increase in domestic credit (and in the money supply) prior to the program and during its first weeks, which certainly contributed to sharp reductions in the monthly nominal interest rate, from 30 to 6 percent. The initial monetary expansion primarily accommodated the increase in money demand resulting from the reduction in the opportunity cost of holding money in a low-inflation environment. Despite its size, the monetary expansion did not in the long run create an excess supply of money, although the capital inflows that occurred during the first two weeks of the program were estimated at $300 million.[5] A policy of easy money would have led to capital outflows. The overall evidence indicates that the government followed a reasonable monetary policy during the *very early* stages of the program. However, as will be discussed later, monetary policy remained sound for only a very short span.

Desagio. A rapid and unanticipated reduction in inflation will, in general, result in a redistribution of income (and wealth) from debtors to creditors. At times when inflation is high, interest rates also tend to be high in order to maintain a constant real interest rate. In high inflation economies, changes in nominal interest rates are primarily determined by changes in the expected rate of inflation. When the Austral Plan was launched, inflation and interest rates were close to 30 percent per month. These interest rates were based on the questionable assumption that inflation would remain at those levels for some time.

The sharp disinflation accomplished by the Austral Plan was an unforeseen event for lenders and borrowers. Nominal interest rates contracted prior to the plan would have resulted in extraordinarily high ex-post real interest rates (close to 20 percent per month). To avoid these effects, the government introduced an ingenious mechanism (the *desagio*), which converted the value of financial agreements originating prior to June 14 with maturities after that date according to a predetermined rule. This was effected through the introduction of a "table" that converted the values of financial obligations maturing after June 14 from pesos into australes. This mechanism was particularly important for the public sector (including the central bank), which was a net debtor at that time.[6] It is conceivable that in the absence of the *desagio* the budget deficit could have been one or two percentage points higher than it actually was during the first months of the program.

Initial Results

By and large this was a well-designed program to combat inflation. It showed an appropriate balance between orthodox and heterodox measures that are necessary to stabilize quickly and without large social costs. The main weakness of the program was on the fiscal side, where the adjustment was extremely fragile. Sustainability of the program required that in the near future the authorities would take a very prudent stance regarding the management of nominal variables, particularly the money supply, and that they would introduce a major fiscal reform aimed at improving government revenues and reducing expenditures on a permanent basis.

The initial results were very impressive. Inflation fell from 348 percent in the first half of the year to 20.2 percent in the second half (see Figure 3.1 and Table 3.1). The adoption of price controls was very important for the sharp disinflation, but despite its effectiveness for controlling prices, it did not lead to shortages in most markets. The initial success was enhanced by an improvement during the third quarter in the current account of the balance of payments and by only a small reduction in the level of economic activity.

The spectacular short-run success was followed by some worrying signs that started to develop in the fourth quarter. While inflation remained at relatively low levels (at 2.5 percent per month), the current account turned into deficit and the economy moved very quickly into an expansionary cycle, mainly propelled by a consumption boom. These events were troublesome, since economic expansion could weaken the anti-inflation effort, and the deterioration in the balance of payments was likely to reduce ability to maintain the fixed exchange rate, lessening the credibility of the program.

Also problematic was the evolution of the monetary variables. Monetary policy was by and large expansionary in the early stages. M1 and M4 expanded, respectively, 64 and 50 percent between August and December 1985. Although part of this expansion was absorbed by increases in the demand for money, its size appears to have been "incompatible" with a serious stabilization effort. At the least, it undermined the credibility of the program,[7] although it accommodated the increase in demand that started in the fourth quarter.

Finally, the persistence of inflation, even at the much lower levels, created problems for the sustainability of the freeze of the exchange rate and prices of public sector enterprises. The initial cushion was slowly being eroded and, in the absence of further reductions in inflation, new policy measures had to be introduced.

Table 3.1 Argentina: Inflation, Devaluation, Interest, and Money

	CPI Inflation	Official Devaluation	Rates of Growth M1	Rates of Growth M4	Deposit Rate
1985					
January	25.1	25.0	19.0	19.8	24.9
February	20.7	20.6	13.3	19.4	20.9
March	26.5	26.4	15.9	18.1	23.5
April	29.5	29.4	19.9	27.0	27.4
May	25.1	32.5	17.2	25.6	31.1
June	30.5	40.2	54.8	36.0	16.8
July	6.2	8.7	47.0	28.2	5.2
August	3.1	0.0	5.1	9.2	5.7
September	2.0	0.0	6.0	8.5	5.3
October	1.9	0.0	10.1	8.5	4.3
November	2.4	0.0	10.4	7.7	4.4
December	3.2	0.0	11.2	5.6	4.4
1986					
January	3.0	0.0	8.8	7.2	4.4
February	1.7	0.0	0.0	6.3	4.5
March	4.6	0.0	–0.5	5.8	4.9
April	4.7	3.3	4.2	5.4	4.4
May	4.0	2.6	8.6	6.8	4.4
June	4.5	2.8	7.0	6.2	4.3
July	6.8	3.4	8.4	6.8	4.6
August	8.8	6.8	1.3	4.7	6.5
September	7.2	8.8	1.6	4.2	6.9
October	6.1	4.1	2.8	7.1	7.9
November	5.3	5.2	7.3	9.0	7.7
December	4.7	5.4	11.8	7.4	8.3
1987					
January	7.6	6.6	2.9	5.4	8.3
February	6.5	7.0	–0.7	5.0	7.5
March	8.2	11.4	5.9	4.4	4.0
April	3.4	0.0	7.4	4.5	7.1
May	4.2	3.2	5.1	5.9	7.7
June	8.0	7.3	6.6	8.2	8.3
July	10.1	11.0	8.2	7.5	10.6
August	13.7	11.7	–0.2	6.5	12.3
September	11.7	16.2	3.3	8.1	15.4
October	19.5	32.0	8.4	10.0	12.4
November	10.3	8.2	11.4	11.3	8.9
December	3.4	0.7	18.3	10.2	12.3
1988					
January	9.1	9.3	6.7	11.1	13.2
February	10.4	12.1	1.2	9.6	13.3
March	14.7	12.2	6.0	14.5	15.7
April	17.2	18.2	11.9	13.0	16.2
May	15.7	17.3	11.1	14.9	17.2
June	18.0	19.8	17.5	17.5	19.5
July	25.6	19.6	19.2	19.7	22.7
August	27.6	24.3	17.6	26.1	10.6
September	11.7	0.0	16.1	20.6	9.1
October	9.0	1.9	14.4	11.3	9.3
November	5.7	3.7	8.5	10.4	10.2
December	6.8	3.6	26.8	16.2	12.2

Sources: Carta Económica and *Indicadores Coyuntura*.

From Success to Failure

The overall situation did not change very much during the first quarter of 1986, except for an increase in the budget deficit. By the end of March, the freeze became unsustainable. The program underwent its first major change in April, when the government announced the beginning of a "flexibilization" stage. On April 4, there was a devaluation of the exchange rate, accompanied by the introduction of a crawling peg system and increases in wages and prices of public sector enterprises.[8] Despite the flexibilization in policies, the government continued to control prices in the private sector, although increases would be allowed in the future when justified by higher costs.

The introduction of the April package was perceived as an acceptance by the authorities that full price stability was beyond their reach and that they were ready to accept the more modest objective of keeping inflation within reasonable bounds. With this acceptance there was also an acceleration in inflation, which reached 6.8 percent in July. The reasons for this acceleration in inflation remain unclear. One possible interpretation is that this resurgence of inflation was caused by a "wage push in June-July and a passive monetary policy from April onwards" (Machinea and Fanelli 1988, p. 142). Indeed, during this period some labor unions obtained significant wage increases, although it is difficult to assess the extent to which these increases merely "officialized" previous wage increases that were already reflected in actual paid (as opposed to contract) wages. According to official figures (INDEC), hourly industrial wages rose by 26.6 percent between March and August 1986, while inflation, measured by the CPI, was 27.1 percent in the same period.

An alternative, more orthodox interpretation puts the emphasis on the continuous and excessive increases in the money supply and the loosening of the budgetary situation. This was probably a more fundamental problem, which to some extent contributed to the wage increases in later months. There was an increase in the budget deficit starting in the first quarter of 1986 (see Table 3.2). The fiscal tightening of the second quarter of 1986, partly driven by seasonal factors (revenues usually increase at this time of the year), fell short of what was necessary to sustain the stabilization effort on a more permanent basis. At the same time, as shown in Table 3.1, monetary growth (measured by M4) remained very high, at a rate that was clearly incompatible with a monthly rate of inflation at the low one-digit level. The larger expansion in the money supply was especially dangerous at a time when nominal interest rates were rising, and hence the demand for money was falling, particularly because the economy was highly monetized because of the expansions of previous periods.[9]

The July inflation rate brought the program to a critical point; the situation was getting out of control and urgent changes were needed to bring it back on course. A new team took control of the central bank at the end of

Table 3.2 Nonfinancial Public Sector: Expenditures, Revenues, and Deficits
(Cash Basis, Percent of GDP)

	Expenditures (1)[a]	Revenues (2)[b]	Operational Deficit (3)	Primary Deficit (4)	Deficit of the Central Bank (5)[c]	Total Deficit (6)[d]
1984	30.6	22.6	8.0	3.1	2.7	10.7
I	31.1	22.1	9.1	4.3	5.6	14.6
II	32.5	22.9	9.6	4.1	6.0	15.6
III	27.7	21.9	5.8	1.4	3.1	8.9
IV	31.7	24.0	7.7	2.5	2.3	10.0
1985	30.4	26.1	4.3	−1.5	2.4	6.7
I	28.8	21.5	7.3	1.4	4.4	11.7
II	28.7	21.8	6.9	0.9	5.0	11.9
III	29.3	27.6	1.7	−3.6	1.2	2.9
IV	34.7	33.3	1.4	−4.8	0.9	2.3
1986	28.4	26.4	2.0	−1.9	1.9	3.9
I	29.2	27.0	2.2	−1.9	1.7	3.9
II	28.4	27.8	0.6	−4.1	1.3	1.9
III	26.9	26.9	0.0	−2.7	2.2	2.2
IV	29.2	24.1	5.1	0.9	2.1	7.2
1987	29.2	24.1	5.1	1.3	0.9	6.0
I	27.2	24.2	3.0	−0.1	1.8	4.8
II	31.3	25.5	5.8	1.2	1.7	7.5
III	29.1	25.2	3.9	0.7	1.4	5.2
IV	29.5	21.9	7.6	3.2	−1.2	6.4
1988[e]	23.0	18.7	4.3	0.4	1.6	5.9
I	24.3	18.0	6.3	2.0	2.8	9.1
II	22.7	19.3	3.4	−1.3	1.3	4.7
III	20.5	18.4	2.1	−0.2	0.5	2.6
IV	24.2	19.0	5.2	1.0	2.0	7.2

Sources: Ministry of Economy; Central Bank of Argentina (column 5, 1984 I–1987 IV); The World Bank (1988 I–IV).
[a]Includes national and provincial governments, social security, system, and deficits of public enterprises.
[b]Excludes current revenue of public enterprises.
[c]Central Bank estimation.
[d]Column (6) = column (3) + column (5).
[e]Figures are preliminary and exclude provincial government.

August and immediately adopted a very tight stance regarding expansions in M1 (see Table 3.1).[10] This program (the Plan Primavera) did not introduce measures to deal with the fiscal imbalances (since according to the authorities the fiscal situation was fundamentally sound). Instead, it placed its emphasis on the problems created by inertial forces, establishing ceilings (3 percent) for monthly increases in prices in the private and public sectors and setting limits on wage increases.

The Plan Primavera had limited success in controlling inflation, which, despite receding, remained at relatively high levels for the rest of the year. The underlying situation was not conducive to attaining price stability. Despite tight money and higher interest rates (the nominal interest rate almost doubled in August), real wages, industrial production, and consumption remained relatively high, although at somewhat lower levels, and the external situation continued to deteriorate. Although there is disagreement among observers about the fiscal situation in the third quarter, there is no question that the fiscal and monetary accounts greatly deteriorated in the last quarter of 1986.[11] By December, the underlying forces were calling for an increase in inflation, although it remained relatively low, partly as a result of the maintenance of price controls.

Despite this situation, the acceleration in inflation that took place in January 1987 and spread into February was considered a surprise. This increase in inflation was particularly troublesome, since it took place at a time when monetary policy was tight, as measured by the growth of M1 (see Table 3.1) or by the expansion of the monetary base (which contracted in January and February). Once again, the authorities resorted to a price freeze to regain control over the inflationary process. This policy response indicates that the authorities were under the impression that the underlying "fundamentals" were in place and that inflation was accelerating as a result of other forces. This interpretation could have been reinforced by the fact that inflation was increasing at a time when monetary policy was tight.

Three remarks are useful for the interpretation of these events. First, although monetary policy was tight in January and February, it had been very expansionary in the last two months of 1986. Second, an important fiscal imbalance in the last quarter of 1986 remained in place in the first quarter of 1987 and was likely to continue for the rest of the year. The existence of a large fiscal deficit made the stabilization policy less credible and, more importantly, it also threatened the sustainability of tight money, which eventually had to give in. Third, firms could have overreacted in their price adjustments in January and February (once the price controls were partly relaxed) and increased their prices in excess of what was warranted by the "fundamentals." Their apparent goal was to hold a cushion for the eventual imposition of a new rounds of price controls (to which the authorities had already shown some addiction).

Inflation was becoming a major liability for the government, and the problem was particularly acute because 1987 was an election year. Something had to be done to deal with inflation before the situation got completely out of control. The government, responding with a new round of direct controls, introduced a price/exchange rate freeze, which was supplemented by a step adjustment in wages and public sector prices (to compensate for past inflation) followed by a freeze. Once again, no effort was made to provide a long-term solution to the underlying fiscal problem.

The February program, like most of the others, had some transitory gains on the inflation front, with inflation falling substantially in April and May (see Table 3.1).[12] Direct controls can be effective in the short run. However, this time the success was much shorter, because the imbalance in the underlying fundamental variables was complicated by political problems that eventually led to mismanagement of nominal variables.

The main political development was the appointment in April of Carlos Alderete, a union leader, as secretary of labor. This led very quickly to a change in policy, particularly regarding wages, which was announced on May 9. The new measures were the result of an agreement (the Acuerdo del 9 de mayo) between the economic team, led by Juan Sourrouille and Alderete and included increases in wages and public sector prices. Prices in the private sector would continue to be subjected to government controls, but under a more flexible policy.

From that time on, the overall economic situation underwent a steady deterioration. Loose monetary management and large budget deficits led to a new acceleration in inflation, which reached 13 percent in August and 19.5 percent in October, when the government launched a new ministabilization program. Like the previous ones, it had an important component of price controls. The main difference was that this time the authorities introduced measures to provide some longer-term relief to the fiscal imbalance and to initiate a structural adjustment process in the economy. Most of the reduction of the budget deficit was going to take place through increases in taxes; there were basically no attempts to reduce government expenditure of the central government. On the other hand, there was an announcement of a firm commitment to privatize some public state enterprises and to start a process of trade liberalization.

The outcome of this program, not surprisingly, was a transitory reduction in inflation (while the controls were in effect), followed by an increase in inflation once the controls were relaxed (in January 1988). From that time on, inflation continuously accelerated from 15 percent in March and 17 percent in April to almost 30 percent in August.

The Plan Primavera, the last stabilization effort by the economic team that implemented the austral, was a response to these events. Once again the program relied on controls of public and private sector prices and public sector wages. This program allowed more flexibility on nominal variables in the sense that controls consisted of ceilings on monthly increases as opposed to an outright freeze.

The Plan Primavera, as could have been anticipated, suddenly collapsed in early February, propelled by an exchange rate crisis. By January 1989, the new "Summer" Plan would take effect. The black market exchange rate experienced a rapid depreciation and the economy entered the hyperinflation stage. Inflation continues to be major problem in the economy.

Lessons and Policy Implications

The failure of the Austral Plan raises questions regarding the feasibility of the strategy and the soundness of its implementation. As was discussed in the previous section, the overall package in the original plan was consistent and could have worked if the authorities had been persistent in pursuing price stability. The initial success was hindered by a lack of decision to address the fundamental structural problems, the eagerness to move into an expansionary cycle after several years of stagnation, misleading readings of the underlying inflation forces, and unfavorable external developments.

Reasons for the Failure

The fiscal situation at the time of the Austral Plan was very fragile. Nothing was done on government expenditure during a period when most of the increases in government revenues were of a transitory nature. The authorities should have introduced a fiscal reform soon after the implementation of the Austral Plan to sustain the level of government revenues and reduce the distortions of the prevailing tax system. Drastic measures should also have been taken on the expenditure side, particularly on government enterprises. This, however, was not done, and the authorities paid a dear price for this lack of action.[13]

A related problem was the quick recovery of the economy in the fourth quarter of 1985. The Austral Plan was launched while the economy was experiencing a recession. This trend continued in the third quarter but was quickly reversed in the final quarter of the year. Although the reasons for the recovery are still unclear, it did not seem advisable to accommodate an expansionary cycle in the very early stages of a stabilization program. The authorities should have used the available policy instruments to slow down the economy, at least while prices were subjected to controls. Instead, monetary policy was overexpansionary, and although the budget deficit remained low, there was a sharp increase in government expenditure (from 28 percent of GDP in the second quarter to 33 percent of GDP in the fourth quarter).

This expansion of the economy worked against the disinflationary program. Price stability can be fully credible only in an environment of freely determined prices. Price controls can be deceiving since they conceal any underlying inflationary pressures; it is never clear to the agents whether low inflation will continue once the controls are lifted and the exchange rate freeze abandoned. For this reason it was very important to maintain a lid on aggregate demand during the early stages, at least until price controls were removed. In Argentina, the early loosening of demand management preceded the relaxation of price controls; this was a basic mistake and became an major reason for the eventual failure of the program.

It is difficult to assess the extent to which the external situation complicated the stabilization effort. It is clear that the service of the external debt introduces an additional burden to the fiscal adjustment. The external situation was complicated by a significant deterioration in the terms of trade in 1986 and 1987. Although it would be unfair to attribute the failure of the program to the service of the external debt, its burden has certainly complicated the management of government finances and the use of the exchange rate as nominal anchor. A serious future stabilization plan would greatly benefit from adequate foreign financing.

Policy Lessons

Important policy lessons from the Austral Plan can be useful in designing and implementing future heterodox stabilization programs. First, it is clear that a stabilization effort needs to be persistent and comprehensive. In countries where inflation has become a chronic problem and where agents have witnessed the collapse of almost every stabilization attempt, additional efforts are required to build credibility. This process is likely to be lengthy, and the authorities should be ready to maintain fiscal and monetary discipline throughout the transition to low inflation.

Second, the Argentine experience is particularly illuminating regarding the advantages and disadvantages of price controls. They were very effective initially to break the inertial forces as the economy moved from high to low inflation. Indeed, it is unlikely that the rapid reduction in inflation at the beginning of the program could have been achieved in the absence of price controls. Price controls, however, serve a very specific purpose: controlling the inertial aspects of the inflation process. To be effective, they must be used cautiously, on a transitory basis, and should be gradually removed as soon as the authorities perceive that the underlying inertial forces have been contained.

One problem with price controls is that they could send a "wrong" signal about the success of a program. In most cases, price controls are an effective tool to bring down inflation, at least temporarily. Indeed, in Argentina, inflation came down initially each and every time price controls were introduced. Unfortunately, inflation went up each and every time they were removed.[14] Thus, in general, it is very difficult to infer the underlying inflation rate on the basis of the rate of inflation observed during a period when controls are effective. An additional problem is that the short-run effectiveness of controls can lead authorities to use them each time inflation starts to accelerate. This, again, was observed in the recent Argentine experience, where price controls became the primary instrument to control inflation. The repetitive use of controls quickly becomes a tool that works against any stabilization effort. Firms start to engage in "anticipatory" pricing and raise prices above the market clearing level; in that way, be in a "good" position in case the government announces a new freeze. It is for this reason that a price freeze, as an instrument in a stabilization program, should be used only once, and it is most effective when its introduction is not anticipated by the private sector.

Another lesson from the Austral Plan is that tight money cannot be sustained in the presence of a large fiscal imbalance. This, of course, is well known from Sargent and Wallace (1981), and is very clear from the recent Argentine experience. The use of tight money did not have any discernible effect on inflation, and in the few cases in which inflation came down (as in the period August-October 1986), it was mainly because tight money was accompanied by price controls. Notice that the drastic tightening of M1 in August and September 1987 hardly had any impact on the rate of inflation.

Finally, the Austral Plan, despite its failure, provided encouraging evidence for the adoption of heterodox stabilization programs. Inflation fell very sharply initially and remained well below the pre-austral levels for over two years. This reduction in inflation did not produce large increases in unemployment nor a slowdown in economic activity. The major reason for the eventual acceleration in inflation was a lack of persistence in maintaining the fundamentals in place. If they had remained in place throughout the program, it is unlikely that inflation would have returned to pre-austral levels. The heterodox shock could have provided an almost ideal path to permanent price stability; instead, it merely ended up as another lost battle in what has become a permanent war against inflation.

Notes

The views expressed in this paper are my own and do not necessarily reflect the views of the World Bank or its affiliated organizations. I benefited from comments and discussions with Nissan Liviaton and Ernesto Feldman. I am grateful to Jariya Charoenwattana for her valuable research assistance.

1. For a more detailed description of these episodes, see Kiguel and Liviatan (1988) and de Pablo and Martínez (1988).

2. In June 1989, while this paper was being revised, out-of-control inflation in Argentina approached hyperinflation.

3. For a detailed comparison of the two programs, see Blejer and Liviatan (1987). That paper also discusses the similar behavior of macroeconomic variables during the early stages of the stabilization programs.

4. The freeze did not apply to goods with seasonal supplies (mainly meat, fruits, and vegetables), which were instead subject to fixed markups over cost.

5. After that time, capital flows slowed down, mainly because the government imposed additional restrictions on capital movements.

6. Most of the public sector domestic debt was in the form of deposits of the commercial banks into the central bank and other types of "forced"

lending through the banking system. A comprehensive study of these aspects is left for future research.

7. Two facts can be used to question the soundness of these increases in the money supply. First, despite its size, the expansion did not produce any significant reductions in interest rates. Second, in the fourth quarter, the balance of payments turned into deficit after being in surplus for the two previous quarters, thus suggesting that at those interest rates there was not an excess demand for money.

8. For a more detailed discussion of the measures, see de Pablo (1987).

9. This interpretation is consistent with the views of Broda (1987) and *Indicadores de Coyuntura* (1987, various issues).

10. The drastic change in monetary policy adopted at that time was necessary to ensure the consistency of the program. The discrepancies between the economic team (led by Juan Sourrouille) and the central bank authorities (led by Concepción) are well documented in the Argentine press of that period. At the same time, the drastic change in monetary stance in August provides indirect evidence that the mismanagement of money supply was considered, at least at some government levels, as one important force behind the resurgence of inflation.

11. For cyclical reasons, the budget deficit is usually larger in the last quarter of the year. Nevertheless, the increase in the deficit toward the end of 1986 cannot be fully explained by seasonal factors; for one thing, it was much larger than in the last quarter of 1985.

12. There was some reduction in inflation in March as well, but this is not fully relected in the official statistics because of methodological problems.

13. Fiscal measures were introduced in October 1987, including new taxes and changes in the rates of existing ones. This reform, however, came late (it should have been implemented two years earlier) and introduced additional distortions in the economy (i.e., possibly reducing financial intermediation and restricting imports). In addition, the authorities seem to be finally moving in the direction of reducing the size of the public sector.

14. Interestingly enough, there were no widespread shortages in any of these cases. Thus, the acceleration in inflation following the removal of controls cannot be easily linked to the existence of "repressed" inflation due to excess demand pressures.

References

Blejer, Mario, and Nissan Liviatan. 1987. "Stabilization Strategies in Argentina and Israel, 1985–1986." *IMF Staff Papers* 34, no. 3.

Broda, Miguel Angel. 1987. "La política monetaria y fiscal desde el Plan Austral: porque se perdio la oportunidad?," *Anales de la Asociación Argentina de Economía Política* 1, pp. 295–320.

Canavese, Alfredo, and Guido Di Tella. 1988. "Inflation Stabilization or Hyperinflation Avoidance: The Case of the Austral Plan in Argentina, 1985–87." In *Inflation Stabilization: The Experience of Israel, Argentina, Brazil, Bolivia and Mexico*, edited by M. Bruno, G. Di Tella, R. Dornbusch, and Stanley Fischer. Cambridge: MIT Press.

de Pablo, Juan Carlos. 1987. "Transición hacia las urnas, confusión inicial y Plan Austral: Argentina, 1982–87." Mimeo.

de Pablo, Juan Carlos, and Adolfo Martínez. 1988. "Macroeconomic Policies, Crisis and Growth in the Long Run—Argentina Country Study." The World Bank. Mimeo.

Indicadores de Coyuntura. Fundación de Investigaciones Económicas Latinoamericanas, Buenos Aires. Various issues.

Kiguel, Miguel A., and Nissan Liviatan. 1988. "Inflationary Rigidities and Orthodox Stabilization Programs: Lessons from Latin America." *The World Bank Economic Review* 2, no. 3.

Machinea, José Luis, and José M. Fanelli. 1988. "Stopping Hyperinflation: The Case of the Austral Plan in Argentina, 1985–87." In *Inflation Stabilization.*

Sargent, Thomas, and Neil Wallace. 1981. "Some Unpleasant Monetarist Arithmetic." *Federal Reserve Bank of Minneapolis Quarterly Review*, pp. 1–17.

4

Brazil's Inflation and the Cruzado Plan, 1985-1988

Luiz Bresser Pereira

Inflation is chronic in Brazil. During the 1970s, it was about 50 percent a year; in 1979 it went up to 100 percent and stayed at that level for three years. Then, in 1983, it increased to 200 percent, where it remained until 1986, the year the failure of the Cruzado Plan took inflation to a new level of around 600 percent. The so-called Bresser Plan eased the situation somewhat in 1987. So, very high, although relatively stable for given periods, rates of inflation—5, 10, and (in 1988) almost 20 percent a month—characterized the 1980s. This situation prevailed, together with recession due to adjustment efforts, in 1981, 1983, and (to a certain extent) 1987.

The acceleration of inflation in recent years has taken place during the most serious economic crisis in Brazil's industrial history. Income per capita has stagnated since 1980. The investment rate fell from 22/23 in the 1970s to 16/17 percent of GDP in recent years. A structural financial disequilibrium of the public sector, whose basic component is an enormous public external debt, is behind the economic crisis. The acceleration of inflation in Brazil and its present high levels are symptoms of this crisis and an indirect consequence of the fiscal crisis of the Brazilian state.

In this chapter I will discuss inflation in Brazil, particularly what caused it and maintained it at such high levels. There is a brief review of the theory of inertial inflation—a new theoretical paradigm originally developed by a group of Brazilian economists in the early 1980s. Finally, there is a comparison of the two heterodox shocks—the Cruzado Plan and the Bresser Plan—that in 1986 and 1987, respectively, froze prices according to the theory of inertial inflation. Although apparently similar, the two plans were very different in terms of objectives, characteristics, conditions that prevailed when each was introduced, and their outcomes.

Evolution of Inflation Theories

Looking at the monetary figures in the last two decades we see that the money supply increased systematically at less than the rate of inflation and did not provoke either reduction of the interest rate or excess demand. Thus, the monetarist theory about inflation does not help to explain either the acceleration or the maintenance of the inflation level in Brazil. The same applies to a parent explanation based on the public deficit (defined as the operational Public Sector Borrowing Requirements—PSBR); see Table 4.1. In 1983, the public deficit was drastically reduced while inflation soared. The public deficit or, more precisely, the structural financial unbalance of the public sector is the basic cause of the crisis of the Brazilian economy, and it is behind the high level of inflation prevailing in the country. It is, however, a poor direct explanation for inflation in Brazil.

At the beginning of the 1980s, the failure of the old theories to adequately explain inflation in Brazil motivated the development of a new theory. The Latin American structural theory of inflation, developed in the 1950s, was a first step. It stressed the chronic and endogenous character of inflation in Latin American countries, but it could not explain the high rates of inflation in Brazil. Like the Keynesian and the monetarist theories, it explained partially the acceleration of inflation, not its persistent very high levels. In 1963, we have a second important step in the structuralist theory of inflation with Ignácio Rangel's book *A Inflação Brasileira*. Rangel was the first economist to do a comprehensive and compelling analysis of the endogenous character of the money supply. Rangel, whose book was a major criticism of the monetarist theory of inflation, argued that the expansion of the money supply was rather a consequence than a cause of inflation. His structuralist theory of inflation, however, as well as the other theories, were unable to explain the high rates of inflation prevailing in Brazil.

Inertial Inflation

At the beginning of the 1980s, a great intellectual effort took place in Brazil to develop a new paradigm for inflation. The result was the theory of inertial inflation, a neostructuralist theory of inflation based on distributive conflict rather than on expectations, and on the clear separation between the accelerating, maintaining, and validating factors behind inflation.[1]

This separation seems today quite obvious, but it was not obvious a few years ago. Papers and textbooks on inflation written before 1983 contain nothing about it. The previous theories tried to explain the acceleration of inflation. The models always start with the assumptions that prices are stable and the inflation rate is zero; then something happens and inflation starts.

Table 4.1 Inflation and Public Deficit

Year	Inflation (%)	Public Deficit (% GDP)
1978	40.8	—
1979	77.2	8.3
1980	110.2	6.7
1981	95.2	6.0
1982	99.7	7.3
1983	211.0	4.4
1984	223.8	2.7
1985	235.1	4.3
1986	65.0	3.6
1987	415.8	5.5

Sources: FGV (IGP, General Price Index); Central Bank Operational PRSB.

"Let us assume that inflation is zero," the theories say, and then, at a given moment, we have a problem of excess demand, or the money supply increases faster than the national product, or organized labor is able to increase wages above the increase of productivity, or monopolies and oligopolies increase their profit margins, or government decides to devaluate the national currency or correct prices of state-owned enterprises that for some reason lagged behind—and at that moment inflation accelerates.

But in Brazil, at the beginning of the 1980s (and still now), it was necessary to start from another sort of assumption—for instance, that inflation is at the level of 200 percent a year, or at 10 percent a month, or at any other high level. And, from this assumption, we ask what explains this level of inflation and what can change it.

The theory of inertial inflation will explain both what causes and what cures inflation. It is a mistake to think that it is just a theory explaining "the inertial component" of inflation. It is also a theory that tries to explain the accelerating factors of inflation—the supply and demand shocks. These can be endogenous or exogenous factors but they certainly are much more powerful accelerating factors of inflation when inflation is relatively stabilized at high levels.

This does not mean that the theory of inertial inflation applies only to high-inflation economies. You can also distinguish accelerating and maintaining factors of inflation in the United States, for instance, where inflation is about 4 percent a year. You can also relate its causes to distributive conflict. But the rate of inflation is so small that the distinction is not relevant, or is much less relevant.

The idea of distributive conflict is essential to the theory of inertial inflation. Distributive conflict can be considered an alternative proposition to the idea of expectations present in the Keynesian and monetarist theories. This does not mean that inertialists do not take into account expectations. Since political economy—the classical name of our science—is a social science, it deals with people and therefore with expectations. The inertialist theory just asserts that inflation expectations are essentially based on past inflation. The basic assumption is that in the distributive conflict that characterizes capitalist economies, every economic agent—every individual, every firm, every economic and social group—tries permanently to maintain, and if possible to increase, its income share by adjusting its prices.

If inflation is, for instance, at a level of 10 percent a month, every economic agent will increase its prices by 10 percent a month. But they will not do that at the same time. They will do it in turn, one after the other. Let us suppose that there are only three agents in the economy. The first will increase its prices by 10 percent on the first day of the month, the second on the tenth, and the third, on the twentieth, always by 10 percent; and then it is again the turn of the first economic agent to increase its prices by 10 percent. The agents are increasing their prices in turn, because they are passing along cost increases to consumers and because they do not coordinate their actions. Nobody can say who started the process. Inflation is an old and chronic problem in this model economy. Its inertial character, based on distributive conflict, maintains it at a level of 10 percent a month.

It is the same distributive conflict that explains the acceleration of inertial inflation. If one of the three economic agents is able to increase its prices by 12 percent instead of 10 percent—it does not matter if the increase is due to a demand push or cost push accelerating factor—the other two agents will have to do the same to avoid losses, or, in other words, to maintain their income share.

Money Supply and Inflation

Today all these ideas seem quite obvious, but they were not obvious in the early 1980s, when the theory of inertial inflation was being developed. At that time, monetarist economists believed that the only way to control the high rates of inflation in Brazil was to reduce the public deficit and the money supply, thereby cutting public and private aggregate demand. The big recessions of 1981 and 1983 were engineered on this theoretical basis. Because of the recessions and the devaluations of the local currency, the balance of payment was adjusted and big trade surpluses emerged. Actually, as Antonio Barros de Castro and F. E. Pires de Souza (1985) underlined, these surpluses were also a consequence of the huge investments of the 1970s. But, contrary to the orthodox theory, the rate of inflation did not slow down. It doubled in 1983 because of the exchange rate devaluation implemented at the beginning of the year.

Money played a passive role in both the acceleration and maintenance of the inflation level in Brazil during the first half of the 1980s. The increase in the money supply always lagged behind the rate of inflation. The money supply increased to maintain the liquidity of the economic system. If the level of inflation was 10 percent a month, and if the nominal money supply remained constant, the real money supply would decrease almost 10 percent every month, leading the economy to recession.

Public Policy

The necessary consequence of this type of inflation theory is that the conventional inflation-fighting tools—monetarist or Keynesian—will not work when high levels of inertial inflation prevail. The basic policy to control inflation will have to be an administrative one. In these circumstances, two alternatives of administrative policy are left to the policymaker: a gradual one, based on price controls to reduce the rate of inflation, or a price freeze—a heterodox shock. Y. Nakano and I presented this alternative in a paper published in July 1984. We called the freeze "a heroic policy of administrative price controls and the total deindexation of the economy" (1984a, p. 104). A little later, Francisco Lopes, whose contribution to the development of the theory of inertial inflation is essential, formally proposed the freeze and labeled it "heterodox shock" (1984). Almost at the same time, two young and very bright economists, André Lara Resende (1984) and Pérsio Arida (1984), proposed the total indexation of the economy, including the money. That was a very interesting and sophisticated alternative to the heterodox shock, based on the same assumption of a prevailing inertial inflation. Its implementation, however, was complicated and risky.

The new democratic government that took office in March 1985 inherited a high rate of inflation, around 11 percent a month, but it was not ready to impose the total freeze that the inertialists were proposing. Instead, the new finance minister decided on a partial freeze. It was economically absurd. The government froze the prices of the state-owned enterprises and of a few big oligopolistic private enterprises but kept the other prices free. Such a policy was impossible to maintain for long, and it reduced the rate of inflation for only a few months. Fernando Dall'Acqua and I (1985) wrote a paper during the partial freeze, using as a tool the theory of inertial inflation and forecasting that the corrective measures, which would necessarily come when the freeze became unbearable, would lead inflation to a higher level than before. Indeed, in the month before the partial freeze, inflation was 12 percent; it was reduced to around

7 percent during the four months of the freeze (April through July); and in September 1984, on the very day the paper was being published, the government announced for August an inflation rate above 12 percent. It was a significant demonstration of the predicting capacity of the theory.

Finally, on February 28, 1986, when inflation was clearly beginning a new period of acceleration, the government introduced the Cruzado Plan. It was designed by some of the economists who had participated in the development of the theory of inertial inflation (André Lara Resende, Edmar Bacha, Francisco Lopes, and Pérsio Arida). Thus, it was technically very well designed. It profited form the experience of the Austral Plan, which had been based on the same theory and introduced in Argentina a few months before. When the decision was taken, the economic authorities were aware of the size of the public deficit and knew very well the devastating internal consequences of the external deficit; but the impression we have today is that they underestimated those two problems. Besides, the designers of the plan made two mistakes. They unrealistically expected "zero inflation," and they increased real wages 8 percent on the day of the freeze, even though the increase of real wages during 1985 was already pushing inflation upward.

These problems, however, could have been corrected in the following months. The four economists mentioned earlier and Fernão Bracher, then the central bank governor, indeed tried hard to curb the excess demand that began in April 1985. The other economic authorities, to a lesser degree, tried also to introduce the necessary corrections into the plan. But they did not get the needed political support; the president, for example, was entirely bewildered—in effect immobilized—by the economic and political success of the Cruzado Plan. In May, for instance, the finance minister said that he was planning to start freeing up prices, and immediately the president forbade any economic authority even to mention this idea. In July, the strength of the Cruzadinho—a compulsory loan aiming to reduce aggregate demand and curtail the public deficit—was severely limited by a personal decision of the president.

During the first months, the Cruzado Plan was very successful in controlling inflation. But as we now know, it was finally a failure, a big failure, not only because it was unable to eradicate inflation, but also because it provoked deep instabilities and a sharp financial and economic crisis. Before the Cruzado Plan, the Brazilian economy was fully indexed. It was therefore able to get along with high, but almost stable, rates of inflation. With the Cruzado Plan, the indexation system was eliminated. When inflation reappeared in December 1986, the legal interdiction of indexation provoked a financial crisis, accompanied by a record number of insolvencies and bankruptcies in Brazil.

The Cruzado and Bresser Plans

In the middle of this crisis, in April 1987,[2] I was appointed finance minister of Brazil. Inflation, accelerating every month, reached 26 percent in June. On June 12, I was responsible for the second price freeze of the Brazilian economy, the so-called Bresser Plan, which I will call the 1987 Plan. It was again a heterodox shock, based (like the Cruzado Plan) on the theory of inertial inflation. But the 1987 Plan was a very different type of economic policy. It was different in terms of (1) its objectives, (2) its characteristics, (3) the conditions that prevailed when it was introduced, and (4) its outcomes. It is interesting to compare the two plans. Table 4.2 presents the rate of inflation in 1986 and 1987, but it is misleading to base the comparison only on the inflation rate outcomes.

The objective of the Cruzado Plan was to eliminate inflation—to achieve a zero rate of inflation. The statements of the authorities connected with the plan were very clear in this respect. And this was the main reason they were not able to correct the imbalances in relative prices present on the day the freeze took effect. In the case of the 1987 Plan, the objective was only to slow inflation, not to eliminate it, avoiding the clear danger of hyperinflation. We knew very well that imposing an emergency freeze without fixing the exchange rate and without deindexing the economy, in a situation where relative prices were very much out of equilibrium, would never halt inflation. Yoshiaki Nakano and Francisco Lopes, the two economists who, with me, were more directly involved in defining the plan, predicted that inflation would be back to around 10 percent in December 1987.

Actually we had a broader objective. We intended, with the freeze and with a devaluation of the cruzado, to overcome the deep economic and financial crisis that the beleaguered Brazilian economy was facing in the second quarter of 1987. And this objective was basically achieved. There was no intention to "solve definitively" the long-term crisis of the Brazilian economy—a king of fantasy that was very common during the Cruzado Plan; but the objective of overcoming the acute crisis of the moment was essential to the 1987 Plan.

Economic conditions at the beginning of 1986 were very different from those during the second quarter of 1987. In 1986, the process of growth started in 1984 was still going on. GDP increased 8 percent in 1985. The balance of payments was in good shape, the trade surplus was around $1 billion per month, and the current account was balanced. Investments, profits, and wages and salaries were increasing. The only two major disequilibriums in current terms (the external debt is a disequilibrium in stock or structural terms) were the public deficit and the fact that real wages were increasing at a faster rate than productivity, pressing inflation upward.

Table 4.2 Inflation in 1986 and 1987 (Percentages)

Month	1986	1987
January	15.01	16.82
February	17.58	13.94
March	(0.11)	14.40
April	0.78	20.96
May	1.40	23.21
June	1.27	26.06
July	1.19	3.05
August	1.68	6.36
September	1.72	5.68
October	1.90	9.18
November	3.29	12.84
December	7.27	14.14

Source: IBGE (IPC, Consumer Price Index).

In contrast, in April 1987, we were probably in the deepest economic and financial crisis in Brazil had ever experienced. During the week I took office, Celso Furtado, an outstanding Brazilian economist, and Olavo Setubal, a leading banker and politician, said that Brazil had not faced such a crisis since at least 1931. It was not only that inflation was rising out control, but also that wages were down by more than 20 percent since the peak of November 1986;[3] moreover, investment had collapsed, the economy was entering a recession, and small and medium-size firms were collapsing one after the other. Finally, the balance of payments situation was terrible (see Table 4.3). The monthly trade surplus of $1 billion had turned into a deficit, and the international reserves, which were only about $3 billion, tended to disappear, despite the moratorium declared in February on the interests related to long- and medium-term debt owed to private banks. Indeed, on the day I took office, the central bank estimated that, continuing the trend, the Brazilian reserves would be exhausted by August.

So, the basic objective of the 1987 Plan was to reestablish the overall balance of the economy by halting the acceleration of inflation and lowering it somewhat, by stopping the fall of wages, by avoiding a deep recession, by reversing the financial crisis, and by reequilibrating the balance of payments. And all these objectives have been achieved. Wages stopped falling and recovered moderately (see Table 4.6). Retail and (after September) industrial sales increased in a limited but effective way, avoiding recession and a rise in unemployment (see Table 4.4). Aggregate demand was carefully managed to avoid the excess demand problem of the Cruzado Plan and recession. The bankruptcy wave ended. The external current account balanced. Inflation dropped but then began to increase at a rate somewhat higher than expected. In December, instead of an inflation rate of 10 percent, which could be explained by the fact that the exchange rate was not frozen and by the need

Table 4.3 Trade Balance in 1986 and 1987 (Millions of U.S. Dollars)

Month	1986	1987
January	701	(35)
February	628	328
March	1,137	302
April	1,292	502
May	1,340	961
June	1,071	1,430
July	1,010	1,457
August	950	1,429
September	544	1,497
October	(79)	1,193
November	(32)	997
December	(213)	1,108

Source: Finance Ministry of Brazil.

and objective of reestablishing the equilibrium of relative prices (which I followed very explicitly), inflation was at 14 percent. What explains this difference, besides an eventual underestimation of the distortions in relative prices on the day of the freeze, was the wage increases starting in September and the lack of confidence in the government's determination to cut the public deficit.

Comparing the Two Plans

The characteristics of the 1987 Plan were very different from the Cruzado Plan. First, the 1987 Plan was an emergency plan and the Cruzado Plan was not. Second, the Cruzado Plan was introduced with a monetary reform, but the 1987 Plan, given its more modest objectives, was not. Third, the Cruzado Plan was based on the total deindexation of the economy, whereas the 1987 Plan maintained and complete the existing indexation system, since inflation was supposed to resume and since a priority was given to reestablish the overall equilibrium of the economy—an equilibrium to which the indexation system, in an inflationary situation, is essential. Fourth, given the very low level of international reserves, the 1987 Plan did not freeze the exchange rate. On the contrary, a real devaluation of the exchange rate was ensured to reestablish the equilibrium of the balance of payments. Fifth, the Cruzado Plan did not set a termination date for the freeze, but the 1987 Plan defined and limited it to three months. Finally, although for many people the Cruzado Plan seemed to be "the complete and final heterodox response to orthodox economic policy," it was very clear to us that the 1987 Plan was only an emergency measure, given inertial inflation and a financial crisis, and that we would have to return immediately after the freeze to the conventional fiscal and monetary policies—which I do not agree to indiscriminately calling "orthodox"—to ensure the macroeconomic equilibrium of the economy.

Table 4.4 Industrial Production in 1986 and 1987 (Index: January 1986 = 100)

Month	1986	1987
January	100.0	100.0
February	94.3	99.9
March	96.2	103.7
April	100.4	102.7
May	104.8	103.8
June	111.4	106.4
July	120.9	105.9
August	119.9	106.8
September	126.4	112.0
October	132.0	114.7
November	116.7	106.8
December	104.9	94.4

Source: FIBGE (Transformation Industry).

The decision to not undertake the deindexation of the economy surprised many economists because, during the Cruzado Plan, it was common to hear the argument that "the cause of inertial inflation is the indexation of the economy." How, then, would it be possible to eliminate or control inertial inflation without deindexing the economy? The answer to this question is simple. The maintaining factor of inertial inflation is indeed the capacity of each economic agent to deal with cost increases by raising prices. Formal or informal indexation is the mechanism that guarantees this transmission process. But this does not mean that the cause of high rates of inflation is indexation. If inflation is monthly near zero, indexation will maintain inflation at that level; if inflation is about 10 or 20 percent a month, indexation will also maintain it at this level. So, if prices are frozen and inflation is immediately reduced to a level near zero, the fact that formal indexation is not eliminated will not accelerate inflation again; it will maintain inflation at its new level around zero.

Certainly the formal indexation represents a continuous danger, because prices become rigid downward, and so every supply or demand shock will provoke an automatic acceleration of inflation, since compensating reductions in other prices—due to productivity increase, for instance—will be much more difficult to realize. But, because the 1987 Plan was an emergency measure (we knew that the need to reequilibrate relative prices after the shock would cause inflation to resume), we decided not to eliminate formal indexation.

Attempting to Reestablish Equilibrium

It is important at the time the 1987 Plan was implemented to reestablish the overall equilibrium of the economy, ensuring a reasonable rate of profit in the different sectors, than to artificially curb inflation for a certain period at the cost of profound economic distortions. When I decided for the freeze, I knew that relative prices were fully unbalanced, that some prices were very low and others very high, and that some business firms were suffering big losses and others realizing big profits. I assigned priority to reestablishing the equilibrium of the economy to achieve full control of inflation.

I was keenly aware of the imbalances in relative prices that prevailed during the Cruzado Plan and the deep crisis that followed its failure. The financial crisis was particularly serious. The number of insolvencies and bankruptcies in the first semester of 1987 was unparalleled in the history of Brazil (see Table 4.5). They were essentially a consequence of the acceleration of inflation due to the elimination of the whole indexation system. It was essential not to repeat the same mistake. Ten days after the Cruzado Plan took effect, I wrote a column in *Folha de São Paulo* saying that if government did not succeed in balancing relative prices, if it insisted on keeping inflation at zero at the cost of maintaining the distortions in relative prices, the plan would fail (Bresser Pereira 1986). There is no doubt today that, besides excess demand, the other cause of the failure of the Cruzado Plan was the fact that relative prices were allowed to remain out of equilibrium. Actually the distortion of relative prices increased, not decreased, in 1986.

Thus, after the freeze, priority was given to reestablishing the equilibrium of relative prices. The distortions on June 12, 1987, were much greater than on February 28, 1986. So, the corrections would have to be sizable. And these corrections would certainly accelerate inflation, because they would be only upward. For sure, on the day of the freeze, some prices were "behind" and others "ahead." Thus, the correct policy would have been to increase some prices and to decrease others. But this was practically, impossible because there is no way to identify prices above the equilibrium level. Businesspeople never acknowledge that their prices are high. They protest strongly only when their prices are low, below the equilibrium level. Therefore, it was very clear that inflation would accelerate again after the freeze. Our hope was that it would level off, around December, at approximately 10 percent. This would be the cost of reequilibrating relative prices—a cost that had to be paid.

The same kind of reasoning—the priority to reequilibrate relative prices—was behind the decision to not freeze the exchange rate. The minidevaluation on the day of the freeze and the maintenance of the minidevaluations during the following days were certainly accelerating factors of inflation. But we had no other alternative, given the low level of Brazilian reserves. Whereas they were around $7.1 billion on the day the Cruzado Plan began, they were near $3 billion—and with a downward trend—in June 1987. We considered slowing down the daily minidevaluations of the cruzado, but even this was impossible. When I insisted on slowing down the

Table 4.5 Insolvencies and Bankruptcies in 1986 and 1987 (in São Paulo)

Month	1986	1987
January	204	169
February	197	194
March	195	262
April	225	338
May	214	451
June	136	538
July	176	540
August	176	397
September	138	331
October	179	309
November	144	302
December	146	311

Source: Associação Comercial de São Paulo (filed insolvencies and bankruptcies).

minidevaluations, the external sector director of the central bank, a very competent economist, answered that this was too dangerous; he would do that only if he was authorized to start selling the small Brazilian gold reserves. At that point I gave up. I agreed to maintain the minidevaluations according to the effective rate of inflation, and not according to a projected lower rate of inflation.

Temporarily Maintaining Macroeconomic Balance

Besides trying to reestablish the microeconomic balance of the economy through the correction of relative prices, we were also concerned with the macroeconomic equilibrium of the economy. In the design and administration of the 1987 Plan, we always kept in mind the Cruzado Plan's failure to control aggregate demand. We were determined not to repeat the same mistake.

Wage policy was essential in this respect. One of the basic reasons for the failure of the Cruzado Plan was the real wage increase on the day of the freeze and in the following months. So we were very careful about wage policy, so careful that we were misunderstood. Our objective was to halt the sharp decrease of real wages that had occurred during the preceding five months and to partially recover the losses. Wages had been reduced more than 20 percent from the peak of November 1987. Since this peak had proved to be inconsistent with macroeconomic equilibrium, we aimed at a recuperation of about 10 percent. To achieve this objective, given that (1) on June 30 wage earners would receive the last *gatilho* (trigger) 20 percent,[4] (2) in June inflation would go down from around 25 percent to less than 5 percent in July (actually inflation in June was 26 percent and in July 3 percent), and (3) workers tend to spend the wages received at the end of each month during the next month, we decided that the June inflation rate should not be considered in the new wage indexation system. We were sure that real wages would stop decreasing and start increasing. And indeed this happened, as all series of data about real wages in Brazil, including the one collected by SEADE/DIEESE, demonstrated later (see Table 4.6). At that moment, however, I could support my arguments only theoretically. And those arguments were not always understood by the workers, by journalists, by federal judges, and by many economists. After all, they are all wage or salary earners. Consequently, workers protested against "wage compression" (*arrocho salarial*) and pressed for a recuperation of real wages, confusing the losses they had suffered between November 1986 and June 1987 with the 1987 Plan. This workers' reaction was one of the causes behind the acceleration of inflation to a level above the one expected when the 1987 Plan was defined.

The workers' pressure to increase real wages, however, was not the only reason why inflation in December was 14 instead of the forecasted 10 percent. The inability of the government to control the wages and salaries of public officials and employees of state-owned enterprises was certainly a cause of this disparity. After the raise that the employees of the Banco do Brasil received in September, the private sector followed the lead, giving generous nominal wage increases to their workers in October and November. It became clear then that populism is not a fault only of politicians. Businesspeople also are ready to raise nominal wages if they are able to pass on the increase in costs to consumers.

There is, however, another major reason for the acceleration of inflation to a level above that forecasted. Already in August, and certainly in September, the private sector lost confidence when the government decided to restrict the public deficit. The basic strategy of the Macroeconomic Control Plan, published in July to overcome the continuing crisis of the Brazilian economy—a crisis that had kept the country's per capita income stagnated since 1980—was to recuperate the savings capacity of the state and to fight the public deficit. According to the inertial theory of inflation, the relation between public deficit and inflation tends to be indirect. It is direct only when inflation produces excess demand. However, businesspeople, and the general public, influenced by conventional theories of inflation, see a direct relationship between public deficit and inflation. So, when in August the press started saying that the government would not be able to cut public deficit to the 3 percent of GDP defined in the Macroeconomic Control Plan, businesspeople lost confidence in economic policy and began to increase their prices more than was strictly necessary, that is, began to increase their profit margins. The consequence was the acceleration of inflation. In September, the huge wage increase given to the employees of the Banco do Brasil and, in October, to the military and public functionaries confirmed the predictions that the public deficit target would not be attained. It was in October that I

Table 4.6 Average Real Wages in 1986 and 1987 (Index: 100 in January 1986)

Month	1986	1987
January	100.0	94.3
February	92.9	89.2
March	98.8	85.9
April	106.4	79.8
May	105.6	74.6
June	96.2	69.5
July	111.0	68.5
August	111.5	68.9
September	103.2	69.3
October	109.9	71.9
November	108.2	71.6
December	95.2	74.3

Source: SEADE/DIEESE.

decided to leave the government, a decision I was finally able to act on in December.

Conclusion and Recommendations

The basic factor behind the structural crisis that characterized the Brazilian economy in the 1980s was the public sector's financial disequilibrium. The Brazilian state was virtually broken, bankrupted. The continuing fiscal crisis of the state has not only a "flow" aspect—the public deficit, the sharp decrease of the country's savings ability—but also a "stock" character: the public internal and, particularly, public external debt. More than 80 percent of the huge Brazilian external debt is public. Only the interest on this part of the debt represents 2.3 percent of GDP.

The origins of this structural disequilibrium of the public finances are to be found (1) in the "growth cum debt" policy of the 1970s, (2) in the increase of the international interest rate at the end of the 1970s, (3) in the pressure to devaluate the local currency in order to face the balance of payment problems, (4) in the subsidies and incentives to the private sector defined in the 1970s (when public finances were still healthy) and maintained through the 1980s (which means that the burden of the adjustment process fell almost entirely on the public sector), (5) in the practice of holding down the prices of state-owned enterprises in an attempt to control inflation, and (6) in the decrease of the fiscal burden due to the acceleration of inflation. The basic, although indirect, cause of the acceleration of inflation since the end of the 1970s is the fiscal crisis of the state, characterized primarily by the external public debt.

Per capita income has been practically stagnated in Brazil since 1980; per capita income in Latin America in 1987 was at the same level as in 1976. The basic common fact behind this structural crisis is the external debt transformed into a fiscal crisis. Inflation accelerated in Brazil whenever it was necessary to devaluate the currency, or, more generally, when, after a period of holding down artificially some prices (particularly public prices), "Corrective inflation"—the correction of relative prices—became unavoidable. In other words, inflation accelerated in Brazil whenever the external debt and the fiscal crisis of the state required changes or corrections of relative prices.

When I decided on the emergency price shock of June 12, I was convinced that a new shock would probably be needed later to effectively control inflation. In October this need became evident. But it was also very clear to me that a new price shock would be meaningless—in fact, irresponsible—if it was not accompanied by two other "shocks" an external debt shock and a fiscal shock.

In other words, to control inertial inflation, a price shock is still the best alternative. But it will fail if, at the same time, the basic causes behind the acceleration of inflation are not faced. In Brazil these causes are structural—they have a stock character: the financial disequilibrium of the state, whose basic component is the public external debt. So, heroic solutions, radical solutions, solutions that involve political will and courage are necessary.

It is not enough to fight the public deficit by curtailing current state expenditures and firing idle public employees, as many conventional (and conservative) analyses suggest every day in the Brazilian press. Brazil must be able, dramatically and radically, to (1) reduce its external debt, profiting from the existence of a discount in the secondary markets and using its capacity to make unilateral decisions, (2) increase the net fiscal burden, by increasing taxes and eliminating subsidies and incentives, and (3) reduce current expenditures. Otherwise, Brazil will not be able to eliminate inflation and economic stagnation.[5] Brazil faces today the most serious economic crisis of its industrial history—a structural crisis based on an external debt that cannot be devaluated by inflation. Never before in the last hundred years has per capita income remained stagnant for so long. There is little hope that this crisis will be solved by the market, according to the dynamics of the economic cycle. That is why heroic economic measures are necessary, measures that only a strong leader—a person with vision and courage—is able to take.

But, to enact a new price shock and end inflation, and at the same time reduce dramatically the external debt and the public deficit, a third element is necessary: a social pact. I have always been very skeptical about a social pact in Brazil, because first you need a political pact—a broader agreement between the main political forces in the country regarding, besides wages, social reforms. In Spain, for instance, the workers agreed to sign a social pact limiting their wage increases only after a political pact was defined and they obtained the guarantee of minimum social reforms. In any case, it is quite clear today that without a social pact in Brazil, it will be impossible to control inflation. When the Cruzado Plan was decided, I observed that a kind of social pact was implicit, given the enormous popular support for the plan. But an implicit social pact is not enough; an explicit one is necessary. The Cruzado Plan failed in large measure because there was not an explicit social pact, and workers were able to increase their nominal and real wages. In the 1987 Plan, workers were able to increase only nominal wages, but this was a basic cause of the acceleration of inflation, since only real wages did not increase after October because inflation followed, or at least accelerated simultaneously with, the increase of nominal wages.

The 1986 Cruzado Plan and the 1987 Plan, like the Argentine 1985 Austral Plan, were not able to control inflation, whereas the 1985 price shock in Israel was successful. This happened because Israel did not have an external debt like Brazil or Argentina and because it was able to control the public deficit in a much more effective way. But a third basic reason why the heterodox shock succeeded in Israel was the political and social pact the Israelis were able to secure.

In my last week as finance minister, I had a very interesting conversation with Shimon Peres, who was visiting Brazil—a conversation that strengthened my decision to resign. He was prime minister of Israel at the moment of the shock, when inflation was about 1,000 percent a year. In this position he personally—not as finance minister—took the responsibility of securing a social or political pact, a pact involving the workers, the businesspeople, and the government. Each group would have to make a sacrifice. The workers accepted a wage decrease, the businesspeople a price control and income policy, and the government a reduction of the public deficit. The negotiations inside the government, among the ministers, were very difficult. After twenty-nine hours of discussions, with the prime minister present, the budget was finally reduced as necessary. My decision to resign was strengthened at that moment, because it was then very clear to me that a similar social and political pact in Brazil would be impossible with President José Sarney as head of state. I was aware that Israel, in contrast with Brazil or Argentina, counted on external help. But it was clear in the case of Israel that their success in controlling inflation was not only the result of a competent combination of heterodox and conventional economic policies, but also the outcome of effective political leadership.

Notes

1. A full statement of this theory and of its development, including the respective bibliography, can be found in the book I coauthored with Yoshiaki

Nakano, *The Theory of Inertial Inflation* (Boulder, Colo.: Lynne Rienner Publishers, 1987). See also Werner Baer (1987). Three books published in Brazil include the more important papers on the theory of inertial inflation: Bresser Pereira and Nakano (1984b), Lopes (1986), and Arida (1986).

2. I was finance minister of Brazil between April 29 and December 20, 1987.

3. Real wages increased systematically during 1985 and continued to rise until November 1986, when they started falling. In July 1987, they partially recovered their previous level.

4. During the Cruzado Plan, wages were indexed according to a trigger system. They were increased whenever inflation reached an accumulated rate of 20 percent.

5. A very interesting analysis of the relation between the public deficit, the external debt, and the acceleration of inflation in Brazil was made by Eliana Cardoso (1988). According to her view, inflation accelerated in Brazil because of the switch from external to internal financing of the public deficit. The consequence was an increase in real interest rates, which triggered the acceleration of inflation. Thus, the fiscal disequilibrium can be solved only through taxation on capital and reduction of the external debt. Her analysis is consistent with the theory of inertial inflation. It should, however, pay more attention to the role of corrective inflation—particularly to the exchange rate devaluations—in explaining the acceleration of inflation in Brazil since 1979.

References

Arida, Pérsio. 1984. "Economic Stabilization in Brazil." Pontifícia Universidade Católica do Rio de Janeiro, December. Mimeo.

———. 1986. "Inflação zero: Brazil, Argentina, Israel. Rio de Janeiro: Paz e Terra.

Baer, Werner. 1987. "The Resurgence of Inflation in Brazil, 1973–86." *World Development* 15, no. 8 (August).

Bresser Pereira, Luiz. 1986. "A inflação é um fenomeno real." *Folha de São Paulo*, March 11.

Bresser Pereira, Luiz, and Fernando M. Dall'Acqua. 1985. "Congelamento setorial de preços e inflação corretiva." *Economia em Perspectiva* (bulletin of the Conselho Regional de Economia de São Paulo), no. 17 (September).

Bresser Pereira, Luiz, and Yoshiaki Nakano. 1984a. "Política adminsitrativa de controle da inflação." *Revista de Economia Política* 4, no. 3 (July.) Republished in Bresser Pereira and Nakano, 1984b, 1987.

———. 1984b. *Inflação e recessão*. São Paulo: Brasiliense.

———. 1987. "Adminnstrative Policy: Gradualism or Shock." In *The Theory of Inertial Inflation*, edited by L. Bresser Pereira and Y. Nakano. Boulder, Colo.: Lynne Rienner Publishers.

Cardoso, Eliana. 1988. "O processo inflacionário do Brasil e suas relaçoes com o deficit e a dívida do setor público." *Revista de Economia Política* 8, no. 2 (April).

Castro, A. Barros de, and F. E. Pires de Souza. 1985. *A economia brasileira em marcha forçada*. Rio de Janeiro: Paz e Terra.

Lara Resende, André. 1984. "A moeda indexada: uma proposta para eliminar a inflação inertial." *Gazeta Mercantil* (São Paulo), September 26, 27, 28.

Lara Resende, André, and Pérsio Arida. 1984. "Inertial Inflation and Monetary Reform in Brazil." Pontifícia Universidade Católica do Rio de Janerio. Presented at a seminar sponsored by the Institute of International Economics, Washington, D.C., December 1984. Mimeo. Published in Arida, 1986.

Lopes, Francisco Lafayete. 1984. "Só um choque heterodoxo poderá derrubar a inflação." *Economia e Perspectiva* (August). Republished in Lopes, 1986.

————. 1986. *O choque heterodoxo*. Rio de Janeiro: Editora Campus.

5

From the "New Republic" to the Moratorium: Economic Policymaking in Brazil, 1985-1987

Hugo Presgrave de A. Faria

The failed Brazilian Cruzado Plan of February 1986 was fundamentally a shock treatment aimed at eliminating hyperinflationary threats and simultaneously jolting the economy into a sustained growth path. The failure of the Brazilian effort, however, carries many lessons for macroeconomic crisis management. In a comparative perspective, the real-life experiences of Argentina, Brazil, and Israel with heterodox policy shocks illustrate a wide array of policy options and their likely effects. This chapter will stress the specific context of the Brazilian experience, specifically the important role of a domestic political environment conditioned by the return to civilian rule, and the external constraints of carrying the developing world's largest foreign debt.

The international debt crisis, unveiled by the near crash of the Mexican economy in 1982, has proven far more resilient than the short-term liquidity crunch that international bankers and finance ministers of developing nations insisted on characterizing it as at the outset. The complex and deeply rooted causes of the collapse of most of the developing world's external accounts have not been successfully wished away by bottom-line commercial bankers, quick-fix finance ministers, or learned technocrats.

The February 20, 1987, Brazilian debt-service moratorium on the country's more than $68 billion owed to private commercial banks helped to aggravate the dangerous flaw that has plagued the seemingly endless debate over the debt crisis. In international financial circles, the focus of attention has, until quite recently, consistently been on the impact of the crisis on the international financial system, with little notice—beyond obligatory lip-service—taken of the devastating impact of the crisis on developing countries' domestic economies. Conversely, in the economic press of developing nations, the international dimension of the crisis is routinely presented in clearly adversarial terms and fails to attract serious attention. Coverage remains limited to general, albeit domestically persuasive, condemnations of the existing international financial order and of unjustifiable attempts by the representatives of this system to interfere in the sovereign affairs of the indebted nations.

By focusing on the rise and fall of Brazil's *Plano Cruzado* from an integrated perspective of domestic political-economic developments and the external financing constraints, the case brings out a more comprehensive picture of the choices faced by decisionmakers in Brazil, as well as the responses of the major international actors. The picture that emerges from this approach is one that allows analysts to identify patterns and factors useful in addressing Brazil's economic morass as well as the far-from-resolved international debt crisis.

The Political-Economic Context of the "New Republic"

The Coup of 1964

On April 1, 1964, the military overthrew the government of President João Goulart.[1] The military intervened in response to the worsening economic conditions and the increasingly radical political rhetoric of Goulart. Disillusionment prevailed because the economy had been in decline since 1962, after the successes of the 1954–1960 period. In fact, it was time for the country to pay the bill for the expansion of the period from the late 1940s, when the economy picked up and had yet to let down, except for the minor recession of the mid-1950s.

Populism had been the rule of thumb of Brazilian politics since the 1930s. The *Estado Novo*, established in 1937 by President Getúlio Vargas, was in essence a blend of fascist corporativism and populism. The developments of 1945 to 1964—when the rudimentary foundations of a mass society were cast—turned around an uneasy alliance of conflicting progressive and reactionary tendencies mediated by populist leaders.

This moderating role of the populist governments consisted of various contradictory elements. On the one hand, the state took an active role in the economy, promoting infrastructure works and setting up the first state enterprises. On the other hand, the productive sector remained essentially private, and the bourgeoisie became increasingly internationally oriented in spite of the socializing-nationalistic rhetoric (Jaguaribe 1985, pp. 16–17).

The presidency of Juscelino Kubitschek fully capitalized on the populist potential. The growth of the economy in the second half of the 1950s (Table 5.1 provides economic growth data for the 1955–1960 period) and the construction of Brasília attest to Kubitschek's relative success in growing "fifty years in five." The price of this rapid growth was a substantial foreign debt—which would mature almost entirely during the Goulart presidency— allied with a tremendous public deficit as public spending rose steadily to 18

Table 5.1 Annual Change by Sector, 1955–1960 (Percentages)

Year	1955	1956	1957	1958	1959	1960	1954–1960 avg.
Agriculture	7.7	–1.8	7.7	2.0	5.3	3.5	4.3
Industry[a]	10.6	6.9	5.6	16.4	12.9	10.6	13.6
Transportation	4.7	3.4	6.0	5.9	6.8	16.1	8.1
Wholesale & retail	5.0	–0.5	12.3	6.8	9.2	4.7	7.2
Other services (incl. banking)	3.0	3.0	3.1	3.0	3.0	3.0	3.3
Public services (incl. defense)	2.5	2.3	2.5	2.4	2.4	2.4	2.6
Total GDP	6.8	1.9	6.9	6.6	7.3	6.3	6.9
Population	—	—	—	—	—	—	3.2

Source: Compiled from United Nations; *Yearbook of National Account Statistics*, 1957, 1958, 1961, 1962.
[a]Industry includes mining, manufacturing, construction, and utilities.

percent of GDP while revenues totaled only 9 percent of GDP (Jaguaribe 1985, p. 21). Jânio Quadros, Kubitschek's successor, lacked the power and will to enact major changes and suddenly resigned in 1961, allowing Vice-President João Goulart to become president.

In 1961/62 the up-to-then impressive economic performance took a dramatic change for the worse, along with the increased conflict and polarization of the political realm. From this perspective, the coup of 1964 was the military's response to the fears of the elite and the middle classes, aroused by President Goulart's provocative rhetoric in addressing the economic crisis.

The military took over with a joint political and economic mission. For one, it was to be an impartial, honest, and efficient administrator of the national interest in economic development. On the other hand, it was to suppress subversion. When the military came to power, it set out to clean up the political arena itself—it controlled the federal level and also a few of the state governments where it had intervened. Economic policymaking, however, was entrusted to a team of respected technocrats, who would approach the economic morass with businesslike no-nonsense efficiency.

The economic team of Otávio Gouvêa de Bulhões and Roberto Campos as finance and planning ministers, respectively, carried out an austerity program aimed at balancing both the federal budget and the balance of payments, while forcefully attacking the number one public enemy at the time: inflation. Popular participation in the initial period of military rule, allied to the sincere moderate convictions of Castelo Branco, plus the prevailing opinion that the intervention was a routine cleanup maneuver, allowed for checks on economic policymaking.

In addition, the fact that the military by and large saw itself as temporarily in power and that the government derived most of its early legitimacy from this transience, made it impossible for the hard-liners within the armed forces to move against the entire constellation of "subversives." Starting with the elections of 1965—the results of which displeased the military considerably—voices within the military began to advocate a tougher line with dissenters. These hard-liners, however, would have to wait until 1967 to make their moves.

The pressures on the economic team of Bulhões and Campos for a drastic shift away from the stringent adjustment policies had been mounting since the inception of those policies in 1964. The government was happy to proclaim the decline in inflation from the (then) historic high of 86.9 percent in 1964 to the relatively low level of 24.3 percent by 1967 as evidence of both military efficiency and the end of the lean years.

The intervening years had witnessed a severe recession; this economic medicine caused considerable hardship and began to affect the entrepreneurs who originally welcomed the military as the savior of capitalism. The military's support base began to erode and the pressures for a new economic outlook began to mount. Real growth came to a halt from 1963 to 1967, and per capita income fell below the 1962 level. As the military stayed on, the power structure made it easy for those being hurt by economic policy to point a finger at the military; for the first time, the military's image was being affected and so was its unity. It became untenable for the military to continue the adjustment programs without unprecedented repression. The alternative was a rapid change in economic policy that would at least benefit the industrial elites and allow for the fulfillment of some of the middle class's ambitions.

By 1967, with the new fiscal solidity of the nation, it seemed that the traditional role of military intervention had been fulfilled. In fact, the time seemed to correspond to the historic moment when the military, after a "moderating intervention," would return the government to civilian hands as they had done in 1930, 1945, 1954, and 1955 (Stepan 1973, p. 58). However, the hard-line led by General Costa e Silva emerged victorious after a protracted struggle within the military, and with the enactment in late 1968 of the *Ato Institucional* number 5—a decree granting the executive vast extraordinary powers for an indefinite period—the hard-liners consolidated their power (Conceição Tavares and Assis 1985, p. 29).

The military also recognized that if they were to remain in power for a longer period of time than what tradition dictated, they would need allies and visible successes to validate their claim to power. In turning on the engines of growth to both oblige their civilian allies and achieve economic legitimization, they resorted to Delfim Netto, an economics professor from São Paulo. The period that ensued is known as the Brazilian economic "miracle."

The electoral process was never completely abandoned and functioned as the third variable in the military's legitimacy formula—along with economic growth and anticommunism. The results of the elections of 1965 convinced the military that a major overhauling of the party system was needed so that "elections no longer returned the wrong groups to power" (Baretta and Markoff 1985, p. 13). This "clean democracy" was inaugurated with the abolition of all the existing parties, student organizations, and labor unions (Wynia 1984, p. 217). The government then proceeded to set up two parties: one, called the Aliança Renovadora Nacional (ARENA), to harbor all the government supporters, and the other, called the Movimento Democrático Brasileiro (PMDB), to encompass all the accepted moderate opposition. These two parties first met in the 1966 federal elections, when ARENA handily defeated the persecuted and unorganized opposition.[2]

When the hard-liners led by Costa e Silva came to power in 1967, they were unhappy with the extent of military control of government, the economy, and the political scene. This led to an increased authoritarianism of the military, exemplified by the many closings of the congress and state assemblies (Schmitter 1973, p. 222); by the establishing of the mechanism of *Decurso de Prazo*, whereby legislation not voted upon by the congress automatically became law after forty-five days; and by the *cassações,* or stripping of political rights of the most prominent opposition politicians and complemented by the torturing of political prisoners.

By 1967, the influence of the graduates of the Superior War College (ESG) and the officers of the intelligence branch of the army—the Serviço Nacional de Informações (SNI)—was very significant. The connection between the two is clear. The new emphasis on national security necessitated a wealth of information, and the SNI was supposed to fulfill this role. The power of the SNI was, and still is, extremely great, as the cabinet rank of its director demonstrates. Moreover, two of the five presidents general (Emílio Garrastazu Medici and João Batista de Figueiredo) came to power via the SNI directorship.

The "Miracle" Years

The political and economic changes of 1967 marked the beginning of the most phenomenal period of economic growth in Brazilian history. With a growth rate of 11.3 percent a year for seven years, accompanied by a decline in inflation from over 24 percent in 1967 down to around 16 percent by 1973, this six-year period does have a miraculous aura about it. (Table 5.2 provides the figures for GDP growth and inflation.)

It is essential, however, to look at the period from 1967 to 1973 in the context of the extreme recession that preceded the takeoff. The fifteen years leading up to the "miracle" period can be divided into three five-year periods. In the first (1951–1956) GDP grew 35.4 percent; in the second, it grew yet

Table 5.2 Inflation and GDP Growth Rates, 1967–1986 (Percentages)

Year	Inflation	GDP Growth
1967	24.3	4.8
1968	25.4	9.0
1969	20.2	9.9
1970	19.2	8.8
1971	19.8	13.3
1972	15.5	11.7
1973	15.7	13.9
1974	34.5	9.7
1975	29.4	5.4
1976	46.3	9.7
1977	38.8	5.7
1978	40.8	5.0
1979	77.2	6.4
1980	110.2	7.2
1981	95.2	−1.6
1982	99.7	0.9
1983	211.0	−3.2
1984	223.8	4.5
1985	235.1	8.6
1986	60.0 (est.)	8.3

Source: Compiled from United Nations, *Yearbook of National Account Statistics*, and F.G.V. *Conjuntura Econômica*, various issues; estimates, Brazilian American Chamber of Commerce, *Bulletin*, April 1, 1987.

faster at 46.8 percent; but in the third, the five years immediately before the "miracle," the five-year growth rate fell to 18.3 percent (1962–1967).[3]

Internationally, the economy was booming, and recovery in the developed countries demanded Brazilian exports. More importantly, the developed economies were peculiarly liquid at the time. This meant that from 1969 to 1974 Brazil could borrow on international markets to finance its trade deficit.

Two trends are noticeable throughout the "miracle" years. First is the marked trend towards regressive income distribution. Second is the increasing foreign debt. During the 1968–1973 period, foreign capital flows played a key role in steadying the balance of payments. In 1971, the interest rate on foreign loans obtained through local commercial or investment banks was up to 11.5 percent below the rate on loans using national resources (von Doellinger et al. 1974, p. 152).

The effects of this rapid accumulation of foreign debt on Brazil's international accounts are summarized in Tables 5.3 and 5.4. The change in the composition of the debt toward an ever-increasing reliance on less politicized, yet more expensive, commercial loans is clearly evident from the data.

The overfinancing of the current-account deficit raises various questions as to the cost and reasons for such a policy. The official line on the cost of

Table 5.3 External Accounts, 1968–1974 (Millions of U.S. Dollars)

Year	Exports FOB	Imports FOB	Net Non-Factor Services	Factor Services	Gross Loans	Foreign Reserves	Total Debt
1968	1,881	1,855	193	197	963	257	3,820
1969	2,311	1,993	235	184	1,239	656	4,403
1970	2,739	2,507	328	232	1,825	1,187	5,296
1971	2,904	3,245	405	259	2,519	1,746	6,622
1972	3,991	4,325	503	357	4,812	4,183	9,521
1973	6,199	6,192	842	372	4,850	6,417	12,572
1974	7,968	12,531	1,176	500	6,504	5,252	17,166

Source: Data adapted from tables in Pedro Malan and Regis Bonelli, "The Brazilian Economy in the Seventies: Old and New Developments," p. 38, and Edmar Bacha, "Issues and Evidence on Recent Brazilian Economic Growth," p. 63, *World Development* 5, nos. 1/2, (1977). Author's calculations.

Table 5.4 Composition of Foreign Debt, 1968–1974
(Millions of U.S. Dollars, Year-End Balances)

Year	Total Debt	International Organizations	% of Total[a]	Supplier's Credits	% of Total	Commercial	% of Total	Other[b]	% of Total
1968	3,820	1,383	36.2	383	10.0	1,083	28.4	971	25.4
1969	4,403	1,473	33.5	447	10.2	1,605	36.5	878	19.9
1970	5,296	1,703	32.2	611	11.5	2,285	43.1	697	13.2
1971	6,622	1,979	29.9	845	12.8	3,193	48.2	605	9.1
1972	9,521	2,266	23.8	1,136	11.9	5,588	58.7	531	5.6
1973	12,572	2,659	21.2	1,442	11.5	7,849	62.4	922	7.3
1974	17,166	3,782	22.0	1,570	9.1	11,211	65.3	603	3.5

Source: Data adapted from tables in Pedro Malan and Regis Bonelli, "The Brazilian Economy in the Seventies: Old and New Developments," p. 38, and Edmar Bacha, "Issues and Evidence on Recent Brazilian Economic Growth," p. 63, *World Development* 5, nos. 1/2, (1977). Author's calculations.
[a]Percentage totals may not add up to 100 due to rounding.
[b]Includes compensatory loans plus foreign debt generated by the acquisition of foreign assets in utilities, and public foreign debt.

foreign capital basically maintained that it was inexpensive and thus a useful substitute for domestic savings, allowing for continued high consumption. However, the estimates in Table 5.5 suggest that the cost of debt servicing mounted steadily until it became a significant element in Brazil's perennial balance of payments problems.

During the first twelve years of the military regimes income became increasingly concentrated (see Table 5.6). The degree of concentration remains such that, unlike in countries where distribution is the trend, to capture any significant changes, the Brazilian income classification schemes disaggregate at the top and aggregate at the bottom, since the tendency is clearly toward concentration in the top 5 percent.

Table 5.5 Average Cost of Foreign Capital Borrowing
(Millions of U.S. Dollars)

Year	Year End Debt[a] (1)	Annual Interest (2)	Average Cost (%) (2)/(1)
1968	3,780	156	4.1
1969	4,303	204	4.7
1970	5,295	284	5.4
1971	6,622	344	5.2
1972	9,521	489	5.1
1973	12,571	839	6.7
1974	17,166	1,355	7.9

Source: Banco Central do Brasil, *Relatório Anual*, various issues. Author's calculations.
[a]By using year-end debt, the average cost is lower than if average debt was used; hence the real cost is likely to be higher than the present estimates.

Table 5.6 Income Distribution Among the Economically Active Population
(Percentages)

	1960	1970	1972	1976	1980
Bottom 20 percent	3.9	3.4	2.2	3.2	2.8
Bottom 50 percent	17.4	14.9	11.3	13.5	12.6
Top 10 percent	39.6	46.7	52.6	50.4	50.9
Top 5 percent	28.3	34.1	39.8	37.9	37.9
Top 1 percent	11.9	14.7	19.1	17.4	16.9

Source: Luiz Bresser Pereira, *Development and Crisis in Brazil, 1930–1983* (Boulder, Colo.: Westview Press, 1984), p.184. Based on data from the 1960, 1970, and 1980 Demographic Census and the PNAD; data for 1972 and 1976 from the IBGE.

The Slow Progress of Abertura

By 1974, economic fortunes had changed and all was not well. Many analysts of the period believe that General Ernesto Geisel was fully aware of this as he set out on a path of regime liberalization. However, the tortuous process suggests that if General Geisel knew what he wanted, and why, as early as 1974, not all of the top brass agreed with him. The Geisel group advocated a return to the rule of the law, an end to the arbitrary powers of the presidency, and an eventual return to civilian rule.

The developments of the Geisel period reflected conflicting positions within the military. In the words of a former finance minister, Luiz Carlos Bresser Pereira (1984, p. 187), "*Abertura* was a process controlled by the military, giving in to the process of redemocratization, yet at the same time postponing it as long as possible in order to preserve military power."

The annual rate of GDP growth in the *abertura* period from 1974 to 1984 was a mere 4.5 percent compared with the record average rate of 11.3 percent for the "miracle" years of 1967–1973. Given the presidential intentions of political reform, it was imperative to maintain a growing economy to satisfy a minimum of social demands. Moreover, since the regime had thoroughly incorporated the criteria of economic legitimation during the "miracle" period, a significant worsening of the economic situation would immediately undermine the regime's modicum of legitimacy.

At the outset of *abertura*, the congressional elections of November 1974 for two-thirds of the senate, the entire chamber of deputies, and the state legislatures became the country's political focus. The results of the November election showed a clear disapproval of the federal government. The opposition received 50 percent of the total vote versus the 34.7 percent share of the government.[4]

During the Geisel years, a large number of ambitious infrastructure projects were initiated in transportation, steel works, hydroelectric power, nuclear power, and military technology. These were largely financed by foreign loans. From 1974 to 1978, gross foreign debt grew 246 percent to a total of $43.5 billion, while *net* foreign debt increased 413 percent.[5]

The economic expansion of the state was ideologically justified by the doctrines espoused by the Superior War College. The strategic demands of national security explicitly supported the strengthening of the communications and transportation network, the founding and rapid expansion of an armaments industry, the "visionary" projects in the energy field, and the quest for nuclear weapons technology.

In the economic realm, the Geisel government clearly opted to promote growth, based on higher government expenditure and foreign financing through commercial loans. It soon became apparent that the increased role of the state in the economy ran counter to the emphasis on liberalization, while paradoxically allowing for a more controlled transition as it increased the government's overall influence over society. Similarly, as some within the military began to plan the end of their direct control of government, military control of the state machinery was greater than ever (Brigagão 1985, p. 21).

The contradictory aspects of *abertura* dominated the period from 1977 to 1979. The military was split over the choice of General Figueiredo as Geisel's successor, the elites were less determined in their support of the military, and the economy was in increasingly worse shape—all of which amounted to pressures for change and adjustment.

Unlike 1967, when the outcome of the struggle within the military factions resulted in a major shift of economic policy and the political tightening of the regime, Figueiredo's government was a rather direct continuation of Geisel's line. However, the opposition to the choice of Figueiredo as Geisel's successor within the military was strong enough to endanger the entire process of political opening.

By 1977, General Sylvio Frota, the army minister, had become one of the most outspoken representatives of the hard-line within the military. His prominent, and supposedly secure, position indicated the extent of the tensions within the military. Frota considered himself to be the best candidate to succeed Geisel, being a senior four-star general widely respected within the military. The fact that Figueiredo was only a three-star general lent further credibility to Frota's claims within traditionalist military circles (Abreu 1980, pp. 67–70). Moreover, Figueiredo's SNI origins, while giving him an important edge in terms of access to information, was a disadvantage, since some conservative military men, like Frota, did not fully endorse the new emphasis on military intelligence. Frota, however, was effectively isolated by the active intervention of Geisel's supporters at those moments when other officers exhibited indecisiveness. Still, the threat had been very real, and it underscored that liberalization would be accepted by some sectors of the military only if it were, ironically, imposed from above.

Surprisingly, Geisel would also find opposition to Figueiredo's nomination from moderate military men. On January 4, 1978, General Hugo Abreu, President Geisel's chief of staff, resigned (Abreu 1980, pp. 67–70). The issue of seniority raised by Figueiredo's being only a divisional general, not a four-star army general, created a new division within the military between those concerned about the cohesion of the armed forces based on the military's legality and tradition, and those who were willing to sacrifice the regulations for the sake of pragmatism.

This division proved more important in the long run than the pressure from the hard-liners. The conflict over Figueiredo's nomination brought the traditional-legalist heritage of the Brazilian military out of hibernation. Although it is true that Geisel and his chief of staff, General Golbery do Couto e Silva, represented a moderate line committed to liberalization, there emerged a new group dedicated to immediate change. These discontent moderates would eventually launch one of their own as candidate to the presidency, challenging Figueiredo and running on an opposition—PMDB— ticket with extensive civilian support.

Civilian elite opposition was mobilized by the slowing down of the economy to a growth rate of about 5.4 percent. The increasing difficulties in financing the large state-sponsored projects were spilling over into the private sector as contracts for supplies were canceled or redistributed over longer periods. As the profits of the private sector began to decrease (the industrial profit rate was down to 10.7 percent by 1979 from 20.8 percent in 1976—see Table 5.7), the bourgeoisie began to find further expansion of the state sector of the economy objectionable. The share of the state sector in the economy had indeed grown rapidly, from an average of 26.4 percent of GDP in the 1970–1975 period to 44.9 percent in the 1976–1979 period (Bresser Pereira 1984, pp. 197–198).

Much of this civilian opposition supported the challenge to the Geisel line presented by moderates within the military. This crystalized in the PMDB candidacy of General Euler Bentes Monteiro, thus making for the

Table 5.7 Indicators of the Post-"Miracle" Economic Downturn, 1973–1979

Year	Profit Rate (%)	Investment Rate (%)	Marginal Output/ Capital Ratio	Growth Rate of GDP (%)
1973	18.3	23.4	0.50	13.6
1974	21.4	24.9	0.29	9.7
1975	18.2	26.8	0.17	5.4
1976	20.8	26.6	0.33	9.7
1977	18.0	24.9	0.20	5.7
1978	14.3	25.2	0.16	5.0
1979	10.7	24.7	0.26	6.4

Sources: Luiz Bresser Pereira, Development and Crisis in Brazil, 1930–1983 (Boulder, Colo.: Westview Press, 1984), p. 186. Data for GDP growth from Conjuntura, "Contas Nacionais," March 1985.

first two-candidate presidential "election" since 1964. Figueiredo won, nonetheless, signaling the continuity of the gradual Geisel agenda.

With the 1978 elections in mind, the Geisel government enacted the infamous economic reform measures of 1977, known as the Pacote de Abril (April package). The major changes affected the senate, the electoral college, and the procedure for making constitutional amendments; but, above all, they aimed at ensuring an ARENA victory on November 15, 1978. The election brought resounding support to the opposition, but—because of the obstacles carefully erected by the Pacote de Abril—the number of votes did not translate into an opposition majority in the congress.

Economically, it was evident that a period of adjustment and slower growth, accompanied by at least token measures of income redistribution, was inevitable. The planning minister, Mario Henrique Simonsen, insisted on the need for a slowdown and major changes. The grim news that Simonsen carried was deemed to be unnecessary pessimism, and Delfim Netto—then serving as minister of agriculture following a profitable diplomatic tour of Paris (which some insist on calling his "exile")—was quick to mount a circle of intrigue, which led to Simonsen's resignation in August of 1979. Some sectors of the industrial elites and Figueiredo expected that Delfim would momentarily engineer part two of the "miracle."

Indeed, for five months Delfim produced what some optimists called a "minimiracle." In December, Delfim disillusioned his followers with the announcement of a 30 percent maxidevaluation of the cruzeiro vis-à-vis the dollar. This was particularly unwelcomed by transnational corporations, as it seriously hurt their profit reports for calendar year 1979. At the same time, he enacted a number of anti-inflationary measures aimed at curbing a galloping inflation of over 77 percent. However, the federal deficit continued to grow, and the foreign debt rose to $49.9 billion, with reserves rapidly falling. Not surprisingly, the second oil shock of 1979 did not help the current account situation.

In 1981, per capita income fell in Brazil for the first time since 1966. Worse yet, the reason for the fall was not a low growth rate, but actually negative growth of −1.6 percent.[6] This dismal performance led to a drop of 4 percent in per capita income. The economic deterioration, however, helped guarantee that the transition to democracy would continue. The military found it increasingly difficult to legitimize their rule as the deep recession led to a variety of economic demands that could not be met.

The harsh economic reality hit home in August 1982. The Mexican moratorium came at a particularly unpleasant time, focusing the country's attention on the economy just when the military had been desperately working to avoid that, since gubernatorial elections—reinstituted in 1980— were scheduled for November (Skidmore 1984, p. 44). With the Mexican collapse, the pressure of the creditors for a strict IMF adjustment program— the symbol of foreign intervention since Kubitschek—would rise. International reserves were at their lowest levels since 1972, new loans were coming in at a level 20 percent lower than in 1981 and were bound to decrease further, and exports were declining at an annual rate of 15 percent.[7]

For 1982, new loans, a sharp cut in imports, and secret negotiations with the IMF succeeded in buying some time. The year of reckoning was 1983. While the general indicators fail to convey the full extent of the crisis, they do portray a dramatic situation. GDP growth was a shocking −3.2 percent, leading to an unprecedented fall in per capita income of 5.5 percent.[8] Real wages fell by 16 percent over the already depressed levels of 1982. Inflation broke both the 100 percent and 200 percent mark to reach a record 211 percent. Industrial output fell by 6 percent. In the external sector, the gross foreign debt grew by 17 percent to reach $81.3 billion. The trade balance, reflecting a sharp decrease in imports, was the sole bright spot, showing a surplus of $6.4 billion.

The overriding consideration was the country's external obligations. The frequent excursions to New York and the Paris Club by Delfim and his follower Ernane Galvêas, the finance minister, combined with the countless violations of the equally numerous letters of intent to the IMF humiliated the entire nation. This experience significantly contributed to further characterizing the IMF, as the instrument of foreign intervention in the Brazilian economy, opposed to the country's domestic interests.

Within this rapidly deteriorating economic picture, certain groups within the military actually favored a firmer course and increased repression, if need be, to return the country to the path of law and order. These hard-liners, mainly from the intelligence community, resorted first to manipulation within the military and eventually to terrorism. Right-wing intimidation of the more vocal supporters of redemocratization included the early-morning confiscation of progressive newspapers and magazines and intimidation of newsstand owners. Yet, not all their activity was so moderate, for example, a letter-bomb was sent to the Brazilian Bar Association—which throughout the military regimes upheld democratic values—killing the secretary who opened the letter (Skidmore 1984, p. 44). The most extreme attempt by the far right to disrupt the redemocratization process was the bombing of a May Day concert on April 30, 1981. Two bombs went off. The first damaged one of the convention center's power plants, and the second exploded inside a sports car in the parking lot killing one of its occupants and maiming the other. The unexpected twist was that the dead man was a sargeant in the DOI-CODI, the infamous political police, and the second victim was a captain in the same force. The power of the reactionaries was still considerable, for after this fiasco they not only succeeded in getting a burial with military honors for the sargeant-terrorist, but General Golbery do Couto e Silva eventually resigned from his post as presidential chief of staff when his efforts to investigate the bombings were blocked.

The orchestrations for an "acceptable" transition had gained momentum in August 1979, when Petrônio Portella, the then justice minister, led a governmental "democratic offensive" in the form of an amnesty (Skidmore 1984, p. 38). The moves towards redemocratization were accompanied by occasional crackdowns, which were a reminders of the military's presence. However, by September 1981, it became clear that redemocratization would arrive, sooner or later. President Figueiredo suffered a heart attack, which took him to Cleveland for a coronary bypass operation. This situation was particularly propitious for a coup by the hard-liners. The fact that no coup was attempted (and that the civilian vice-president, Aureliano Chaves, was acting president for eight weeks) was convincing proof that the reformist group within the military had firm control of the helm.

In the elections of November 1982, the government's "new" party, the Social Democratic party (PDS) was soundly defeated. The opposition won 59 percent of the popular vote. It gained control of the governorships of Rio de Janeiro (Leonel Brizola as the candidate of the Workers' party [PDT]), São Paulo (Franco Montoro of the PMDB), Minas Gerais (Tancredo Neves also of the PMDB), and six other states. The opposition-controlled states accounted for nearly 70 percent of the population and about 80 percent of GDP. The popular vote notwithstanding, the electoral reforms of 1981 guaranteed a PDS majority in the senate, a slim majority—in alliance with the conservative Brazilian Labor party (PT)—in the lower chamber, and a supposedly comfortable thirty-eight-vote majority in the 680-member electoral college, which would choose Figueiredo's successor in 1985.

The Birth of the "New Republic"

From the Diretas Já to Tancredo's Death

Though Brazil's return to civilian rule is the product of the long and tortuous *abertura* process, the "New Republic" was ushered in by the 1984 *Diretas Já* campaign.[9] Popular demands for a return to full democracy crystalized in the massive *Diretas Já* campaign, which called for the direct elections of the president who would succeed Figueiredo. The demonstrations of more than a million people in the streets of São Paulo, and even proportionately larger numbers in all the other major cities of the country, constituted the largest popular demostration movement in Brazilian history. However, the campaign died with a whimper. The congressional initiative to have direct elections—the Dante Oliveira amendment—was defeated in the congress, consequently, the indirect selection process would remain for the time being.

Despite its failure, the *Diretas Já* campaign strengthened the hand of those opposition figures negotiating the transition with the military. Foremost among these were Tancredo Neves (the PMDB's governor of the traditional political breeding ground of Minas Gerais) and Ulysses Guimarães (the PMDB's indefatigable president). The military demanded an indirect election through the PDS-dominated electoral college, preferably with at least three candidates, in order to split the opposition vote. The major concession on the military's part would be to nominate a civilian candidate; however, the opposition articulators began to spoil the military's plan by producing Tancredo Neves as the single challenger in the race.

The ex-governor of São Paulo, Paulo Salim Maluf, emerged victorious from the PDS's national convention. The military were unhappy with the choice of Maluf, and their failure to actively support him clearly demonstrated their disapproval. Moreover, numerous civilian supporters of the military, including Figueiredo's vice-president, Aureliano Chaves, and the ex-president of the PDS, José Sarney, refused to cooperate with Maluf.

When major figures of the PDS voiced their preference for Tancredo, PDS congressmen defected to the opposition by the dozen. By late 1984, the Tancredo candidacy was strengthened by the selection of the PDS's former president, José Sarney, as the vice-presidential candidate, and it was apparent that the Tancredo-Sarney ticket would win. Certainly one of the key factors in consolidating the support for Tancredo had been the recognition by both the military and large numbers of PDS politicians that the so-called Aliança Democrática, composed of the PMDB and its allies, such as the Liberal Front party (PFL), could provide a viable, moderate alternative to Maluf.

On January 15, 1985, the electoral college elected Tancredo Neves to succeed General Figueiredo; José Sarney was elected vice-president, bringing the PMDB-PFL coalition to power. However, the final twist to the indirect election of Brazil's first civilian president in twenty-one years was the tragic death, as a result of sudden intestinal complications, of Tancredo Neves, the president-elect, in April 1985. On April 21, 1985, fate, it seemed, made an ex-PDS man president of Brazil when José Sarney assumed the presidency, a position he had held in a provisional capacity since March 15.

Sarney's Political Inheritance

At first, the death of Tancredo Neves appeared to seriously jeopardize the transition to civilian rule. Tancredo had been the major articulator of the negotiations. A popular and politically strong leader, he used his extensive political experience and solid conservative credentials in his dealings with the military, and his charisma and his promise to carry out fundamental reforms won him unqualified popular support. He successfully assured the military of the moderate course of his government. At the same time he presented himself as a credible reformer who could lead Brazil through the crisis and complete the liberalization process.

With Tancredo's death, Sarney inherited a number of commitments and alliances that had been personally coined by the president-elect. These were embodied in his ministerial cabinet. The cabinet included representatives of the entire political spectrum, illustrating the intricate pattern of compromises behind Tancredo's election. In the economic sphere, for example, Francisco Dornelles, the finance minister, was a technocrat of conservative neoclassical leanings as well as Tancredo's nephew. Balancing this perspective was the planning minister, João Sayad, an economics professor and a representative of the São Paulo PMDB. Antônio Carlos Lemgruber, the president of the central bank, completed the economic trio. Lemgruber's monetarist persuasions gave the conservative side a numerical advantage, but Sayad was in charge of the Planning Ministry, which in the preceding period had been the true seat of policymaking power.

The configuration of the rest of the cabinet posts followed this encompassing approach. While new people were brought into the government, a number of politicians with strong ties to the recent military past—starting with Sarney himself—were placed in high-ranking posts. This was also the case of Aureliano Chaves, Figueiredo's vice-president, who became minister of mining and energy, a powerful position directly connected to many of the largest state corporations.

Even the previously excluded popular sector was represented. Two energetic and widely respected reformers, Almir Pazzianotto in the Labor Ministry and Nelson Ribeiro in the newly created Ministry of Agrarian Reform and Development, represented to some degree many of the demands of the masses. The cement of this heterogeneous congregation seemed to be Tancredo Neves; thus, when Sarney was confirmed as president, many questioned his ability to execute the delicate moderating role Tancredo had envisioned for himself.

Sarney began his presidential term with the support of two parties, which soon after the inauguration were no longer cooperating. The difficulties were compounded by the increasing strength of various other parties and an extremely fluid electoral panorama. On the other hand Sarney had, as columnist Newton Rodrigues (1986, p. 607) noted, the confidence of the military "with which he had gotten along very well in the previous phases [to the transition]."

Sarney's tenure began—as most presidents' do—with a reasonably short-lived honeymoon period. The national mood was one of euphoria tempered by mourning for the deceased president-elect. During the initial months of the Sarney presidency, the government attempted to give shape to the ideals behind the transition to civilian rule and the drafting of a so-called "democratic agenda." Here, a constituent assembly, to be entrusted with the drafting of a new charter to replace the Constitution of 1967, had a prominent place from the outset. The convocation of a constituent assembly was a constant theme in popular demands throughout the last years of the transition period and became an important symbol of the full return to democracy.

The political arena was dominated by broad agreement as to the need for changes in the landholding system, the fiscal system, the state bureaucracy, and the management of the foreign debt; the specifics, however, were slow in the making. In agrarian reform, for example, a detailed and moderate plan was proposed in May 1985; by the time it became law six months later, in October, the project fell short even of the timid goals of the military's own land reform program known as the *Estatuto da Terra*. The crucial difference was that this time the project had been widely discussed, and criticized, both within the government and by Brazilian society at large.

The Economic Legacy of Military Rule

In these early days of the "New Republic," it became clear that for the sake of the country's economic well-being and the future of democracy, some changes could not be postponed much longer. The tremendous concentration of income, the highest in the world,[10] received increasing attention from academics and technocrats alike as a pressing and potentially explosive problem. The management of the foreign debt took an equally prominent place in both public and government debates.

Extreme concentration of income, the developing world's largest foreign debt, the threat of hyperinflation, and a tradition of case-by-case, reactive economic policy were the most obvious elements of the Brazilian economy in early 1985. However, the expectation of most Brazilians that the new government would swiftly return the country to a growth path *and* concomitantly address the grave social issues facing the country was crucial.

By the end of May, as the nation emerged from the shock of Tancredo's death, the new government came under conflicting pressures and demands for action. Tancredo had left no clear-cut economic strategy; to a significant degree he had envisioned the first six months of his government to be a period of evaluation of the country's situation. This period was to be a time during which the key economic ministries would take stock of the country's situation before moving ahead with reforms.[11]

Saddled with a cabinet picked by the late president-elect and faced with rapidly mounting expectations, Sarney cast aside this nonpolicy without substituting any clear guidance of his own.[12] The transitional nature of the period; the emerging rifts within the cabinet; the mounting—but still not unbearable—pressures from business groups, union leaders, and politicians; and the prospect of nationwide mayoral elections in November 1985 all contributed toward a period of indecision as Sarney emerged from his brief honeymoon with the Brazilian people. As he searched for support to constitute a cabinet and policies of his own—and as he acquired a taste for popularity—his calls for a socially responsive, growth-oriented policy became the only guideline for the "New Republic's" economic policy. The economic decisionmaking process of the Sarney government evolved largely in response to this amorphous embodiment of popular aspirations, subject to the constraints of Brazil's political and economic heritage from the military years and the transition period, in particular, as well as to the new dynamics of incipient civilian rule.

Decision point 1. At this juncture the Sarney government had a wide array of policy choices available. What were these choices? Which groups pressured for what alternative policies?

The Road to the Cruzado Plan

Sarney's Economic Cabinet Takes Shape

In its first month, while Tancredo Neves was still alive in the hospital, the new administration took only a few steps in the field of economic policy, with no fundamental change in orientation from the last years of military rule. These measures reflected to a significant extent the views of Finance Minister Francisco Neves Dornelles. Dornelles had expected to be the strongman on the government's economic team. These expectations stemmed largely from his family ties with Tancredo and his solid conservative-technocrat credentials.

Tancredo had certainly planned for significant changes in social policy during his administration, but economic policy was to be run essentially on orthodox lines under the Finance Ministry's guidance. In the words of the planning minister, João Sayad, "Tancredo envisioned the Planning Ministry as something ornamental, . . . [Dornelles] arrived with a menu ready, and went ahead despite proposals for alterations, complaints, and arguments against that path."[13] Meanwhile, Sarney refrained from playing an active role in any aspect of policymaking, choosing to remain in the shadow of developments until a few weeks after the death of the president-elect.

The Sarney administration's first economic package consisted of (1) a cut in the government's fiscal budget, (2) a slowdown of operations at federal credit institutions, (3) alterations of the indexation methods and greater reliance on government bonds to increase the public debt, and (4) strenghtening of the Interministerial Price Council (CIP) guidelines, amounting to a short-term price freeze. These measures did not constitute any shift in terms of economic policy design; in fact, they were fundamentally the same measures that had been unsuccessfully implemented many times before. Public reaction to the package was generally unenthusiastic. Scholars and businesspeople pointed out the well-known limitations—in terms of conception and particularly in terms of their implementation by the Brazilian government—of the austerity measures and the price freeze. The only point that raised some criticism was the change in the process of calculating the exchange rate and the *Correção Monetária*—the key index that periodically readjusts most financial prices.[14] Despite the lack of promise and confusion that marked the first two months of the new administration the prevailing public attitude was to give the government the benefit of the doubt and to allow it time to enact more energetic reforms.

Sarney, however, remained uncomfortable with a cabinet that was clearly not of his choice. Indeed, the cabinet members acted as if they controlled the president, and not the reverse: "In the beginning of the government, [Sarney's] office was often invaded by his unannounced collaborators. [His ministers] addressed him in the familiar *você* and presented papers for his signature as if he was a clerk."[15] Sarney (1986, p. 103) insisted that he was troubled and unprepared to assume the presidency: "I prepared to be a discreet and circumspect vice-president, without ambition." By early June 1985, Sarney had clearly decided to stay on and attempt to take control of the presidency. Economic policy remained far from the president's mind, however, as he focused attention on the crucial issues of convoking the Constituent Assembly—which would determine the duration of his mandate as it formulated a new national charter—and of enacting cabinet reform.

While Sarney mustered sufficient strength to make changes in the cabinet, he created a "cabinet within a cabinet," composed of personal friends working as presidential advisers. This inner circle consisted initially of Célio

Borja (as primarily a political adviser), Rubens Ricupero (as counsel to the president on foreign relations), Marcus Vilaça (as special adviser with a broad mandate for "cultural affairs"), and Luís Paulo Rosenberg (as the president's personal adviser on economic matters) (Bardawil 1985a, p. 28). In the economic arena, Mr. Rosenberg's role was "almost of cabinet rank."[16] Considering that Rosenberg enjoyed the president's friendship and trust, and also held a quasi-cabinet bost, it is likely that he outstripped both Finance Minister Dornelles and Planning Minister Sayad in terms of influence with the president.

Differences among President Sarney's economic staff became increasingly public by the end of May 1985. The rift between Dornelles and Sayad widened as the government came under greater pressure to act. The São Paulo private sector, represented by the presidents of the São Paulo Federation of Industry (FIESP) (Luís Eulalio de Bueno Vidigal), the Commerce Federation (Abram Szajman) the State Commerce Association (Guilherme Afif Domingos) the Agricultural Federation (Fábio Meireles), and the Brazilian Rural Society (Flávio Menezes), promised support for the continuation of Dornelles's economic program (Lage 1985, pp. 31–32). Meanwhile, Sayad (1987) went public with some of his disagreements. During this period, Sayad soared in public support, benefiting greatly from his PMDB affiliation and the appealing path of adjustment with growth that he proposed.

Sarney was caught in the middle, between his two economic ministers. Because of the mildly expansive economic climate and his temporarily successful attempts to associate himself closely with the heritage of Tancredo, Sarney gained popularity. Sarney recognized the need for both popular support and continued support from the senior partner in the governing Aliança Democrática (the PMDB) in order to govern and to carry out any sort of cabinet reform. In terms of increased popular support, Dornelles's recessionary policies—as well as his links to the tenure of former planning minister Delfim Netto—held little political utility for Sarney. This conflict of priorities and orientation between Sarney and Dornelles soon generated rumors of a cabinet shakedown. Later, Dornelles (1987) accused Sarney of "simply start[ing] to spend without any list without any description," after Tancredo's death. While Sayad did not offer Sarney a free-spending economic policy, he did propose a controlled growth and adjustment strategy.

Dornelles's departure was precipitated by the remarks of a high-ranking Finance Ministry official, Marcos Vital, speaking as an official representative of Minister Dornelles. The cautious pessimism of Vital—typical of the attitudes prevalent in the Finance Ministry at the time—during an address to a gathering of Brazilian bankers clearly did not please the president (Bardawil 1985b, p. 28). Sarney, encouraged by Sayad, preferred an economic course of moderate growth with inflationary control, but within this orientation Dornelles and his followers could not find sufficient maneuvering room. Dornelles resigned at the end of August along with the central bank president, Carlos Lemgruber.

The new finance minister, Dilson Funaro, and the new central bank president, Fernão Bracher, were more closely aligned with Sayad's adjustment-with-growth strategies than with the monetarist orientation of their predecessors. The choice of Funaro, a São Paulo businessman—neither an economist nor a traditional technocrat—and Bracher, a well-connected banker, brought a much-needed boost of confidence to the government's economic team from businesspeople and bankers—both domestic and foreign—who had become uneasy over the confrontations between Sayad and Dornelles.

The Decision to Implement Reforms

In the aftermath of the first cabinet changes of the "New Republic," one uncertainty remained over President Sarney's economic team. It was widely rumored that Sayad might also be removed to allow Sarney to take control of economic policy through "his" ministers, as opposed to the cabinet inherited from Tancredo. These rumors, combined with the natural transition period from one minister to another in the Ministry of Finance, yielded a two-month policy void. This interlude, however, gave Funaro and Sayad the opportunity to get acquainted and to forge a good working relationship.

Sayad and Funaro recognized the need for major economic reforms that would (1) bring inflation under control, (2) provide for continued economic recovery, and (3) promote gradual income redistribution. Funaro also became an advocate of deindexation as an essential ingredient for solving Brazil's chronic inflation. Deindexation would amount to the elimination of the well-established mechanisms (instituted since 1964) of periodic adjustment of nearly all prices (financial rates and wages among them) based on the official inflation index. This economic outlook left external debt policy, considered by many foreign critics to be a necessary key element in addressing the country's economic morass, as a residual, deriving from domestic priorities. To Brazil's foreign creditors, the insistence of the new economic team on not sacrificing growth for the sake of the country's external obligations, signaled that changes in the debt-servicing arrangements were forthcoming. Beyond these broad points of agreement, the specifics on both the domestic and the foreign front were slow in developing.

By mid-1985, there was little question that the economy had finally emerged from its deepest recession in recent history and was gaining momentum quickly. In the nine months from January through September 1985, consumer purchases skyrocketed in relation to the same period in the previous year. Car sales increased 27.4 percent, supermarket sales were up by 25.6 percent, and building material purchases went up by 7.6 percent.[17] This demand boom rapidly returned industrial output to near capacity level, with positive implications for employment, all of which fed into a virtuous growth cycle; however, it was also feeding into an inflationary cycle. The monthly inflation rate in September reached 9.1 percent, with a slight decline to 9.0 percent in October. Still, the inflationary pressures indicated that the 10 percent threshold would be easily surpassed in November.[18]

The government responded to the mounting inflationary pressures with a consumer credit reform in the last week of October. Reiterating the government's top priority of economic growth, Finance Minister Funaro stated that "we continue to desire economic growth, but we want it to be orderly and lasting." The basic effect of the new measures was that the maximum maturity for consumer credit for durable consumer goods would be shortened from twenty-four to twelve months. The credit reform met with the general approval of the entrepreneurial classes as voiced by Abílio Diniz, head of Pão de Açucar, the country's largest retailing group: "It was only a signal from the government to avoid an explosion of demand." The president of the São Paulo Federation of Industry, Luís Eulálio de Bueno Vidigal, was more explicit when he stated that "the industrial sector supports this measure, because supply is indeed not adjusted in relation to consumption"[19]

On November 15, 1985, nationwide elections for mayors of former "national security areas"—including all state capitals—were held. The results were mixed, as the Aliança Democrática parties (PMDB and PFL) split in various states. The PT (Worker's party) elected the mayor of Fortaleza; in Rio de Janeiro, Leonel Brizola's PDT elected Saturnino Braga; in Sarney's home state (Maranhão), the battered PDS defeated a divided Aliança Democrática; in São Paulo, the conservative PTB allied to the PFL elected the former president Jânio Quadros against the PMDB's Fernando Henrique Cardoso. Elsewhere, however, the PMDB and the PFL fared better. After the elections, national attention quickly shifted back to the economic arena as the November monthly inflation rate reached 15 percent and rumors of major economic reforms permeated the media.

Decision point 2. The building expectation of reform set the stage for the government's moves; both domestically and internationally Brazil's future was depicted as hinging on the government's ability to take charge of the economic situation. What were the reform options available? How real was the perceived tradeoff between external adjustment and economic growth? Which groups, foreign and Brazilian, pressured for specific alternatives?

On Monday, November 25, President Sarney resorted to what was generally thought to be his strongest weapon in taking control of the government, by announcing that a cabinet shake-up was the next item on the political agenda. After eight months in power, Sarney believed that it was time for him to nominate his own cabinet. While several cabinet positions would change hands (the chief of staff, the justice minister, and the foreign minister most prominently), something even more important would happen over the coming months: Sarney would accept a bid for radical economic reform. In late November, the national weekly *Veja* wrote off Sayad's cabinet seat as a result of the mayoral elections and Sarney's announced cabinet shuffle:

> Minister João Sayad, who was already weak before the municipal elections, became even more exposed after them. Sarney feels obligated to give the Minas Gerais governor, Hélio García, a share in the federal government, earned by his capacity to pacify the party and lead it to a spectacular electoral show in the state capital. This share would be exactly the chair today occupied by Sayad.[20]

Still, Sayad remained in his post and emerged as one of the principal articulators behind the intense efforts to devise an economic strategy that was supposed to lead the country to the desired path of adjustment without recession. Developing the reforms that became known as the *Plano Cruzado* sidetracked all other issues. The foreign debt, cabinet reform, the constituent assembly, and eventually the elections of 1986 all became a function of this economic formula. Before the plan was announced, however, Funaro and Sayad—and their teams of economists—still needed to fine-tune their ideas.

On November 27, Minister Funaro announced a new package of reforms, which consisted of the same tired and unconvincing measures: higher taxes and government austerity.[21] This package was received with the usual cynicism by the public and sharply criticized by tax specialists, small business leaders, and labor leaders. One part of the package, however, attracted even more attention than the naturally controversial issue of tax reform. Funaro announced a change in the calculation of the official inflation index and the establishment of a sole index for all price adjustments—wages, monetary correction, and the exchange rate.[22] The public outrage arose because the new index set the November inflation rate at 11.1 percent, whereas the old index set the monthly rate at 15 percent; this difference clearly opened the government up to charges of manipulating the index.

The issue of indices has been a traditionally sensitive one in Brazil. Throughout the dictatorship years, the government was accused of manipulating indices, ranging from inflation to budget figures. In the first nine months of the "New Republic," there were *three* changes of indices (including this one). Minister Sayad had championed a change from the Fundação Getúlio Vargas's (FGV) index—which had been used for forty years—to the more broadly based, and therefore arguably more representative, index of the Instituto Brasileiro de Geografía e Estatística (IBGE). The two indices differed widely in their bases, but neither was consistently lower than the other. In fact, in January 1985, the IBGE's inflation figure was 14.6 percent, whereas the FGV's was a *mere* 12.6 percent. Sayad had been advocating such a shift for months, and Funaro also supported a single index for all prices as part of his aim to deindex the Brazilian economy.[23] In the midst of the public outcry, the former planning minister, Mario Henrique Simonsen, clearly outlined the essence of the problem surrounding the change in indices: "The substitution of the IGP [general price index], of the Fundação Getúlio Vargas, by the IPCA [broad consumer price index], of the IBGE, as the parameter for the calculations of monetary and exchange rate corrections is a defensible measure, but it was taken at the wrong time."[24] The issue of timing was crucial. However, the fact that Funaro personally ordered the change of index illustrated a hitherto unnoticed side of the minister's character: his almost dictatorial behavior once he had made up his mind and a sense of "mission," which he held above all other considerations. While this particular trait would not play an important role in the coming months, it certainly influenced the economic policymaking climate in the months after the collapse of the *Plano Cruzado*.

In late November 1985, Funaro announced in Washington that Brazil would seek a new renegotiation of its foreign debt without the IMF.[25] Funaro argued that Brazil was one of the few debtors to be up-to-date on interest payments; in return, easier debt-servicing terms were expected in the future. As if to drive home the point, the government broke with the long tradition of honoring the unguaranteed debts of private banks by liquidating three commercial banks, including the sixth and twelfth largest private Brazilian banks, which owed a total of $455 million in bank-to-bank loans abroad.[26]

On Wednesday, December 18, 1985, a *Folha de São Paulo* headline brought out into the open the debate that had been raging among the government's economists: "Planning Ministry does not reject the use of heterodox shock." The instruments of the then recent economic reforms in Argentina and Israel (June and July 1985, respectively) embodied the concept of a "heterodox shock." The policy mix that yields a heterodox shock is based on an underlying belief that the high inflation rate is a result of "inertial inflation," and it usually includes orthodox internal and external adjustment measures (currency devaluations, restrictive fiscal and monetary policies, as well as deindexation), combined with unorthodox elements such as monetary reform (the creation of a new currency), wage and price freezes, and pegged exchange rates.[27]

The possibility of deindexation was first raised outside closed meeting rooms by the interim planning secretary, Andrea Calabi, while João Sayad was out of the country on a trip to Washington. The reactions to Calabi's remarks were immediate. The black market dollar exchange rate shot up 8.9 percent over the previous week's level, the stock market went on a downward slump, and nervous attention was focused on the projected monthly inflation of 18 percent for January 1986. Sayad immediately called from Washington, demanding explanations from Calabi and sending him on a damage control mission. Calabi, however, did not manage to quiet the mounting speculative debate despite his claim that he had spoken only in theory and that while a heterodox shock was not discarded as a policy option, it could only take place in May or June of 1986 and only if the inflation continued to gain upward momentum.[28]

Decision point 3. What impact did publicity and public pressure over the issue of a "heterodox" reform have on the range of choices available to Sarney's economic ministers? What role may the perceived success of the Argentine and Israeli experience have on Brazilian decisions? Was a "heterodox" strategy necessarily confrontational with regard to IMF policy preferences, and how would this affect the negotiations on Brazil's foreign debt?

In retrospect, Minister Sayad was characteristically candid: "Calabi made a mistake. He needed to have taken the same postion that we all did at the time and lie," that is, deny any knowledge of the impending reforms (Sayad 1987). The government's economic team had been fully aware of developments in Israel and in Brazil's southern neighbor, Argentina; both the nature of their original troubles and the success of the policies made "heterodoxy" attractive. Calabi's declaration allowed the press to attribute to the interim planning minister what had been on nearly everybody's mind: that Brazil was ready to opt for radical changes in economic policy.

On December 17, the same day on which Calabi became the focus of the economic press, declarations by Finance Minister Funaro further exacerbated the debate. While in Uruguay, Funaro stated that economic policy for 1986 would not be recessionary and that the possibility of price and wage freezes had been discarded. Also of interest was Funaro's comment that Israel's heterodox shock recipe, based on a consensus among the government, unions, and industrialists was preferable to Argentina's reform-by-decree formula.[29]

A further complicating factor related to the nature of Funaro's trip to Montevideo for a meeting of Latin American finance ministers regarding the region's foreign debt. Upon his return to Brazil, Funaro attempted to cool the heated debate about imminent reform: "At no time did I defend freezing prices and wages."[30] On that second crucial issue of foreign debt, the finance minister was less cautious: "Economic growth will not be interrupted in 1986, even if it requires postponing payment of the foreign debt."[31] From this point on, both economic ministers consistently placed the servicing of Brazil's foreign debt in the context of the administration's unswerving commitment to domestic economic recovery. (Table 5.8 presents the development of Brazil's foreign debt situation in the period preceding the Cruzado Plan) The year 1985, and the first nine months of the "New Republic," ended with December inflation running at a record annual rate of 235.1 percent, while economic growth had recovered to a 8.6 percent yearly level—the highest in ten years (see Table 5.2).

In February 1986, under the shadow of nonstop rumors about economic reform, President Sarney finally felt that he had the opportunity to shift around his cabinet. The cabinet shake-up amounted to a redistribution of forces between the two Aliança Democrática parties: the PFL and the PMDB. While the PMDB—to which Sarney officially belongs—ended up with fifteen cabinet positions, the PFL—in which observers believed Sarney felt ideologically more comfortable—picked up five. Still, the numerical division of the positions did not reflect the muscle of the ministries, budget-wise the five PFL ministries outnumbered the fifteen PMDB cabinet members' spending power 2.5 to one.[32] However, the crucial reforms were yet to come; the PMDB would rebound in the political battle against the PFL with the initial smashing success of the Cruzado Plan engineered by its economic ministers.

The *Cruzado* Era

The Dangerous Overnight Success of the Cruzado

The conservative shift in Sarney's cabinet did not eliminate the growing speculation over the heterodox path of impending economic reform. Indeed, the innovative Cruzado Plan, announced on February 28 at 9.30 a.m. by President José Sarney on nationwide radio and TV, was far from conservative. The plan's essential features were the following: (1) deindexing of the economy, beginning with the elimination of *Correção Monetária*—used for indexing wages, savings accounts, and other financial instruments; (2) immediate and indefinite price freeze of over 80 percent on goods and services; (3) redenomination of the currency from cruzeiro to cruzado, to be converted at a rate of 1,000 to one; and (4) a 33 percent increase in the minimum wage and an 8 percent bonus to wage earners. The government estimated that the inflation rate, which had reached 255 percent annually in February, would fall to zero in March.[33]

The reforms enacted by the Cruzado Plan went beyond the wildest optimistic projections in promoting growth and boosting the government's popularity. In the polls immediately following the announcement of the

Table 5.8 Brazilian Foreign Debt, 1980-1985 (Millions of U.S. Dollars)

	1980	1981	1982	1983	1984	1985
Total external debt	70,236.7	79,978.4	91,304.2	97,854.8	103,520.4	106,729.9
Long-term debt[a]	56,710.7	64,657.4	73,303.0	81,006.5	87,835.0	91,093.6
Short-term debt	13,526.0	15,321.0	17,451.0	14,204.0	11,500.0	11,017.0
Commitments	9,006.0	12,602.9	12,519.5	8,608.6	7,866.6	3,013.9
Official creditors	1,853.4	2,435.7	2,567.6	3,134.8	1,346.2	1,971.0
Private creditors	7,152.6	10,167.2	9,951.8	5,473.8	6,520.4	1,042.9
Disbursements	8,121.8	9,982.8	10,293.3	8,023.5	9,615.5	2,502.5
Official creditors	1,162.6	1,481.1	1,976.2	2,505.2	2,666.8	1,494.5
Private creditors	6,959.1	8,501.7	8,317.1	5,518.3	6,948.7	1,008.0
Principal repayments	3,848.9	3,924.4	4,167.3	1,946.2	2,208.6	1,496.7
Official creditors	507.8	562.7	961.0	919.3	1,164.6	1,036.8
Private creditors	3,341.1	3,361.8	3,206.3	1,026.9	1,044.0	460.0
Net flows	4,272.9	6,058.4	6,125.9	6,077.3	7,406.9	1,005.8
Official creditors	654.9	918.4	1,015.1	1,586.0	1,502.2	457.8
Private creditors	3,618.0	5,139.9	5,110.8	4,491.4	5,904.6	548.0
Interest payments	4,190.8	5,146.1	5,937.2	5,089.6	5,304.8	6,279.5
Official creditors	437.0	488.7	580.8	600.9	792.6	899.2
Private creditors	3,753.8	4,657.3	5,356.4	4,488.7	4,512.2	5,380.3
Net transfers	82.1	912.3	188.7	987.7	2,102.0	-5,273.7
Official creditors	217.9	429.7	434.3	985.1	709.6	-441.4
Private creditors	-135.8	482.6	-245.6	2.7	1,392.4	-4,832.3
Total debt service	8,039.7	9,070.5	10,104.6	7,035.7	7,513.4	7,776.2
Official creditors	944.8	1,051.4	1,541.9	1,520.2	1,957.2	1,935.9
Private creditors	7,094.9	8,019.1	8,562.7	5,515.6	5,556.3	5,840.3

Source: World Bank, *World Debt Tables*, 1987.
[a]Includes only public and publicly guaranteed long-term debt.

monetary reform, Sarney's approval rate reached 95 percent,[34] and Minister Funaro was congratulated and applauded in the streets. Economically the measures engineered an unprecedented consumption explosion. The real wage hike, which resulted from the concomitant 33 percent increase in the minimum wage (plus the across-the-board 8 percent pay bonus), and the price freeze amounted to the largest real buying power gain in decades. The April sales index, in relation to the same month in the previous year, went up a whopping 36.2 percent in Rio de Janeiro and a similarly impressive 29.5 percent in São Paulo (see Table 5.9).

As the consumption rise that had begun in mid-1985 developed into an unquestionable consumption boom by April 1986, the need to safeguard the long-term prospect of the recovery and to ward off inflationary pressures became acute. Shortages of consumer goods (particularly food items such as:

Table 5.9 Sales Index
(Percentage Variation Over Previous Year, Same Month)

		Rio de Janeiro	São Paulo
1985	January	3.4	−2.9
	February	−10.8	−11.3
	March	−6.1	12.4
	April	5.2	−3.9
	May	14.0	22.6
	June	5.3	8.8
	July	28.9	6.0
	August	24.6	17.5
	September	28.4	0.7
	October	32.1	21.1
	November	32.3	19.6
	December	16.9	18.2
1986	January	20.5	19.6
	February	17.8	25.7
	March	14.1	14.5
	April	36.2	29.5
	May	27.8	34.4

Source: Conjuntura (July 1986), p. 7.

potatoes, eggs, milk, meat, and poultry), consumer durables (new cars most noticeably), intermediate goods (steel), and raw materials (electricity) all became commonplace by June. Demand pressure led to the beginning of a black market in most of the scarce consumer items, taking the form of the payment of an *ágio,* or surcharge. On the positive side, employment levels and production rose steadily.

In its editorial, "The Giant Goes Back to Shopping," dated July 15, 1986, the widely respected *Conjuntura* magazine warned of the dangers ahead:

In this new phase of the *Cruzado* Plan, the Government will have to face many challenges. The moderation of consumption and the incentive to save are certainly two of them. . . . The economic surgery carried out by the de-indexation program was successful. The important point, now, is to care for the economy's post-surgery health. The clearest symptom that the patient still requires attention is the exacerbation of consumption. This, however, has its roots in the recently adopted expansionary policies, and in some of the measures enacted by the Monetary Reform. Without appropriate correction, the excess of consumption will inhibit investment due to the shortage of financing, will reduce the exportable surplus and increase the already existent price distortions. In the end, there would be left inflation and the need to apply even more restrictive economic measures. . . . Thus, there still remains much to be done.[35]

Meanwhile, the external context had shifted significantly, reflecting both the effects of the Cruzado Plan and exogenous developments in the international trade and finance environment. The trade balance soon became the most pressing concern. The enviable trade surplus that Brazil had maintained since 1983 quickly collapsed as a result of the simultaneous decrease in exports and the increase in imports brought about by excessive consumption, (see Table 5.10).

Decision point 4. This is a crucial point in the process of monetary reform. The range of options open to the Sarney government has shrunk significantly with the enactment of the Cruzado Plan, and the options concerning the future of the plan itself are becoming increasingly limited with the exacerbation of consumer pressures and the approaching nationwide elections of November. Government action is further constrained by the rapidly deteriorating external account situation. What are the political factors influencing Sarney's considerations? What is the outlook for the international trade situation and the impact which this may have in the near future on the country's need for external financing?

Last Chance to Save the Cruzado

After the unexpected smashing success of the Cruzado Plan, the Funaro-Sayad team stumbled onto the plan's shortcomings without producing the needed solutions. Minister Sayad stated that from May 1985 onward the "principal problem was the supply of goods" (Sayad 1987). The pressure on prices could not be ignored. On July 23, the so-called Cruzadinho Plan was announced, ostensibly as a set of measures to control consumption and provide for continued growth, with the goal of, in Sarney's words, "eliminating misery by the year 2000."[36] Critics accused the plan of being a mere stopgap decree to raise revenue for the government to finance the increasing public deficit it had failed to curb.

The package consisted of (1) a 28 percent compulsory deposit on gasoline and alcohol (for motor vehicles), which would be returned to consumers, with market interest, three years later based on average consumption; (2) compulsory deposits on car purchases: 30 percent for new cars, 20 percent for cars up to two years old, 10 percent for cars up to four years old (shares of the newly formed National Development Fund [FND] were to be issued for the value of the deposit and could be traded within three years); (3) a 25 percent tax on international airline tickets and dollar purchases for foreign travel, with the proceeds also going to the FND (this tax, however, would not be returned to consumers); (4) an end to government-set interest rates for savings accounts and the introduction of floating rates; (5) the creation of the FND to administer both the new

Table 5.10 Trade Balance (FOB), 1984–1987 (Billions of U.S. Dollars)

	1984 Quarter				Year Total	1985 Quarter				Year Total
	I	II	III	IV		I	II	III	IV	
Trade balance	2.39	3.60	3.62	3.48	13.09	2.02	3.49	3.63	3.34	12.48
Exports	5.54	7.01	7.36	7.10	27.01	5.12	6.50	6.76	7.26	25.64
Imports	3.16	3.41	3.73	3.62	13.92	3.09	3.02	3.13	3.93	13.17

	1986 Quarter				Year	1987[a] Quarter		
	I	II	III	IV		I	II	1st Semester Total
Trade balance	2.47	3.70	2.50	(0.32)	8.35	0.58	2.88	3.46
Exports	5.82	6.46	6.17	3.95	22.39	4.14	6.50	10.64
Imports	3.35	2.76	3.66	4.27	14.04	3.57	3.61	7.18

Source: Banco Central do Brasil.
[a]Preliminary data. Totals may not add up due to rounding.

revenues, estimated at Cz$35 billion for 1986 (US$2.5 billion at the official rate, $1.4 billion at the black market rate), and 33 percent of government pension funds, valued at Cz$38.8 billion in 1986 ($2.8 billion at the official rate, $1.55 billion at the black market rate)—the FND was created to invest in state-owned enterprises and long-term infrastructure projects; (6) income-tax free government bonds; and (7) increased taxation of short-term financial investments (open-market, overnight, and thirty- to sixty-day certificates of deposit), gradually increasing in inverse proportion to the length of the investment (Nassar 1986).

The Cruzadinho package was a clear demonstration of the limits of the Sarney government's power, particularly clear in an election year. The measures were by no means a radical alteration of economic policy, however, wage compression was ruled out, and the measures implemented aimed at the top layer of consumers rather than at the mass. While this approach was consistent with Sarney's espoused socially responsible economic policy, it also reflected the needs of the PMDB in view of the November elections for the entire lower chamber of Congress, two-thirds of the Senate, and all governorships.

Preelection Paralysis

Despite the clear political constraints, pressures still existed within the government for alterations to the Brazilian "heterodox" model. In the debate, however, political considerations prevailed, and proposals to switch from a blanket price freeze toward a system of administered prices—such as that in place in Argentina at the time—were swept aside. Sayad (1987) explained that

> as far as the price freeze was concerned, which was the most criticized aspect of the plan, there was a perception within the government that it was a barrier, a wall, a dam that could not have any gaps or otherwise everything would collapse. So the government took a position, on the President's orientation, of inflexibility. . . . My position which maintained that [the price freeze] was not working, lost force in face of the two arguments which stated that the problem was about to be solved [presented by Funaro], and the other which said that we cannot open or otherwise everything will come crashing in.

This tension within the government remained largely confined to the Monday, Wednesday, and Friday morning, closed-door cabinet discussions. Meanwhile, the PMDB presented an unprecedented united face, basking in the positive aspects of the program. However, at the end of July, Planning Secretary Sayad and the president of the Brazilian Institute of Geography and Statistics, Edmar Bacha, publicly clashed over the issue of inflation indices. Sayad, with the support of President Sarney and Funaro, requested that the official inflation index exclude the effects of the taxes and compulsory deposits enacted by the Cruzadinho. Bacha, trying to preserve the respectability of his institute's index—which had been the official index for only eight months—insisted on including the effects of the government's measure in the official index. In the spirit of an election year, a compromise was reached whereby two indices were published by the IBGE, one containing the effect of the July 23 reforms, the other purging that effect.

In the only other major attempt to address the building inflationary pressures, the government opted for the traditional approach of suppressing the symptoms rather than addressing the causes of the problem. Throughout the first three weeks of August, the Federal Police cracked down on the dollar black market as the surcharge reached 90 percent. The dollar black market, as well as the black markets rapidly developing for other items in short supply, allowed a glimpse of the true state of inflationary trends. Rumors of imminent major exchange reforms abounded. Reflecting the rising speculation and expectations of future price increases, inflation climbed to its highest level since the beginning of the Cruzado Plan. The reversal of the downward price trend of foodstuffs was the main cause of the inflation surge, leading to a 2.24 percent monthly rate in the São Paulo area (1.1 percent was the purged index).[37]

For the average consumer, the supply of beef and milk reached a crisis situation during the months preceding the November election. This condition led the government to a few token moves against cattle raisers hoarding produce. But, when a confrontation—perhaps even an armed confrontation—with well-connected and powerful growers became a distinct possibility, the government stepped down. Once again plainly demonstrating its lack of enforcement infrastructure and to some degree its lack of political will, the government opted for the nonconfrontational, costly, and inefficient option of importing thousands of tons of European beef.

The decision to open the door to imports—not only beef, but a wide range of foodstuffs and consumer goods then in short supply and a number of luxury items such as foreign beers, salmon and caviar—was justified by the government as necessary measures to preserve the integrity of the reforms from the economic sabotage of cattle raisers and other elements of society who were hoarding goods. The government's critics condemned the liberalization of imports as catering to the electioneering interest of the PMDB and the PFL in face of the coming elections. Whatever the actual motivations behind the importing spree, it amounted to an increase of about $1.3 billion in the country's import bill, or roughly 25 percent of the nation's international reserves at the time.[38] The confrontation over the supply of beef discredited the government's economic team more than any other single episode since the inception of the reforms; still the government and the PMDB, in particular, succeeded in focusing national attention on the tremendous increase in real purchasing power—even with goods in short supply and with black market surcharges.

To counter the calls—both domestic and foreign—for austerity in the country's external accounts, the government pointed to supposedly exogenous factors that were continuously restricting the range of options available to the country. Foremost on the government's list of adverse international factors was the unwillingness of the financial markets to offer new money. The success of the country's adjustment with growth necessitated consistent, if diminishing, injections of new foreign loans, which in the uncertain environment of mid-1986 were not forthcoming. Another crucial, and related, issue raised by government economists was the shift in foreign investment trends in Brazil. In 1985, for the first time in decades, net foreign investment in Brazil had been negative, and the figures shaping up for 1986 were even more worrisome (see Table 5.11). Both the unavailability of new loans and the net foreign investment flows augured ill for the prospects of a sustained recovery.

The PMDB swept the November 15 nationwide congressional and gubernatorial election, gaining nearly a two-thirds majority in both houses of Congress as well as twenty-two of twenty-three governorships. The major defeat of left- and right-wing parties was seen by many analysts as an endorsement of the Cruzado Plan. However, the consumption boom continued, with shortages ranging from imported industrial inputs to eggs, and from electricity to cars. Most goods that were available sold at a

Table 5.11 Foreign Investment, 1980–1986 (Billions of U.S. Dollars)

	1980	1981	1982	1983	1984	1985	1986[a]
New investment	1.63	1.90	1.51	1.01	1.23	1.06	0.77
Remittances	0.69	0.70	1.00	0.92	0.91	1.40	1.55
Net foreign investment	0.94	1.20	0.51	0.09	0.32	−0.34	−0.78

Source: Banco Central.
[a]1986 figures are estimates. New investment is registered foreign investment in the form of capital, equipment, and debt to equity conversions. Remittances comprise repatriation of capital, as well as profit and dividend remittances, to parent company.

surcharge in the neighborhood of 100 percent over the official government prices.

Too Little, Too Late: The Collapse of Monetary Reform

On Friday, November 21, a mere six days after the elections, Ministers Dilson Funaro, João Sayad, and Almir Pazzianotto announced what quickly became known as the Cruzado II Plan. The new measures included a rash of major price increases which, according to many, dealt the final blow to the price freeze of February 28, 1986. Whereas the subsidies and prices of steel, meat, and milk remained unchanged, the prices of many consumer goods went up: beer and cigarettes by 100 percent; new cars by 80 percent (80 percent of which was to go to the government); gasoline and alcohol fuel by 60 percent; different varieties of sugar by over 20 percent; and, finally, government services such as electricity, telephone, and mail by 35 percent on average.

The second, and perhaps the most controversial, element of the Cruzado II package was a further alteration of the inflation index. The official inflation index would be based on a typical basket of goods, that is, one that might be purchased by a consumer earning up to five times the minimum wage per month (about $280), thus purging the effect of most of the recent price hikes. This latest alteration of the inflation index contributed to the resignation later that same day of IBGE President Edmar Bacha, one of the original architects of the Cruzado Plan.[39] Third, the new package spelled out the mechanism by which an automatic wage adjustment scheme, instituted by the original Cruzado Plan, would function. When the inflation rate reached 20 percent, wage increases of at least 50 percent of the official inflation rate would take effect, after discounting any voluntary pay raises granted over the previous nine months. Fourth, a new policy of minidevaluations (the first one was of 0.26 percent, on November 21) set by the central bank on an almost daily basis would control the exchange rate. Noticeably, this was the sole measure in the reforms that directly impacted the country's pressing foreign account situation.

Fifth, the Cruzado II Plan also included a number of measures aimed at promoting savings (for example, the introduction of a new tax-free retirement fund) and at recapturing some of the money floating in the parallel economy through a fiscal amnesty. Finally, as a further step along the road of deindexation, treasury bills became free of inflation indexing and started to float with interest rates.[40]

In sum, the package was aimed at containing consumption through sales taxes, rather than income taxes, as part of an option for increased revenue rather than major government spending cuts. The new measures had a projected revenue of $11.3 billion—nearly 4 percent of GNP. According to Finance Minister Dilson Funaro, the government's share of the adjustment in the form of cuts and privatization would account for slightly more than 20 percent of the total new revenue. In the words of Funaro, after a month of negotiations within the PMDB and the administration, "We did not have a choice."[41] Minister Sayad, however, would argue that the government did have a choice: "The President had two options before him, one which I presented and another presented by the Finance Minister" (Sayad 1987). Sayad's reform option favoring more sustained structural reforms, and less of a tributary emphasis, however, did not present the immediate impact of Funaro's recipe and required a significantly higher degree of political coordination given their longer-term implementation and operational period.

The split in the economic cabinet echoed that between Sayad and Dornelles in 1985. The solution apparently was chosen on the same grounds as in August 1985: Sarney opted for the politically easier option presented by Funaro. As to the wisdom of the tremendously unpopular alteration of the inflation index, Sayad (1987) stated that "you did not even have to study the situation, all you had to do was look at what had happened in July [with the Cruzadinho]." This lack of attention to the drafting of the Cruzado II Plan, combined with a national sense of betrayal stemming from the de facto end of the price freeze only six days after the election, helped President Sarney's approval rate plunge from a high of 95 percent in April 1986 to a low of 54 percent ten days after the Cruzado II announcement.[42]

Beyond the *Plano Cruzado:* Moratorium

The Debt Service Moratorium

The announcement of the Cruzado II Plan was a brief moment of activity that barely broke the paralysis of economic policymaking that had prevailed since August 1985. The poor reception of Cruzado II, and the government's defensive attitude, heralded a new period of policymaking paralysis. During this five-month hiatus, domestic economic policy came to a complete halt. Instead, the government, partly out of a strategy to buy time on the domestic front and partly out of necessity, resorted to a foreign debt gamble.

Domestically, Sayad became increasingly isolated, while Funaro took charge of a major public relations initiative to obtain public support for the government's actions. During this period, Funaro's deep conviction that he had the definitive role to play in placing the Brazilian economy "back on track" was evident. Time and time again, Funaro reiterated that recessionary policies were not an option and that Brazil would grow in 1987 at levels comparable to those of 1985 and 1986. However, it soon became clear that the strength of the minister's rhetoric and personal motivation was not matched by political coordination or support. At the second eschelon of the government, disarray prevailed without direction from above, and many of the "fathers of the Cruzado" resigned their government positions and returned to private or academic life.

In the midst of despondency and confusion, Funaro attacked the issue of the country's foreign debt as if it held the key to Brazil's economic future. Funaro addressed the U.S. Congressional Summit on Debt and Trade, held in New York City on December 5, 1986, and kicked off his foreign debt crusade:

> After strenuous, prolonged attempts at convincing our partners through reasoning, we have now reached a point where all parties involved have to assume their responsibilities. We also have our shareholders. They are the people of Brazil and they number 135 million. . . . The strategy of pumping unprecedented trade surpluses out of developing economies only to ensure the payment of interest has run its course. Debtor developing countries can no longer continue to be net capital exporters in these staggering amounts. *If the debt is to be paid, it will have to be serviced at a much lower cost in the years to come.* . . . We shall be prepared to negotiate what is negotiable, and this does not include the growth of our economy (author's emphasis).[43]

This populist line, even if rooted on solid economic ground, did not go over well with the international banking community. Funaro's intention to utilize a significant portion of Brazil's scheduled debt-service payments—up to $6 billion in 1987—for domestic adjustment would be realizable only with the agreement of the country's creditors or through a unilateral moratorium. Governor Brizola, of the PDT, and the PT's leader, Lula, were the two leading public advocates of the latter course. Funaro, however, was not ready to call for a moratorium. Relying on the country's foreign reserves and hoping for the support of other major debtors such as Mexico, Argentina, and the Philippines (all countries that were either already negotiating substantial reschedulings or were about to do so), Funaro pressed for concessions from the banks.

Funaro won a minor victory when the IMF notified the official creditor nation group—known as the Paris Club—that Brazil's economic adjustment program was workable. This tentative IMF endorsement was crucial not only for the Paris Club rescheduling, but more importantly for the upcoming commercial bank rescheduling. In addition, the IMF "go ahead" in the absence of an orthodox IMF austerity program was a victory for the Brazilian government, which had refused to negotiate an adjustment program with the IMF.[44] The IMF backing yielded some positive results when the Paris Club agreed to the rescheduling of $4.1 billion in official credits on January 21, 1987. Still, the creditor nations stressed that they "would reconsider their action if Brazil [did not] receive a 'favorable report' from the IMF during annual consultations [in] July."[45] This partial victory brought a brief period of deceiving calm to the debate. During December 1986, Brazil had managed a meager trade surplus of $156 million; in January 1987 the surplus fell further, down to $129 million, while inflation threatened to take off once again, reaching 15 percent in January. Faced with the consummated fact of the return of inflation, the government finally acknowledged it by officially lifting the price freeze on February 5, 1987.

Decision point 5. What are the links between the deteriorating inflation, trade balance, and political pictures? How is the pressure applied by domestic and foreign interest groups constraining the government's ability to design and implement activist policies? How will the divisions within the cabinet and the ministries affect policy making? Is the tradeoff between domestic growth and meeting the country's foreign obligations, emphatically presented by Funaro, real or imagined? How does the range of options available differ from that of early 1986 before the announcement of the Cruzado Plan?

The gravity of both the domestic and foreign economic picture for Brazil was undeniable by February 1987; the resignation on February 10 of Fernão Bracher, the central bank president, added one further element of instability. In time, it became known that the major reason behind Bracher's resignation was his disagreement with Funaro over the then impending unilateral suspension of debt-service payments. President Sarney announced the de facto moratorium on February 20 in a brief fifteen-minute address on national television. He revealed that Brazil's reserves had shrunk to a low of $3.9 billion and that to safeguard a minimum ability to pay for essential imports, he had decreed a suspension of interest payments on $67 billion in commercial foreign debt.[46]

Sarney and Funaro expected that the moratorium would serve as a rallying point for public support of the regime. In addition, there was a clear hope that at least one of the other major debtors—probably Argentina—would join Brazil to force the comercial banks to accept terms more favorable to the indebted countries. Neither proved true. Popular support was negligible. Headlines were grabbed by Governor Brizola and PT president Lula, both criticizing the moratorium because it had been taken from a position of weakness—when reserves were nearly exhausted—rather than from a position of strength, as would have been the case in March 1986. Internationally, Funaro engaged in a fruitless world tour of major OECD capitals in an attempt to establish government-to-government debate on the debt as a preliminary step to eventual negotiations with the banks.

On March 16, Funaro recognized that none of his recent efforts had yielded significant results, and that "perplexity" dominated the economic climate.[47] The following day Planning Minister João Sayad resigned. Sayad's resignation, for one fleeting moment, seemed to open the door to new and cohesive policies. However, Sarney opted to place a close personal friend with little economics training, Anibal Teixeira, as the new planning minister. The choice of Teixeira clearly left Funaro in control of the economic policymaking machinery of the government. Despite the cabinet shuffle, Funaro continued to be consumed by the developing confrontation over the foreign debt. Meanwhile, the proposals for reform that had been made by Sayad before his resignation were similarly dismissed, leaving the country once again without any firm policies.

Funaro's Fall

During the month after Sayad's resignation, the economic outlook deteriorated further. Inflation persisted at 15 percent a month, and the trade surplus for the first quarter of 1987 totaled a mere $526 million—compared with $2.41 billion for 1986.[48] In addition, the prospects for renegotiation of the foreign debt were dimmer than ever, with all of Brazil's possible debtor nation allies signing on with the banks, or about to do so. Minister Funaro was the natural center of attention.

For months, and particularly since the February 20 suspension of foreign debt payments, there had been repeated calls for Funaro's dismissal, both domestically and internationally. On April 9, the three most powerful PMDB governors—Orestes Quércia of São Paulo, Wellington Moreira Franco of Rio de Janeiro, and Newton Cardoso of Minas Gerais—publicly demanded Funaro's removal.[49] However, on April 12, Ulysses Guimarães, PMDB governor Miguel Arraes of Pernambuco, and other party leaders called for party unity and support of Sarney's cabinet and criticized the group of governors for attacking Funaro while he was in Washington.[50] This unexpected outburst of PMDB support for Funaro further clouded the political scene. Nonetheless, this political storm, combined with the cool reception of Funaro's economic proposals by the country's creditors, meant that Funaro's days on Sarney's cabinet were numbered.

Funaro's fall, however, did not come as quickly or as easily as some had been predicting as early as November 1986. The delay in Funaro's removal reflected more than confusion over the future course of economic policy; it was a product of the entire economic decisionmaking process of the Sarney government. While public opinion—and in this case international public opinion as well—made itself heard loudly and clearly, the key decisions were taken by a very limited number of decisionmakers for reasons often not related to those current in the media. Indeed, Funaro's dismissal brought out into the open the essence of high-level decisions in the Sarney government.

Sarney's indecisiveness, the difficulty of the PFL in standing up to the PMDB—when it acted in a united fashion, Ulysses's power within the PMDB, and São Paulo's place of honor in economic policy all conspired to both delay Funaro's exit and determine his successor. The price charged by the PMDB for removing Funaro, who had once been the party's most popular minister, included the dismissal, on April 22, of Sarney's staunch ally and PFL leader, Marco Maciel, from his position as the president's chief of staff.[51] Not only was Maciel's removal from that powerful position arranged, but Ulysses publicly blocked Sarney's first choice for the new finance minister once Funaro's resignation was announced on April 24. Sarney reached to his native northeast for a new finance chief and chose family friend and businessman Tasso Jereissati, the young governor of Ceará. Ulysses vetoed this choice and instead offered a short list of alternatives to Sarney. The least controversial, and to the president most palatable, name on the list was São Paulo entrepreneur-economist Luiz Carlos Bresser Pereira. This embarassing cabinet reform—which started with Bracher's resignation in February—concluded the convoluted first two years of the Sarney government's frustrated attempts to create an economic policy for the "New Republic." Guilherme Afif Domingos (PFL-SP), the federal deputy who received the largest number of votes in the November 1986 elections, stressed the importance of the dramatic conclusion of the Cruzado cycle: "this week will be remembered as the beginning of the fall of President José Sarney."[52]

Notes

1. This background section draws heavily on my "Political Economy of Military Rule in Brazil, 1964–1985" (Senior Essay, Yale University, Fall 1985). Most accounts of the coup of 1964 give March 31 as the date of the coup. However, as General Hugo Abreu describes in his book *Tempo de crise* (Rio de Janeiro: Nova Fronteira, 1980), the final preparations took place on March 31, but the actual coup was on April 1.

2. See Bolivar Lamounier, "Eleições e abertura política no Brasil: notas

para uma interpretação," draft of chapter published in Alfred Stepan, ed., *Democratizing Brazil: Problems of Transition and Consolidation* (New York: Oxford University Press, 1989). Table 1 reproduces electoral results for 1966, 1970, 1974, 1978, and 1982 from the Tribunal Superio Eleitoral.

3. United Nations, *Yearbook of National Account Statistics*, various years.

4. Lamounier, "Eleições," Table 1.

5. Data are from *Conjuntura Econômica*, July 1985.

6. Ibid.

7. Ibid.

8. Ibid.

9. See Alfred Stepan, *Os militares: de abertura à nova república* (Rio de Janeiro: Paz e Terra, 1986), for a thorough and concise account of the *abertura* process.

10. For detailed Brazilian income distribution data, see Table 5.5 and the World Bank's *World Development Report*, 1986 (New York: Oxford University Press, 1986), Table 24, pp. 226–27. Data for income distribution are particularly difficult to find; however, of those countries for which reasonably reliable data are available, Brazil holds the dubious distinction of having the highest income concentration.

11. Former Finance Minister Dornelles stated that Tancredo's first intention was that "in the first six months each ministry [take] stock of the resources available, and set priorities in order to establish an investment policy." However, Dornelles added: "Once Tancredo died and Sarney took over, he did not want to wait some six months of greater austerity in order to take inventory and establish priorities. He simply started to spend without any list without any description." Interview with Francisco Neves Dornelles, Rio de Janeiro, March 13, 1987.

12. Minister Dornelles's statement quoted in the preceding note is but one insider's view of President Sarney's lack of guidance in economic matters. The next part of this chapter discusses in greater detail Sarney's role in shaping economic policy.

13. Sayad, minister of planning in the Sarney government from March 1985 to February 1987, made these remarks during an interview conducted by Hugo P. Faria at the Park Lane Hotel in New York City, April 21, 1987.

14. The following three articles discuss in detail the "New Republic's" first economic measures: Celso Luiz Martone, "As novas medidas," *Informações FIPE*, no. 60 (April 1985), p. 3; José Roberto Mendonça de Barros, "As recentes medidas de política económica e a conjuntura," *Informações FIPE*, no. 60 (April 1985), p. 1; Instituto Brasileiro de Economia, "Primeiras medidas, últimas intâncias," *Conjuntura* (April 1985), pp. 7–10.

15. This observation appeared in an article, "Sarney toma biotônico," in the national weekly *Veja*, November 27, 1985, p. 37.

16. Francisco Neves Dornelles, who was a federal deputy (PFS-RJ) in the Constituent Assembly and minister of finance in the Sarney government (March 1985 to August 1985), described Rosenberg's role during an interview conducted by Hugo P. Faria at the Fundação Getúlio Vargas, Rio de Janeiro, March 13, 1987.

17. "Com o pé no freio," *Veja*, November 6, 1985, p. 93.

18. "Inflação: no mesmo tom," *Veja*, November 6, 1985, p. 95.

19. "Com o pé no freio," *Veja*, November 6, 1985, p. 93.

20. "Sarney toma biotônico," *Veja*, November 27, 1985, p. 37.

21. Um pacote enfeitado," *Veja*, December 4, 1985, p. 36.

22. "Um outro termômetro," *Veja*, December 4, 1985, p. 45.

23. Ibid.

24. Mario Henrique Simonsen, "Um pacote bem embrulhado," *Veja*, December 4, 1985, p. 50.

25. *The Economist*, November 30, 1985, p. 83.

26. Ibid. The banks that were liquidated were Comind (no. 6), Auxiliar (no. 12), and the smaller Banco Maissonave.

27. Francisco Lopes, *O choque heterodoxo* (Rio de Janeiro: Editora Campus, 1986). Two brief, but interesting, discussions of the issues are: "Hyperinflation: Taming the Beast," *The Economist* (November 15, 1986), pp. 55–64; and Peter T. Knight, F. Desmond McCarthy, and Sweder van Wijnbergen, "Escaping Hyperinflation," *Finance & Development* (December 1986), pp. 14–17.

28. "A última cartada," *Veja*, December 25, 1985, pp. 64–65.

29. Ibid., p. 65.

30. Ibid.

31. Ibid., p. 66.

32. "Um PFL vale 2, 5 PMDB," *Veja*, February 19, 1986, p. 21.

33. A vida e a nova moeda," *Veja*, March 5, 1986, pp. 28–34.

34. "Sarney sai da retranca," *Veja*, December 10, 1986, p. 37.

35. Instituto Brasileiro de Economia, "O gigante volta às compras," *Conjuntura* (July 1986), pp. 7–9.

36. José Sarney, announcement of economic reforms on nationwide Brazilian television, July 23, 1986.

37. "FIPE registra pressões no custo de vida em SP," *Folha de São Paulo*, August 20, 1986, p. 23.

38. "Escandalo da carne," *Senhor*, September 8, 1987, pp. 41–42.

39. "Deserções no cruzado," *Veja*, November 26, 1986, p. 50.

40. "O governo enche o bolso," *Veja*, November 26, 1986, pp. 42–47; and Roger Cohen, "Brazilian Effort to Moderate Economy, Improve Trade Surplus Draws Criticism, *Wall Street Journal*, November 24, 1986.

41. "O governo enche o bolso," *Veja*, November 26, 1986, p. 43.

42. "Sarney sai da retranca," *Veja*, December 10, 1986, p. 37.

43. Dilson Funaro, "Statement by Mr. Dilson Funaro, Minister of Finance of Brazil," U.S. Congressional Summit on Debt and Trade, The Waldorf Astoria, New York City, December 5, 1986, pp. 3–5. Mimeo.

44. "IMF Agrees to Back Brazil Economic Plan," *Wall Street Journal*, December 11, 1986.

45. "Brazil Wins Rescheduling of $4.1 Billion in Payments to Its Government Creditors," *Wall Street Journal*, January 22, 1987, p. 35.

46. "Brazil to Suspend Interest Payment to Foreign Banks," *New York Times*, February 21, 1987, p. 1.

47. Dilson Funaro, "Perspectivas da econômia brasileira em 1987." Address delivered at "Brasil 87: O Desafio Econômico," Copacabana Palace Hotel, Rio de Janeiro, March 16, 1987.

48. "Brazil Trade Surplus Shrank to $136 Million in March," *Wall Street Journal*, April 24, 1987, p. 21.

49. John Barham, "Leaders in Brazil Demand Funaro Quit His Post," *Wall Street Journal*, April 10, 1987, p. 19.

50. "Brazilian Ruling Party Voices Support for Funaro," *Wall Street Journal*, April 13, 1987, p. 18.

51. Roger Cohen, "President Sarney's Staff Chief Quits: Shuffle May Ensue," *Wall Street Journal*, April 23, 1987, p. 29.
52. Roger Cohen, "In Brazil's Political Theater, Sarney Could Face an Early Exit from Stage," *Wall Street Journal*, April 30, 1987, p. 26.

References

Abreu, Hugo. 1980. *Tempo de crise*. Rio de Janeiro: Nova Fronteira.
Bardawil, José C. 1985a. "Um gabinete no gabinete." *Senhor*, no. 220 (June 5).
———. 1985b. "Sarney deu a volta." *Senhor*, no. 233 (September 4).
Baretta, Silvio R. D., and John Markoff. 1985. "Brazil's Abertura: A Transition from What to What?" University of Pittsburgh, May. Mimeo.
Bresser Pereira, Luis. 1984. *Development and Crisis in Brazil, 1930–1983*. Boulder, Colo.: Westview Press.
Brigagão, Clovis, 1985. A militarização da sociedade. Rio de Janeiro: Jorge Zahar Editor.
da Conceição Tavares, María, and J. Carlos de Assis. 1985. *O grande salto para o caos*. Rio de Janeiro: Jorge Zahar Editor.
Dornelles, Francisco Neves. 1987. Interview by Hugo P. Faria, March 13, Fundação Getúlio Vargas, Rio de Janeiro.
Jaguaribe, Helio. 1985. *Sociedade de política*. Rio de Janeiro: Jorge Zahar Editor.
Lage, Ana María. 1985. "Tudo se decide na guerra da economia." *Senhor*, no. 219 (May 29).
Nassar, José R. 1986. "Crescimento Complusório." *Senhor*, no. 280 (July 29).
Rodrigues, Newton. 1986. Brasil provisório. Rio de Janeiro: Editora Guanabana.
Sarney, José. 1986. "Brazil: A President's Story." *Foreign Affairs* 65, no. 1 (Fall).
Sayad, João. 1987. Interview by Hugo P. Faria, April 21, Park Lane Hotel, New York City.
Schmitter, Philippe C. 1973. "The Portugalization of Brazil?" In Stepan, *Authoritarian Brazil*.
Stepan, Alfred. 1973. "The New Professionalism of Internal Warfare and Military Role expansion." In his *Authoritarian Brazil*. New Haven: Yale University Press.
Wynia, Gary. 1984. *The Politics of Latin American Development*. 2d ed. New York: Cambridge University Press.

6

Israel and the Success of the Shekel: The Key Years, 1984-1987

Emanuel Sharon

Hyperinflation in Israel, which started in the third quarter of 1983, reached its peak at the end of 1984 and subsided when a comprehensive stabilization program was launched in July 1984. Inflation, or price instability, is only one dimension of the economy, a thorough analysis of which would require a very complex study. However, it might be worthwhile to compare some aspects of the takeoff stage of hyperinflation in Israel and the dynamics of the disinflation process.

At least four different and independent attempts are apparently now under way to thoroughly analyze the four hyperinflation episodes in Israel in recent years and the stabilization programs that followed. As a result, we reach a better understanding of the economic phenomenon. Researchers who were not involved in the decisions affecting the economy and who can sit back and analyze the situation after two or three years, have, of course, the advantage of objectivity. On the other hand, persons like myself, who were in the center of the activity, have more insight into the mechanisms, the political and administrative environment, and the reasoning, right or wrong, that led the decisionmakers to do whatever they did. Therefore, I shall try and stress these aspects in my account.

Background Statistics

The area of Israel is about 21,000 square kilometers, which is 0.25 percent of the area of Brazil. The cultivated area is about 4,000 square kilometers, of which 2,000 are irrigated. Over half the area of Israel is desert. The country's population is approximately 4.5 million, about 3.7 percent that of Brazil, and the work force is 1.4 million. In 1988, Israel's GNP was $2 billion, over $5,000 per capita. During the 1950s and 1960s, the rate of growth was about 10 percent per annum. Since 1973, Israel has experienced a long stagnation period, and the annual average growth rate has been only 2 percent, roughly equivalent to population growth.

Israel exports $12 billion and imports $16 billion in goods and services. The goods and services deficit is about $4 million, including defense, and is financed partly by U.S. aid, partly by unilateral transfers, and partly by borrowing. The main items of export are processed diamonds, metal and electronics, chemicals, agricultural products, processed food, and textiles. Some 40 percent of the exports are directed to Europe, 25 percent to the United States, and the balance to other parts of the world. Note, first, the size of the foreign trade relative to GNP and, second, the size of the goods and services deficit. These figures demonstrate both the dependence of the country on foreign trade and the sensitivity of local process to external price shocks and exchange rates.

Another unique feature of the Israeli economy is the size of its defense expenditures. In addition to the military aid that Israel receives from the United States in the form of grants, which amount to $1.8 billion a year, Israel spends 15 percent of its GNP on defense.

In many respects, Israel may be regarded as a developed country. The quality and availability of health and education services are among the best. Israeli agricultural sciences and technology are known throughout the world. In some high-tech areas, Israel competes against Silicon Valley and Route 128. On the other hand, in many respects Israel is a developing country and therefore shares the problems of developing countries.

Inflation in Israel

Inflation in Israel passed through four distinct phases. The first, which lasted until the third quarter of 1983, was characterized by increases in inflation by steps. Throughout the 1960s, the annual inflation rate was 5 percent. In 1971/72 it jumped to 12 percent, in 1973–1978 to 33 percent, and in 1978 and 1979 to 63 percent; then, for four years annual inflation stood at about 140 percent. The second phase was the takeoff phase, which lasted from the end of 1983 to the end of 1984. The third was an attempt to contain inflation through social pacts between the government, unions, and employers. The fourth phase began with the stabilization program implemented in July 1985.

To look at a country's inflation process over time without paying proper attention to the structural, fiscal, and monetary causes of the inflation is an injustice to economic analysis. Nevertheless, I would like to concentrate on what I call the takeoff period, the social pact (which we called package deal) period, and the stabilization program. Aspects of those periods that played a role later on will be emphasized. Without trying to explain *why* the step function of inflation over time emerged, I will analyze what it did to the economy.

Wage Indexation

Wage indexation started in Israel even before the establishment of the state in mandatorial Palestine during World War II. In the 1950s and 1960s, when inflation was small, wages were partly indexed once a year. Then, cost-of-living increases were paid twice a year; in 1979 frequency of payment increased from biannually to quarterly, and the rate of indexation increased from 70 to 80 percent. During the takeoff period, cost-of-living payments were made when inflation passed a certain threshold, and if inflation was high enough, the rate of indexation was 90 percent. Consequently, during 1984, cost-of-living payments were made monthly.

Monthly wage increases based on past performance create a technical problem in any disinflation program, since disinflation may mean an automatic substantial increase in real wages. Of course, the opposite is also true, but the whole system of compensation was adapted to take care of inflation. Disinflation requires special attention. This part of a disinflation program is especially tricky, mainly because neither the public nor the unions fully understand the problem and, moreover, do not believe that disinflation will be sustained.

Indexation of Financial Assets

As inflation grew over the years, so did the indexation of financial assets—to the point where even liquid assets were indexed and the publication of the cost-of-living index once a month was not good enough because people wanted to protect the value of their money even for a few days. The solution was to establish bank deposits linked to the exchange rate of foreign currencies. The trade in actual foreign currencies is, by the way, restricted and regulated. The banks, in turn, set up their foreign-currency-linked accounts with the central bank to protect them against devaluation. In the first quarter of 1985, 60 percent of all liquid assets were foreign-currency-linked. This system provided full accommodation of devaluation for business and households.

In the stock market, one type of stock generally kept its value relative to inflation and the dollar, namely, bank shares. There was a popular belief and understanding that the shares were a conservative investment, since the banks, the central bank, and the government would not allow their value to fall.

Profits and Money Illusion

Not only were ordinary citizens at a loss as to what their income was worth, so were the companies they worked for. Accounting methods fail to measure in an inflationary world. The inflation-adjusted reporting rules, which were introduced in the late 1980s, can cope with one-digit inflation, perhaps. But, when presented with triple-digit inflation or more, we have no proper measure for flows of revenues and costs. As a result, efficiency of management is adversely affected. Financial officers take the lead in their firms, and most management effort is directed to financial manipulations aimed at trying to preserve the value of money.

The task of budgeting in a commercial firm became even more difficult when contracts started being indexed. First, long-term contracts were indexed, and later on even the shortest-term contract was either index-linked or dollar-denominated. The net result was that businesses truly did not know if they were making profits or losing money. Many businesses honestly believed that they were in good shape until they collapsed after the disinflation took place.

Taxation

The inadequacy of the accounting system to record profits in a time of hyperinflation is even more obvious when records are kept for income tax purposes. If a business is able to delay payments and meanwhile keep its working capital in the form of some linked short-term asset, it may end up not having to pay income tax at all. During the period of hyperinflation, even the transaction-oriented taxes like value-added tax, which were paid once a month, were paid in money that, by the time of payment, was valued less. In a 10 percent-per-month inflation period the Treasury lost 10 percent of the tax, and in 20 percent-per-month inflation, the Treasury lost 20 percent. This is the well-known Tanzi effect. The payer meanwhile held the money in a foreign-currency-linked account. Companies even traveled to little branches of banks in obscure places in the Gaza Strip to pay their taxes, because it took the bank two additional days to process the transactions. The cost of inflation to the tax authorities was not a minor issue. Prior to the launching of the stabilization program, that cost was estimated to be about 2 percent of GNP. This was taken into the Ministry of Finance calculations when it proposed in the frame of the stabilization program to cut the budget by a certain specified amount. Later estimates were that the Tanzi effect was closer to 4 percent of GNP.

Public Sector Expenditures

Finally, the same problems created in the private sector applied to the public sector as well. The use of budgets expressed in nominal terms became less and less practical, and eventually the nominal budget was abandoned. Budgets were specified in theoretical prices, which were updated periodically by the

Bureau of Budgets in a somewhat arbitrary way. The indexation of the budget completed the cycle. With the indexation of contracts, wages, financial short-term assets, and the budget, we achieved a full accommodation of any price increase.

The importance of balance of payments to the Israeli economy must be underscored. A deficit in balance of payments contributes to an increase in the external debt, and an increase in the external debt causes increases in the debt service and the deficit. All governments in Israel have regarded exports as a national priority. The size of imports relative to GNP and, in particular, the size of imports of consumer goods also tie the exchange rate directly to the cost-of-living index. Roughly, a devaluation of 1 percent increases the price level by 0.6 percent. The government of Israel, to maintain the competitiveness of the industry, devaluated whenever export profitability fell below a certain threshold. The immediate effect was an increase in prices followed by an increase in wages, which necessitated a new devaluation.

In mid-1982, when inflation started to increase, it became evident that the government must take steps to curb the growth of inflation. In September 1982, the Ministry of Finance announced a new plan to synchronize the rate of inflation by setting up an annual target of 80 percent inflation and devaluating by 5 percent a month, increasing by 5 percent a month the prices of goods and services that were either supplied or regulated by the government. The theory behind this plan was that the inflation was a "bubble inflation," fed by expectations, and that the government, by following a systematic price increase, would change expectations and gradually start leading a downward trend in inflation. No compatible steps were taken in either the fiscal or monetary policy of the government. Some six months later it became apparent that this policy had failed. A new policy was then conceived, which later received the name "The Dollarization Plan." The idea was that, because most financial assets were linked by that time to the dollar and because most prices started to be dollar-denominated and dollar-quoted, Israel might stop inflation by one bold move—making the dollar the legal tender in Israel.

The cooperation of the U.S. government was needed, and talks started between the two governments. The plan was aborted even before it was specified in detail. The abortion of the plan, plus a crisis in the stock market when the value of the previously mentioned bank shares crashed, caused the minister of finance to resign. The policy of the new minister was to work only on the real side of the economy. He tried to cut the budget by 9 percent, but the cut was never implemented. Part of the failure was because the budget, being nominal, was not a suitable instrument to curb government expenditures and because, with wages and contracts indexed, most expenditures could be reduced by a fixed percentage.

The minister was also very active in encouraging exports through subsidies and the exchange rate. The net result was an increase in budget deficit, mainly due to subsidies on the one hand and increases in the rate of inflation on the other. The policy that stressed only the real side of the economy regarded inflation as a regulator that decreases real wages. This policy succeeded in improving the current account, but failed in other aspects and was one of the reasons for the takeoff of hyperinflation.

In May 1984, due to an internal political crisis, the cabinet fell and the Knesset (Parliament) decided to hold elections at the end of July. As a result of the elections, a new coalition government was formed with equal representation for the two big political blocs. Retrospectively, the inability of the government to handle the economic problems and the general feeling that the economy was running amok contributed to the crisis and to the change of government. During the election campaign, both parties promised to stop inflation through a "package deal"—a kind of social pact between workers, employers, and the government—to restrain inflation by imposing a voluntary or nonvoluntary freeze on prices, restrain wage demands, and keep prices of subsidized commodities and exchange rates in line. Implicitly, the theory behind a package deal approach is that inflation is created only by expectations.

Package Deals to Fight Inflation

About a month after the new government was sworn in, the Ministry of Finance presented to the prime minister the first version of the stabilization program. Comparing the two documents, the one presented in October and the one presented in July, one can find many similarities, except that the July program was much more refined and complete. The October program can be regarded now as the first draft of a program. The commitment to the package deal concept of the parties that constituted the government was too strong, and consequently this proposal was rejected in favor of the first package-deal. Before elaborating on the first package-deal, I will review briefly the economic situation at that time.

The oscillations of the monthly inflation rate during 1984 were the result of typical seasonal fluctuations in inflation plus the fact that the index of building and housing services, which constitute 20 percent of the general cost-of-living index, is measured only every quarter. But the fluctuations in 1984 were stronger than in previous years. Transfers of foreign currency by the private sector, particularly the banking system, is a good indicator of public expectations. The public did not give the government good marks for economic performance during 1984. Israel's foreign currency reserves, which result from private transfers, public transfers, and the ability to secure loans abroad, are an instructive indicator. We saw a dangerous decline in reserves between 1982 and 1987. The reserve situation, though a crude indicator, is a factor in the political decisionmaking process.

First Package Deal

The first package deal was signed, after very long political deliberations and negotiations, on November 2, 1984. It was an agreement to last for three months. The main items in the package were a price freeze on all goods and services for over 60 percent of the goods and services on the market. A follow-up committee, composed of representatives of the government, the unions, and the association of employers, was authorized to amend the prices with mutual consent. The government agreed to freeze all tax rates for the same period and the unions agreed to give up one-third of the cost-of-living allowance to which they would be entitled during the period. The government agreed to pay special compensation to employees who earned less than a certain income. The price freeze also included subsidized goods and services provided by the government. These goods and services amounted to 25 percent of the typical consumer's shopping basket. This meant that the Government had to bridge the difference between price and cost by increasing subsidies.

The immediate result of the agreement was a drop in the inflation rate to 4 percent. When wage indexation is based on past inflation, you have the effect of increase in real wages when inflation goes down. Nevertheless, the private sector could maintain the three-month freeze, mainly because, prior to the agreement, in anticipation of the price freeze, it had increased prices above what was "normal." The follow-up committee worked day and night trying to keep the economy functioning and to solve the hundreds of practical and legal cases that arose.

Second Package Deal

At the end of the first package deal, the second package deal was signed. By that time the expenditure on subsidies was enormous. The second package deal was to be effective for eight months. It was agreed that the government be allowed to increase prices of subsidized goods and government services by not more than 12–13 percent in real terms per month and that the private sector not be allowed to increase its prices by over 3–5 percent. The unions agreed to restrain their wage demands. They also announced that any price increase over 5 percent a month would be regarded by them as a breach of contract. Much power was given to the follow-up committee, which decided both on individual price increases and on general price increases. Two months later, inflation reached a level of 20 percent a month, and a third pact was reached, this time for four months. According to the new agreement, there was to be a general price increase and then a freeze of two months, followed by yet another general increase and a freeze for two months.

It became apparent that the inflation rate was on a rising trend, with very sharp oscillations due to the different package deal agreements. It was also clear that the package deal regime had seriously disrupted the whole structure of relative prices in the economy. During the period October 1984 to June 1985, work was progressing, confidentially, on a comprehensive economic plan.

Comprehensive Economic Plan

In October 1984, the prime minister visited Washington and decided, together with the U.S. President, on a joint economic group between the United States and Israel; it would meet at least twice a year to discuss ways to stabilize the economy. The group, composed of officials from both governments, assisted by private U.S. and Israeli economists, was chaired by Allen Wallis, the U.S. undersecretary of state for economic affairs, and myself. The private economists, H. Stein and S. Fischer on the U.S. side and E. Berglass, Michael Bruno, and N. Liviatan on the Israeli side, played a very important role in the discussions. With Wallis and M. Bailey on the staff of the State Department, the discussions and deliberations of this group resembled more a seminar in the department of economics of a good university than bilateral negotiations between countries.

The first draft of a plan was presented to the prime minister as early as October 1986. This plan was very much influenced by papers and ideas generated in the research department of the Bank of Israel, headed by M. Frenkel. Contributors were Bruno, Liviatan, and Fisher (to early works on inflation) and bank researchers Frenkel, Ben-Bassat, Pitterman, and Sokoler. Following the U.S.-Israeli joint group discussion, the Israeli delegation, which consisted of ministry representatives as well as private economists, started to act informally as a planning team.

When the second package deal was signed, the Israeli Ministry of Finance conducted three distinct planning efforts. The main one worked on the stabilization program, the second worked on an alternative idea, which was closer to the dollarization plan, and the third one, which worked on a program we have called "Doomsday," was mainly concerned with the possibility of an economic collapse before the implementation of a comprehensive plan or following the implementation.

Early in June 1985, when it became apparent that package deals were not going to lead anywhere, the ministry officials and private economists who had worked together informally were officially appointed to present a plan.

The work was to be conducted confidentially and reported only to the prime minister and minister of finance. On July 1, 1985, the government was called to decide on the plan. The meeting lasted for twenty-five continuous hours and, at the end, the government voted with a small majority for the plan, which was announced on July 2. The announced goal of the plan was to stop hyperinflation, without increasing the internal and external debt, and set the economy on a normal track. The following were the major elements of the program.

Fiscal

1. A deep cut into the subsidies that had increased the prices of some consumer goods and services by 25 to 100 percent. The goal was to reduce the subsidies, which at the time of the plan were 7 percent of GNP, to 1.5 percent of GNP.
2. Reductions of regular expenditures of approximately 2 percent of GNP.
3. Reduction by 3 percent of the public service work force.
4. Various changes in taxes, direct and indirect. The aim of the changes was not fiscal; it was rather to offset price increases that had followed other steps and also to distribute the impact of the program among various segments of the population.

Exchange Rate

In addition to a 7 percent devaluation in June, an additional devaluation of about 20 percent took place, after which the dollar/shekel exchange rate was to be stabilized for a time at IS 1,500 = U.S.$1.00.

Wages and Prices

1. Increase of all prices (which had been controlled since the first package-deal) by 17 percent.
2. A freeze on prices thereafter for three months.
3. An increase of all wages by 14 percent and a freeze thereafter. The idea was that the government, for a specified emergency period, would regulate the level of real wages. This meant that the agreements between employers and the employees would be void for the duration of the emergency period. The union opposed this step fiercely, and it was never implemented. A complex of agreed-upon wage adjustments followed. As a result, real wages eroded more than planned during the first six months following the plan, but then increased again to well above the plan's figures.

Monetary Policy and Capital Markets

1. Abolition of foreign-currency-linked deposits that mature in less than one year.
2. A restrictive monetary policy featuring high real interest rates.
3. Reforms in the capital market.

The program dealt simultaneously with the fiscal deficit, exchange rate, monetary policy, capital market income, and prices.

It was decided to launch the program on July 1, because that date was judged to be in the middle of an economic oscillation caused by the package deals, and when relative prices would presumably be less distorted. The planners carefully calculated price level, exchange rate, interest rate, and wage levels, trying to reach a set of prices that would keep the economy more or less in equilibrium. In that way, after the price freeze was lifted, market forces would be able to reach an equilibrium not far from the artificial prices imposed by the planners. When calculating the budget cuts, planners took into account the Tanzi effect, both for expenditures and for revenue.

The length of the cabinet meeting indicates that the politicians were not enthusiastic about the plan, to put it mildly. The media were skeptical, and the unions opposed it openly and bitterly. But the public at large received the plan very positively. As a result, the media, and later the unions, had a change of mind. Two years later, it was difficult to find anybody who did not claim fatherhood.

The price control regime played a major part here. Price control was not meant to suppress prices. It was meant to stabilize expectations. As a result, an enforcement organization was hardly necessary. The public itself was monitoring the prices. The government launched a public relations campaign in the papers and on TV stressing the role of the public in maintaining price stability. Maximum prices were established for some 40 percent of all goods and services, and the list of prices was printed and distributed free so that the public could compare prices in the market to the list. The fact that many of the transactions were carried out through chains of department stores and supermarkets helped in this aspect. Throughout the period there were no shortages and no black markets.

Beginning in July 1985, controlled prices were changed by a special committee and controls were gradually lifted by that same committee. Once a week the prime minister's economic adviser and representatives from the Ministry of Finance, the Ministry of Economy and Planning, the Ministry of Industry, and the Bank of Israel met for two hours in my office. We were the monitors of the plan. We checked weekly the economic indicators, and when we saw danger signs of problems areas we went, as a monitoring body, to the prime minister and the minister of finance (who appointed us) and made them aware of the danger. This practice has continued since I left the Ministry of Finance in November 1987.

Results of Plan

As a result of the comprehensive stabilization program, inflation dropped to about 20 percent in 1986 and 16 percent in 1987. Inflation did not increase even after we devaluated the shekel by 10 percent in January 1987. The adjustment of the exchange rate was required mainly because our inflation rates were still higher than the inflation rates of the countries with whom we trade. We managed to compensate the price effect of the devaluation by decreasing the payroll tax and reaching an agreement with the unions, according to which the unions agreed to postpone indefinitely part of the cost-of-living allowance due them. The tax decrease compensated for part of the permanent increase in the revenue from taxation that resulted from disinflation.

In terms of fiscal performance, the government's domestic deficit went down from 13.2 percent of GNP in 1984/85 to 2.8 percent of GNP in 1986/87. This decrease was due to the restrictive monetary policy, reflected in real interest rates. The high interest rates, though not popular in the business community, were an absolute must to complement the fiscal policy and ensure the success of stabilization.

When asked by the ministers about the dangers in launching the stabilization program, the planners answered that they were concerned that, as an immediate result of the budget cut and the monetary restrictions, unemployment would increase in the short run. Unemployment is a very sensitive social variable in Israel. Any rate above 6 percent is considered high. As can be seen from Diagram 8, unemployment increased along with inflation beginning in mid-1983. The package deal regime was followed by reduced unemployment, which started to increase after a short period and reached a peak of 8 percent in July 1987. To our surprise and delight, this did not happen following the comprehensive plan. Unemployment went down for five months, went up again for half a month, and then decreased to a more or less stable percentage of 5.5–6 percent.

What about the role of the U.S. grant of $1.5 billion given in the two years following the stabilization? For sure, it had a very definite role. It made the decision to launch the program easier for the decisionmakers, it was perceived by the international financial community as an implicit endorsement of the plan, and it saved Israel considerable sums of money in interest payments. On the other hand, the trend in foreign currency transfers reversed. Positive transfers would have solved our reserve problems even without the grant. But this, again, was a development we anticipated.

In sum, the stabilization program had two goals: (1) to stabilize the economy in a short time, and (2) to keep the economy stable for one to two years to permit structural changes. We were fully successful in achieving our first objective. The relative stabilization of the program and the structural change we sought to achieve are yet to be assessed.

7

The Political Economy of the Israeli Inflation

Richard Weisskoff

The period of accelerating inflation in Israel, which lasted roughly from 1978 to 1985, presented one of the greatest internal challenges to the survival of the state since its founding. Today, the effects of both the inflation and the anti-inflationary policies are still being felt.

The inflation in Israel was triggered by the spending programs of the Likud party, which had won control of the state in 1977 but faced uncompromising opposition by the Labor party–dominated trade union and its business enterprises. To establish its own patronage and consolidate its political position, the government invested heavily in West Bank infrastructure and settlements, waged war in Lebanon, and supported rising wages and consumer benefits. Locked finally into a coalition government with neither party in absolute control of the state, Israel entered a period in which economic policy became a tool of irresponsible political promises and ambitions. The result was hyperinflation, which compelled citizens and enterprises alike to alter their business conduct in order to survive during this period. Finally, as Emanuel Sharon has written, the Finance Ministry was able to convince the prime minister of the [grave danger] if the situation were to continue. The two parties reached a package deal or "social compact," slashing expenditure in every field in mid-1985, freezing prices and wages, and temporarily deindexing the economy.

Undercutting the living standard across the nation had varying effects on different segments of the population. The more protected workers in Israel suffered a temporary decline in living standards but weathered the transition with the safety net of the social welfare system. The anti-inflationary policies, however, cut the bottom out of the migrant Arab work force from Gaza and the West Bank. This jolt, coupled with the reaction to the militarized occupation, acted as the economic trigger for the uprising of the poorest segment of Israel's working class; this uprising has become known as the *intifada*.

This chapter has three goals. The first is to update the experiences of

Argentina, Brazil, and Israel through the end of 1989 and to reflect on these events and the role of inflation. The second goal is to compare the underlying structural features of these economies in order to highlight both their singularity and their similarity to Israel's experience. The third goal is to analyze the political economy of Israel, the consequences of its apparent success in stopping the inflation, and the policies that now must be pursued if price stability is to be translated into true social peace. I conclude with alternative guidelines, especially relevant today in light of events occurring in the Soviet Union and Eastern Europe.

Inflation in Argentina and Brazil, 1986–1990: New Plans and Presidents

The Record—Argentina

By the beginning of 1990, only Israel was sustaining a stable price level. "The heterodox hypothesis has been tested in Argentina, Brazil, and Israel," Rudiger Dornbusch wrote. "The Israeli experience . . . can be pronounced a full success."[1] The evidence is even more compelling after four full years.

In Argentina, the Austral Plan had effectively cut the inflation rate from 672 percent in 1985 to 90 percent by 1986 (see Table 7.1). But by 1987 the inflation had picked up to an annual rate of 132 percent, and by 1988 it had reached 343 percent. In February 1988, the IMF and foreign creditors suspended financial support for the Austral Plan because of noncompliance. By September 1988, the government responded with a new Primavera Plan, a pact with business and labor to fix wages, prices, and public service rates. Backed by a U.S. Treasury bridge loan for $500 million and World Bank loans of $1.25 billion, the Primavera Plan did arrest inflation for several months. By year's end, unemployment rose to 6.3 percent and GDP fell 1.1 percent, despite the successful 1988 grain harvest and higher international prices for grains due to the drought in the U.S.

By early 1989, the growing black market rate of the dollar signaled pressure on imports, the official exchange rate, and local interest rates. Between late February and April, the Primavera Plan was discarded, and rising exchange and interest rates forced an upward revision of prices, salaries, and pensions. The monthly inflation rate, which had been contained at less than 10 percent since November 1988, rose to 33 percent by April 1989.

The collapse of the Primavera Plan ushered in the presidential campaign, the election on May 14, and the inauguration of President Carlos Saul Menem in July 1989. His initial program under conservative minister Nestor Rapanelli cut the inflation from 200 percent in July to 6 percent in October. A standby agreement was signed with the IMF in October for $1.4 billion.

Table 7.1 **Average Annual Inflation Rates, 1965–1989**

	Argentina	Brazil	Israel
1965–1980 (average)	78.3	31.3	25.2
1980–1986 (average)	326.2	157.1	182.9
1985	672.1	226.9	304.6
1986	90.0	145.0	48.1
1987	131.6	229.8	19.9
1988	342.7	682.3	16.3
1989	3,700[a]	1,765[a]	(17.6)[b]

Sources: World Bank, *World Development Report 1988*, Table 1; IMF, *International Financial Statistics*, January 1990, lines 64, 64a; *New York Times*, February 11, 1990, p. E-3. Israel, *Statistical Abstract 1989*, p. 274.
[a]Entire year, est.
[b]Through October 1989

By December, prices started rising again, the austral was devalued by 35 percent, and Antonio Erman González replaced Rapanelli as economics minister.

A new program introduced on December 15 allowed the austral to float and removed price controls. The prospect of "dollarization"—tying the austral to the dollar—led to even greater speculation, driving the exchange rate up from 1,000 to 3,800 by New Year's Day 1990. On January 3, Minister González surprised the nation by transforming the popular *plazo fijo*, the seven-day interest-bearing savings certificates, into ten-year government bonds with interest and principal guaranteed in dollars. By the end of January, these were selling at less than half their face value. The program had effectively reduced purchasing power by confiscating $2 billion worth of private savings, driving up the black market price of the remaining dollars as a store of value.

With private spending power reduced by a third and the government unable to borrow australs again domestically, business, consumers, and the state all face a liquidity squeeze. This may force the government to print more money or to follow Mexico's path and settle its debt with U.S. Treasury Secretary Brady in quest for fresh financing from abroad. President Menem may also take on a reform of the tax system and a cut in the government deficit, confronting the very interests that placed him in power.[2]

In May 1989, the Brazilian Institute of Economics published some well-intentioned advice to the future Argentine president which might still be relevant today. "At all costs," the editors wrote, "avoid economic solutions that are too original; there's no such thing as invention in Economics. Don't allow the interests of a privileged minority to outstrip the interests of the rest. There are no 'neutral' economic steps in economic evolution. Things either advance or deteriorate."

"Argentina has everything," the advice concludes, "to make it the model for the next century. . . . Argentina suffers at her own will; her people needn't cry any longer."[3]

The Record—Brazil

In Brazil, the first Cruzado Plan, which began in early 1986, had succeeded in reducing the annual inflation rate from 227 percent in 1985 to 145 percent. But by late 1986, the Cruzado Plan was falling apart to be replaced by the Cruzado Plan II of Minister Bresser Pereira in mid-1987, which cut the budget deficit and attacked the inflation through an incomes program. By late June 1988, Brazil negotiated a rapprochement with the IMF with a $1.5 billion standby arrangement and in August rescheduled its bilateral debts with the Paris Club. In September, Brazil rescheduled its $61 billion debt with private banks, obtaining $5.2 billion in new money and $14.4 billion in trade and interbank lines of credit.

But President Sarney failed to back Minister Bresser Pereira's efforts in 1988 to achieve further budget cuts. By December, inflation had reached 28 percent, an annual rate of 1,900 percent. Treasury bonds (OTN), fully indexed and of short maturity, replaced the cruzado as a store of value and medium of exchange. The domestic debt measured in current monetary terms "soared" from 31.4 percent of GDP in 1987 to 48.5 percent of GDP in 1988.

On January 16, 1989, the government announced its Summer Plan of wage and price controls with a new currency ("new cruzado"), 17 percent devaluation, and abolition of the OTN in favor of indexed passbook savings with a real monthly yield of .5 percent. The real interest rate was maintained to discourage capital flight, several ministries were to be consolidated, and plans were made to privatize state enterprises and dismiss 90,000 government workers.

Aside from the temporary price freeze, little of this was actually carried out by the Congress. By the winter 1989, most prices and wages had been freed from controls, and the scramble to "catch-up" triggered new rounds of inflation in both the private and public sectors. Monthly inflation rates by July 1989 had reached 30 percent, or nearly 2,000 percent on a yearly basis. The grain harvest of 1988/89, however, was a record high, and production levels in general had been sustained. The November 14 election, the first under the new 1988 Constitution, gave conservative Fernando Collor de Mello about the same number of votes as the populist Luis Ignacio ("Lula") da Silva. Collor has emerged president in the runoff, and 1990 now finds Brazil set for a new economic policy.[4]

One Chilean journal summed up the failures of the Argentine and Brazilian programs as having lopsidedly focused on fixing incomes and prices to stop the escalator-like inertia of the systemic inflation.[5] In the end, the budget deficits were never effectively reduced, and the central banks continued to finance government operations. In Israel, on the other hand, the rate of inflation seemed to stabilize around 20 percent in 1988 and 1989.

Underlying Issues

The underlying issue in the inflationary countries is the use of the economic system as the means to play out civic and social conflict, which under the military had been managed by decree and constrained by force. Prices and the price level do not simply measure value as a thermometer measures the temperature of a patient. Prices themselves represent the command of actual resources. Hence, struggles between classes, regions, sectors, or groups of firms, and rivalries between employees and owners and between the state and the private sector are fought out on economic turf. The government itself has become, along with workers and private industry, a major sector as both employer and employee. In addition, the state tries to play protector and referee for the entire system. By being also monopolist-producer of the key commodity (money) and both spender and collector of *all* the people's taxes, the government has become an enormous locus of power and privilege.

The state under the military in both Argentina and Brazil suppressed wage demands of workers by breaking strikes through force and repression. With prices rising, this alone reduced the real standard of living. The fall in the share of wages in national income in Brazil from 1959 to 1970, John Sheahan writes unambiguously, "could hardly have been done without blocking the right to strike."[6] The military regime that came to power in Argentina in 1966 promoted industry and agriculture by driving down the average real wage in the industrial sector. Following the ending of the Perón era in March 1976 by the military, real wages were suppressed by 40 percent over the next two years, and then followed four more years of enforced economic discipline, extreme repression, brutal disappearances, and a war with England in 1982.

The subsequent return of civilian rule to Argentina in 1982 and to Brazil in 1985 has meant the restoration of the electoral process, sensitivity to worker rights, and the loosening up of the economic system as the means of reasserting civilian power. Shares of the pie would be henceforth determined by economic conflict and by the state through the price-wage system rather than through police action. An occasional halt in this conflict, the freezing or "time out" to breathe easily, has become known as "incomes policy." An alternative to this conflict, as Sheahan writes somewhat naively, would be to tie an increasing standard of living to real productivity gains and minimize the social strife. "That would have meant," Sheahan concludes, "a corresponding limit on the rate of gain of the winners in the power contest."[7]

Simply turning the economy over to "market forces" away from an authoritarian bureaucratic state has also highlighted the importance of concentrated market power in the hands of protected oligopolies and strong labor unions. "Inflation is a battle between dominant groups for a larger share of the economic surplus," Bresser Pereira states simply.[8] Who loses? The workers, managers, and small firms in the competitive sectors. Who gains? The dynamic and politically stronger sectors. "From this point of view, inflation in Brazil is a way of transferring income . . ." from the politically weaker to the stronger sectors, made possible only with a cartel-like organization of the major oligopolies and the collaboration of the state with the powerful interests.

Thus, with the return to civilian rule, the price level—the inflation—has become both the mechanism and the arena of social conflict. It not only *measures* the gains and losses; it *is* the civil war. Jeff Sachs reminds us that economic policymaking in Latin America—indeed, everywhere to some degree—remains a battleground of populist strife.[9] In earlier decades, these battles had been fought between regional agencies or between rival governors' claims on the federal treasury. These were the classic issues of land reform, urban-rural migration, import substitution, industrial policy, and export promotion. Today, in circumstances of a generally rising price level, these battles must be fought on the very steps of the inflationary escalator. And if the escalator stops, or even slows, *all* the passengers are jolted.

All the instruments of the state—the Congress, the ministries, the military budget, the "public" corporations—become tools for redressing the economic balance of power. In Brazil especially, great numbers of people survive at very low levels of health and education. Brazil's mortality rate for children under five, which is UNICEF's single most comprehensive measure of child welfare, was estimated at eighty-seven deaths per thousand in 1987, compared to thirty-eight for Argentina and thirteen for Israel.[10] Similarly, adult illiteracy in Brazil in 1985 was held to be 20 percent, compared to 4 percent in Argentina and 5 percent in Israel. Only 20 percent of first-graders in Brazil completed primary school between 1980 and 1986, compared to 66 percent in Argentina and 97 percent in Israel.[11] Oppressed by their reduced share of private and public resources and barely surviving at minimal health standards, the masses exert their claim through the electoral process, and the candidates play, and possibly pay, for their allegiance.

The informal or invisible sector, estimated in Brazil to add 30–50 percent to recorded economic activity, is a parallel economy that grows avoiding government interference and anti-inflationary controls. Tax avoidance, underbilling, double-ledger bookkeeping by professionals and firms, and capital flight all cut government revenue and put more of a burden on regressive consumption taxes.[12]

The state, despite these circumventions, carries on its own program of practical activities and governs by popular, not repressive, mandate. It must collect and then disperse its own considerable economic pie, keeping the next elections in mind. First the public sector and then the entire economy are affected by policies of the Treasury, Central Bank, Economic Ministry, and Congress. The price level becomes both prize and weapon of rival interests.

It is unfortunate that we have learned little of the substance of these rivalries as they are thrashed out in the quiet lobbies and noisy legislatures. Frontline battles are fought within each firm in shop-by-shop labor negotiations and the constant effort to protect the real wage. With prices rising daily outside the factory or office, it is the fault of neither worker nor employer that the money wage must be vigilantly negotiated and renegotiated, elevating labor conflict as a major activity for each company.[13] The final scorecard of these battles, from plant floor to congressional pie, is summarized monthly in the price level.

Comparisons of the Three Countries

Earlier chapters in this book have examined the inflationary experience and policies of each country. It may be helpful now to evaluate these experiences in the light of the particular economic character and structure of each nation.

Israel, the smallest of the three countries whose population of 4.4 million is 14 percent the size of Argentina and 3 percent that of Brazil, has achieved the highest per capita GNP and, until 1988, had been growing moderately (see Table 7.2, lines 1-4). Israel's total external debt (line 5) in absolute terms is half that of Argentina and less than a quarter that of Brazil, but as a share of GNP, Israel's exceeds them both. This has presented less of an immediate political concern, as Israel's debt is held mostly by the U.S. government and has a longer-term structure. Hence, Israel must devote a relatively low share of her exports to pay for debt service—19 percent—compared to 33 percent for Argentina and 52 percent for Brazil.

The most striking characteristic of Israel's economy is, of course, the 30 percent share of the total budget spent on defense (Table 7.2, line 9). A much smaller country, Israel spends in *absolute terms* three to four times more than each of the other countries spends on the military. Some of this is offset by the high levels of foreign aid that Israel receives (Table 7.2, lines 10-11), but for the most part, it reflects plainly the near-war conditions in the Middle East and their economic cost.

Table 7.2 Economic Comparisons: Three Countries, 1986–1988

	Year	Argentina	Brazil	Israel
1. Population (million)	1987	31	141	4.4
2. GNP (per capita) (US $)	1987	2,360	2,020	6,810
3. Inflation rate (%)	1988	343	682	16
4. GDP growth rate (%)	1980–86	2.7	–0.8	1.1
	1987	1.6	3.0	3.6
	1988	–1.1	–0.3	0.0
5. Total external debt ($ billion)	1987	56.8	123.9	26.3
6. Total external debt/ GNP (1986) (%)	1987	76.6	43.5	88.4
7. Debt service/ exports (%)	1986	32.2	52.2	18.9
8. Government deficit/ GNP (%)	1986	11.6	8.0	3.5
9. Defense/total budget (%)	1986	3.1	5.2	30.1
10. Foreign aid/ GNP (%)	1986	0.1	0.1	6.8
11. Foreign aid per capita ($)	1986	1.3	2.8	450.0

Sources: World Bank, *World Tables 1988-89*, pp. 37, 105, 157, 329; *World Development Report 1988*, Tables 17, 19, 22, 23; IMF, *International Financial Statistics*, January 1990, line 64, country entries; IDB, *Social and Economic Outlook 1989*, Statistical Profiles; Israel, *Statistical Abstract 1989*, p. 188.

In comparing these three nations, it may be helpful to keep in mind a simple structural model that is the foundation of all economies. These are, first, the work force; second, the distribution of income that the people command; third, the pattern of consumption that the people demand; and fourth, the structure of the industry that produces to meet those demands.[14] Money, and the value it represents, serves as the circulatory medium that connects and nourishes these pieces. Money is also a commodity like any other and can be watered down or adulterated, diluted or debased, by its producer.

When the industrial structure does not produce what its people need or fails to employ its own work force, then the economic pieces may seem not to fit harmoniously together. The economy is said to be "disarticulated," and attempts to fashion major policies, such as cutting public employment or the government deficit, may result in even further disjointedness.

Let us turn to the first piece, the labor force. All three economies experienced considerable decline in the share of agricultural employment from 1960 to 1980 (see Table 7.3), reflecting the great migratory shift from country to city and the resulting pressures on public services, education, and the urban food supply. Israel had begun with the smallest (17 percent) share of its labor force in agriculture, compared to 44 percent for Argentina and 52 percent for Brazil, and today retains but a token of its own work force in the rural area. Striking also are the comparable labor force shares in industry (24%) for Brazil and Israel, smaller than Argentina's 35 percent. The major difference between Israel's labor force and those of the two South American economies is her 70 percent share engaged in services compared to 46–47 percent in Argentina and Brazil in 1980. This underscores Beveridge's preference for the term "social service" to "welfare" state, as Israel Katz reminds us.[15]

The profile of incomes generated by this labor force is also markedly different for the three countries (see Table 7.4). While the available data are from the earlier decade for Argentina and Brazil, it is likely that an even greater deterioration in equality for these countries has occurred during the past twenty years due to repression and hyperinflation.[16]

The degree of inequality is the most extreme in Brazil and the least extreme in Israel. The poorest 20 percent of families in Israel received 5–6 percent of household income in the 1970s, which is 1.4 times the share received by the bottom quintile in Argentina and three times the share of Brazil's poorest. At the other end of the social pyramid, Israel's richest 10 percent received 23–24 percent of the national pie, two-thirds the size of the share received by the top Argentine decile and less than half the share of Brazil's top 10 percent.[17]

Comparing the shares of the poorest to the richest *within* each country, we note that Brazil's top quintile claims thirty-three times the income share of the nation's poorest. In Argentina the top quintile receives eleven times the poorest and in Israel from five to six times from 1975 to 1986.

These income structures suggest that although Argentina and Brazil *on the average* have only a third of the per capita income of Israel (Table 7.2, line 2), the rich of those poorer countries have reached international levels because of their large claim on their nations' incomes. Israel, on the other hand, as a matter of policy and practice, has tolerated neither extreme wealth nor extreme poverty generated by the nation's economy. The state undertook responsibility for production and delivery of many goods and services, and aside from a few clearly visible fortunes, has succeeded in leveling incomes across broad segments of the economy.[18]

The level and distribution of income also imply different national

Table 7.3 Labor Force Structure, 1960–1980

	% Agriculture		% Industry		% Services[a]	
	1960	1980	1960	1980	1960	1980
Argentina	44	18	29	35	27	47
Brazil	52	30	15	24	33	46
Israel	17	6	23	24	60	70

Source: *Statistical Abstract of Latin America*, Vol. 25, p. 230; *Statistical Abstract of Israel 1987*, p. 7.
[a]Services include construction.

Table 7.4 Distribution of Income to Households by Quintiles

		Argentina	Brazil		Israel	
Quintile (20%)		1970	1972	1975/76	1979/80	1986/87[a]
Poorest	I	4.4	2.0	6.1	5.4	8.4
	II	9.7	5.0	12.6	11.6	12.4
	III	14.1	9.4	18.2	17.6	17.2
	IV	21.5	17.0	24.4	24.9	23.2
Richest	V	50.3	66.6	38.7	40.6	38.8
(top 10%)		(35.2)	(50.6)	(22.9)	(24.3)	(23.2)

Sources: *Statistical Abstract of Latin America*, Vol. 28, p. 278, for Argentina, Brazil; Israel Central Bureau of Statistics, *Family Expenditure Survey 1975/76* and *1979/80; Statistical Abstract of Israel 1989*, pp. 290-291.
[a]Not strictly comparable to earlier years.

patterns of private consumption (see Table 7.5). Israel generally has spent a smaller share of total household consumption on food and clothing and much larger shares on transport, appliances, and services than Brazil. Both spend similar shares—a quarter—on housing. The difference between the 23 percent share of spending on services and the 71 percent employment in services for Israel (see Table 7.3) suggests that public subsidies underwrite a large part of this sector and that services have become the employer of last resort.

The differential structure of consumption *within* each country (see Table 7.6) gives us an x-ray of how different levels or classes of people live. These patterns measure differences due, for example, to income, status, occupation, region, and ethnicity. They also indicate how each class would be affected by a differential increase in prices or changes in subsidies.

The basic patterns, in comparing the bottom, middle, and top classes in Israel and Brazil, reveal the decline in the shares of spending on food and the

Table 7.5 Average Spending Patterns for Brazil and Israel

	Brazil 1975	Israel 1975/76	Israel 1979/80	Israel 1986/87
Percent spent on:				
A. Food, beverages, tobacco	39.9	24.0	23.5	23.3
B. Clothing	8.9	7.5	6.4	7.3
C. Housing (services)	25.5	29.9	30.0	25.2
D. Transport & household furniture	14.8	19.0	19.0	20.8
E. Services (medical, personal, other)	11.4	19.6	21.0	23.4
1. Average expenditure	21,234[a]	3,925[b]	2,311[c]	1,865[d]
2. Average income	—	5,281[b]	3,419[c]	2,078[d]
3. Ratio expenditure/ income	—	.74	.68	.90
4. Family size	5.0	3.8	3.4	3.5
5. No. families (millions)	19.1	.8	.9	1.1
6. No. people (millions)	94.7	2.9	3.0	3.8

Sources: Brazil: *Anuario Estadístico do Brasil, 1980*, p. 696. Israel: *Family Expenditure Survey, 1975/76* and *1979/80*, Special series 711, pt. B, Table 2. *Statistical Abstract of Israel 1988*, p. 300.
[a]In Cr$ per year at current prices.
[b]In Israeli lira per month at average prices of survey period.
[c]In Israeli shekels per month at average prices of survey period.
[d]In New Israeli shekels (NIS) per month of average prices of survey period.

rise of the shares spent on housing, transport, and services. The variation between the Brazilian classes is by far greater than in Israel because of the wider range in income in Brazil.

The inclusion of the 1973/74 Survey of the West Bank and Gaza in these comparisons (See Table 7.6, cols. 7–8) suggests a submerged population similar to the lowest class in Brazil, but with a share of service expenditure more similar to Israel's lowest quintile. Recent official Israeli statistics suggest that for the last five years, the *average* consumption per capita in Israel has been three times that in the West Bank and 4.5 times that in Gaza, which puts the *average* level in the territories at about half the living standard of the *poorest* quintile in Israel.[19]

Structural inequality, as reflected in incomes and consumption within each nation, takes on crucial importance under conditions of hyperinflation because of the escalated level of social conflict required in the defense of each group's economic position. Some classes may have been able to protect themselves more effectively by indexing their wages and safeguarding their assets. Other groups are "pinched" at both ends; their money incomes, if unindexed, fail to rise with the general wage rates, and their consumption basket may consist most heavily of those goods and services whose prices are raised as government subsidies are cut.

In the unionized sectors, strikes, talks, and negotiations are the means by

Table 7.6 Consumption Pattern by Income Class for Israel & Brazil

Income Class:	Brazil 1975 Income Groups			Israel 1975/76 Quintile			Territories 1973/74		Israel 1979/80 Quintile			Israel 1986/87 Quintile		
							West Bank	Gaza Strip						
Expenditure category:	1	4	7	1	3	5			1	3	5	1	3	5
A. Food	56.2	35.8	13.6	29.6	26.2	18.0	46.5	57.7	42.2	23.5	15.8	36.2	23.7	17.2
B. Clothing	7.8	9.8	9.1	5.6	8.9	6.5	7.6	7.1	7.3	6.2	5.4	10.2	7.4	5.8
C. Housing	18.6	25.2	43.2	36.5	27.7	31.6	8.5	6.2	24.1	30.8	33.1	21.0	25.4	26.9
D. Transport & furniture[a]	9.8	15.3	18.3	12.0	17.7	23.3	10.2	8.8	10.6	19.1	22.6	13.7	20.2	24.3
E. Services	7.6	13.9	15.8	16.3	19.5	20.6	27.2	20.2	15.9	20.4	23.1	18.9	23.3	25.8
1. Ratio Expenditure/ Nat. Aver.	—	—	—	.48	.97	1.61	—	—	.54	.97	1.50	.63	.95	1.49
2. Ratio Expend./Inc.	—	—	—	—	—	—	—	—	.96	.74	.51	1.35	.99	.69
3. Family Size	5.4	5.4	4.5	5.5	3.7	2.9	6.9	7.1	4.2	3.3	2.6	4.6	3.4	2.7
4. No. families (million)	4.4	1.5	.2		.777		(29.6)[b]	(49.6)[b]		.893			1.092	
Population (million)		94.7			2.985		.556			3.038			3.822	

Sources: Anuario Estadístico do Brasil 1980, p. 69b; Family Expenditure Survey 1975/76 and 1979/80, Special Series 711, pt. B Table 2; Statistical Abstract of Israel 1988, pp. 296-299; Family Expenditure Survey in the Administered Territories 1973/74, Special Series 532 (1976), p. vii.
[a]Includes appliances.
[b]In thousands.

which wage and profit shares are ultimately decided. In the unorganized sectors, that is, the lowest classes, the forms of protest and social tension may be more diffused and chaotic because the channels of expression fail or are shut down. Thus, Sheahan could write that both Brazil and Argentina "relapsed at different crucial points" into intense political repression for substantial periods of time rather than deal more openly with their economic and social strains.[20]

These consumption differences—in level as well as form—measure both social tension and the precariousness of life. They also reflect the readiness of the populist politician to grant concessions when groups within the structure are threatened by price changes or by budget cuts.

In summary, then, the greater share of labor in Israel engaged in services and the country's greater homeogeneity may have made the achievement of a social compact between combatants more feasible. In Argentina and Brazil, the range of incomes, living standards, and occupations is so vast that to arrange a truce between the contestants would compromise the state's own position as both employer and focus of political power. In the light of this structural background, we turn now to analyze the Israeli hyperinflation—the circumstances of its appearance and the aftereffects of its disappearance.

The Israeli Economy and the Hyperinflation

The success of the Israeli economy from its founding until the inflationary period had resulted from its policies of building an "independent" or "self-sufficient" economy. In my opinion, the economic crises of the last decade, especially in Israel's wrestling with hyperinflation, have grown out of the abandonment of those principles.

Historical Background

The early Jewish settlements in colonial Palestine under the Turks and the British mandate had been founded on principles of self-sufficiency. Aid was accepted, indeed relied upon, to finance the building of roads, schools, clinics, the *kibbutz*, the *moshav*, and the towns.

"The revival of Palestine during the past quarter century," Robert Nathan and associates wrote in 1946, "is commonly regarded, in Western countries, as a charitable enterprise. . . . This view is erroneous. The established population of Palestine is fully self-sustaining."[21]

Guided by a settler Zionist vision, the immigrants wanted to avoid replicating the social structure of the nations they had left. A new form of economy was to be established, based on collective or cooperative working of the land, a strong trade union, and working-class ownership of the important enterprises. The leading firms in banking, wholesaling, produce marketing, construction, and home building were owned by the trade union organization (Histadrut). The successful formation of an independent economy preceded statehood and made political independence viable.[22]

With the departure of the British, the state of Israel assumed the economic tasks involved in nation-building, such as forming a regular army, establishing a system of taxation, regulating the money supply, constructing the society's infrastructure, and providing social services. The government also took over or initiated new enterprises, such as the railroads and public utilities, chemicals and minerals, shipping and ship repair, the airlines, and weapons production and development. While the government and its enterprises today share the work force almost equally with the private and Histadrut-owned firms, the state supplies three-fourths of the capital of the entire economy. It is thus through the government budget and control of the state apparatus that resources are distributed throughout the society.

During its first two decades (1948–1967), the Israeli economy concentrated on producing food, housing, manufactures, and services for its immigrant labor force, and on creating jobs and providing for the physical needs of the newly arrived population. A new nation based on the in-gathering of a dispersed people, the state of Israel was to avoid the pitfalls of other Third World or newly independent peoples. It was to avoid generating extremes of wealth; it would not tolerate abject poverty.

The state, the Histadrut, and private enterprises divided the economic tasks. And in this division of labor, the identification of the Labor party with the state and the Histadrut was almost complete. Except for the proliferation of minor opposition parties, the dominance by the Labor party of the state and trade union was thought to be incontestable.

In the period following the Six Day War in 1967, the economy of Israel began to undergo a second or "maturing" transformation. In weapons production, it was to become self-sufficient, reducing its reliance on foreign suppliers. New, technologically more sophisticated industries were built, leading to a change in the labor force. Agriculture declined as a leading export sector, and the demands of capital formation gave way to demands for higher levels of consumption. The once isolated and relatively backward village economies of the West Bank began to disintegrate, especially after 1973, as the local product markets and labor supply of the territories[23] were absorbed into the main economy of Israel.

The Likud victory in the 1977 elections marked the end of the Labor party's monopoly of the state and its enterprises, but not of the Histadrut and its enterprises. This electoral mandate may be seen also as a reaction to the changing economic structure, a protest by the growing Sephardic lower and middle classes to blocked social and political opportunity. The Likud's programs of making consumption goods more widely available, constructing settlements in the territories, and, finally, its initiative to invade Lebanon were not halted by the Labor opposition. As a result of these altered national priorities, investment in native industries has decayed, traditional jobs have been displaced, and the basic labor force has been undercut by Arab labor recruited from the territories.[24]

Changes in opportunity and mobility may indeed have occurred for the top- and middle-income groups with a shift in the control of the state. But on a national level, Israel began taking on a character of greater dependence and less self-sufficiency. Competition between the Likud party–dominated government, together with its enterprises, and the Labor party–dominated Histadrut, with its enterprises, resulted in a spiral of government spending and wage hikes, strikes and price increases, yet higher wages, and more government spending. The government could not control the Histadrut, and the Labor party could not effectively sabotage the government's programs. The subsequent electoral contests of 1981 and 1984 were too close to be conclusive.

During the periods 1967–1973 and 1974–1977, when Labor dominated the government, prices rose on the average 8 percent and 39 percent per year, respectively. (See Table 7.7, line 1 for inflation and line 3 for election results.) But prices rose on the average 120 percent per year from 1978 to 1981 and 218 percent per year from 1982 to 1984, periods of Likud domination. The election of 1984 proved a standoff. The parties joined in an alternating coalition, and the frenzy of hyperinflation continued.

Inflation in Israel was triggered by the overspending by the government following the 1977 triumph of the Likud in the national elections after thirty years in the opposition. It accelerated after 1981 and 1984 because of the near balance between the two parties and the more equal division of the government. In order to overcome the opposition of the Labor party entrenched in the major economic institutions, the state undertook endeavors beyond its fiscal capabilities. It waged a war in Lebanon; provided a new infrastructure of roads, factories, and settlements in the West Bank; and, at the same time, raised the standard of living of the Israeli electorate through higher wages and a wider distribution of imported consumer durables.[25]

Economics became the tool to secure the voters' allegiance, and economic intransigence became the opposition's defense. Without sufficient foreign and domestic resources to carry out these ambitious programs and unable to compromise, the Treasury simply printed money, and the economy inflated.

Social disarray had been averted only through the built-in escalators and indices that insulated the wages, savings, and pensions for most of the working class from the losses due to rising prices and the eroded real value of their money. Government revenues based on income taxes declined as rising prices and costs made true "income" and "profit" almost impossible to

Table 7.7 Changes in Prices, Exchange Rates, Elections, and Other Measures, 1967–1988

	1967–1973	1974–1977	1978–1981	1982–1984	1985	1986	1987	1988
1. Consumer prices (aagr)[a]	8.2	38.6	120.1	218.3	304.6	48.1	19.9	16.3
2. Exchange rate (IS/US$)	.37	.89	7.15	260	1,176	1,494	1,591	1,599
3. Elections (% votes Labor/Likud)	(2.1)[b]	1.3[c]	.74[d]	.91[e]	1.1[f]	—	—	.96[g]
4. GDP/capita (% aagr)	6.3	0.7	1.9	0.0	2.1	2.0	3.6	0.0
5. Govt. expenditure (% aagr)	—	—	-6.4[j]	-1.5	4.1	-9.9	16.9	-2.4
6. Priv. consumption (% aagr)	— (13.4)[h]	— (1.9)[h]	-12.6[j] (3.3)[h,i]	3.7	0.5	14.2	8.4	3.0
7. Capital formation (% aagr)	15.2	-4.7	-1.1	5.9	-10.6	10.4	3.3	-2.1
8. Imports (% aagr)	17.1	-0.3	4.2	4.0	-0.7	8.9	19.3	-3.0
9. Wages (% aagr)	6.3[k]	1.9	4.6	1.7	-9.0	7.8	7.9	6.0
10. Unemployment (rate)	2.6[k]	3.4	4.1	5.1	6.7	7.1	6.1	6.4
11. Workdays lost in strikes (average annual days, thous.)	375[k]	235	652	1,262	540	406	996	516

Sources: Statistical Abstract of Israel 1987, 1988, 1989.
[a] aagr = average annual growth rate
[b] Election 1969
[c] Election 1973
[d] Election 1977
[e] Election 1981
[f] Election 1984
[g] Election 1988
[h] Refers to private consumption plus government
[i] Refers to 1978–79
[j] Refers to 1980–81 only
[k] Refers to 1973 only

compute. Companies, delaying their tax payments, could earn more through speculation and financial manipulation than through real employment and investment. The unpredictable yet inevitable devaluations rewarded funds kept in liquid form, free to move abroad and back again depending on real rates of interest. Skillful money management became a source of incredible profit; only the salaried working person was locked into regular tax payments through the withholding system.

The state, short on cash, taxed consumption, tourism, travel, and imports, in order to extract revenue from the population. The public sought to protect its earnings by demanding imported durables, and the government supplied them to secure voters' allegiance and collect the taxes on the goods themselves, on the importer's deposits and markups, and on the complementary products, such as fuel and spare parts.[26]

By making foreign exchange available at a highly favorable rate, the state opened up a new era of conspicuous consumption for the electorate by diffusing more widely dollars for appliances, automobiles, and foreign travel which, under the earlier Labor governments, had been severely restricted to the most privileged groups. This, of course, diverted scarce foreign exchange to consumption and away from production and investment, indebting the country further and forcing Israel to rely more on foreign largess to provide the crucial dollars for the system to continue.

Local employment suffered as funds sought speculative, rather than productive, activity. Money and people fled the country, and from 1980 to 1983 and again in 1985, more people left Israel than entered.[27] The black market flourished, and even the Bank of Israel is reported to have supplied dollars to these markets at times.

In short, the moral confidence in the government as an honest broker, the keeper of the people's currency, was greatly undermined. Just as the medieval princes "clipped" the edges of silver coins to provide themselves with additional revenue, so the modern nation state debased the value of its money, diluting its real content. By simply printing enough money to cover its desired expenses, which exceeded the quantity of available resources, prices began to rise and then wages, and all interconnected and interlocking escalators for a substantial share of the citizenry.

The inflation also covered up real investment mistakes, rewarded ruthless financial manipulation, and made honest bookkeeping impossible and obsolete. Rather than caring for productive efficiency and existing plant and equipment, the rapid inflation distracted entrepreneurial activity into financial wizardry and converted working people into petty speculators, contractors, importers, and super-consumers. The public investigations that followed the stock market crash in the fall of 1983 revealed for the first time the full extent of the manipulation and collaboration of the banking community and their regulators and owners. All were caught up in the speculative bubble: the

Bank of Israel, the Histadrut, the Jewish Agency, and the private banking families. The state, to settle the affair, bailed out the banks and their stockholders, replaced the managements, and ultimately held individuals responsible for having succumbed to the temptations of manipulating a very lucrative stock market under inflationary conditions.

The abrupt halting of inflation, beginning in the summer of 1985, was based on the explicit agreement by the government, the Histadrut, and the Manufacturers Association to cut spending, subsidies, wages, and profits, and to freeze most prices. The agreement had been achieved because of the efforts of the Finance Ministry, as Emmanuel Sharon has informed us, to impress upon the cabinet the importance of such action and the dire consequences of continuing inflation. These efforts too were encouraged by the prospect of the U.S. administration's request to Congress for an additional $1.5 billion if Israel could agree on a plan. Once a price tag was finally put on inaction and compromise sweetened by considerable reward, budget cuts were finally agreed upon.[28] Ongoing aid, which to this day continues to be the prize for collaboration of the coalition government, supplies the cash to continue the basic dollar-based activities that other nations, facing similar inflationary crises, would be forced to curtail.

The decline in the real wage, the reduction of profits, and the removal of subsidies from the basic products and services had been voluntarily negotiated by representatives of all the affected parties. The social welfare system provided the safety net for the poor and for the laid-off workers.

However, the very poorest workers—the Arab noncitizens of the West Bank and Gaza—had no such protective net. The shock of the public cutbacks in services and the sudden contraction in construction, agriculture, and manufacturing meant less need for the marginal workers who were thrown back into their village economy. The severity of the Israeli contraction and the competitive pressure on wages and work opportunities throughout the lower working class heightened social tensions between the Arab and Jewish populations and the military authorities in the territories.

In Venezuela, Argentina, Peru, and Brazil, similar attempts to shock the economy out of its inflationary spiral have been met by riots in the capital city or uprisings in the countryside, a subsequent military response, and the collapse of the program. In Israel, a much smaller and more tightly organized society, the *incorporated* working class cooperated with the shock treatment through their elected leaders, for they stood to regain their economic position if stability and growth could be restored. U.S. aid and the signing of a free trade area agreement with the United States in April 1985 were additional incentives.[29]

However, the lowest portion of the working class in Israel, the almost 100,000 migrant workers and their families in Gaza and the West Bank, remained outside the realm of Israeli minimum wages, incomes, social services, and unemployment insurance.[30] Their work force could not be unionized; their wages and hours were loosely regulated, and legal grievance procedures were undeveloped.[31]

During the period preceding the inflationary spiral, evidence suggests a mixed picture of the decline of the village economy, an increase in real money income because of the incorporation of the territories into the cash wage economy, and a clearly visible disparity between the average migrant wage and the Israeli wage in similar industries. The incorporation of the Arab worker at the bottom end of the wage scale created greater dependence on the migrant condition in both the territories and the Israeli economy.[32]

The abrupt halting of the inflationary expansion and the interruption of that absorptive process led to an increased number of incidents of conflict between settlers, residents, and the military in the territories.

Despite the return of apparent prosperity by 1986, social relations were turning very sour. "The quantifiable facts present an accurate picture of the intensity of the intercommunal strife in the occupied territories," Benvenisti wrote in August 1987. "Between April 1986 and May 1987, 3,150 incidents of violent demonstrations occurred . . . less severe than in 1985-86, but the cycle which started in 1981-82 remained for five consecutive years (1982-87) above the 3,000 mark. By comparison, the average annual occurrence of 'disturbances' between 1977-82, was only 500. . . . The ratio of terrorist to spontaneous acts indicates a new phase in Palestinian resistance and intercommunal strife. . . . There is no doubt about the grass-roots origin of the most violent actions."[33]

Finally, in December 1987, came the explosion, known as the *intifada*.[34] The economic basis of the Arab uprising had been laid first by drafting this lowest laboring class into the Israeli economy, then by maintaining the great disparity between the wages of the two labor forces, and finally by not providing any mechanisms for resolving conflict between the Arab worker and Israeli employer and between residents and settlers. The ultimate frustration was triggered perhaps by the failure of the 1986/87 olive crop in the West Bank, which yielded but 6 percent of the tonnage and 10 percent of the revenue of the previous bumper harvest. The continued integration of the surplus Arab labor into the Israeli economy, labor rendered surplus by the inevitable destruction of the village economy in the face of modern production techniques, has sustained the *intifada* despite the superficial attempts to blockade villages and substitute other foreign workers.

The continuing need of the stalemated Israeli government to support the lifestyles of its own voters has led the state to violate the basic principles of disciplined economic management. Specifically, this has meant favoring present consumerism over savings and investment, imported durables over local manufactures, luxury construction over low-income housing, and new settlements over repair or expansion of existing facilities. It has emphasized the use of foreign exchange for the private automobile, fuel, and spare parts, and of public spending for roads rather than for the improvement of bus and rail transport. In the end, the economy, by importing more of its basic needs and exporting higher-technology equipment and weapons, has been failing to provide sufficient work opportunities for its own skilled and educated work force. The result has been outmigration of large segments of its own ambitious and experienced population to the United States and the readiness of young army veterans to entertain risky mercenary ventures in other parts of the Third World.

What have been the consequences of the inflation? Here are my hypotheses. First, there has been a greater differentiation—a spreading out— of families' consumption among a wider variety of goods, especially for imports and for durables, rather than for local products and savings. This can be seen in the growth and sophistication of the advertising industry in Israel, the emphasis on conspicuous consumption, the distaste for locally made goods, and the rise of automobiles and electronics as depositories of the families' savings.

Second, several "new" industrial complexes have been created at great expense, such as aircraft, metals, communications, high-tech, and armaments. The traditional consumer industries remain undercapitalized in their technical inefficiency and today face steep competition with Israel's entry into freer trade areas of the United States and Europe.

But the *new* industrial complexes are not yet linked with other *local* industries to the same degree as the older ones. They rely on imported raw materials and machinery and export their output. As the older industries close because of foreign competition, their supplier networks too are reduced. The chain of production decomposes, and unemployment becomes a serious structural and ongoing problem.

A new profile of Israeli industry is emerging which needs *fewer* if better trained workers and relies more on foreign capital, techniques, and markets. The GNP continues to rise, but the underlying productive structure has changed and, with it, the structure of the labor force, its skills, and remuneration.

Third, recent evidence suggests that the income distribution has become less equal now than before the inflation began. There may have been no shortcuts in redressing social inequalities through foreign exploits or internal transfers. The basic inequities built into the structures of employment income, consumption, and production had never been addressed explicitly. Policymakers toyed with political demagoguery and justified their actions in terms of imported technocratic theories of inflation and its fancied causes. Insufficient attention had been given to justice, equity, or fairness through work and real production. Economic forecasters had lost touch with their duty to interpret reality in the best interests of the entire nation, to provide a warning system for its working people, and offer fresh alternatives for its political leadership.[35]

The rising unemployment rate and the cut in government subsidies, services, and transfers, together with the fuller integration of the Arab work force at the lower end of the pay scale, all contribute to increased inequality in the most current period. The inflationary years may have also promoted a new ethic in Israeli society as the working family took a beating both in the work place and in the stock market. Indeed, working for a wage came to be seen as "backward" or "old-fashioned" compared to seeking greater rewards through speculation, gift-giving, and favor-seeking.

As the inflation slowed, some of Israel's largest and most respectable firms required bailouts from the Treasury. And the state in turn turned to Washington for its own bailout.

In summary, the Israeli economy has passed through three stages. First was the formation of a national, self-sufficient economy, relying on foreign assistance to finance the infrastructure (pre-1948). Second was the deepening of the linkages within the economy, broadening and upgrading the labor force, and the emergence of class and racial differences (1950-1973). In the third or current stage, as the inequalities of income and opportunity are becoming more glaring, the structure of industry is changing from the production of basic needs and services to weapons and more sophisticated goods. The Arab labor force in the territories has become imperfectly integrated into the Israeli economy, and personal consumption has become more differentiated across the wide range of incomes.

The austerity program cut both government and personal consumption and at the same time made large quantities of consumer imports available to the public at a subsidized exchange rate. This further undermined local durable production and created the need for further imports of fuel and spare parts. The reliance on glamour high-tech exports short-circuits the urgency of retooling the traditional industries and undercuts the complicated sets of their already-established linkages and labor supply.

The destruction of the backward village economy in the territories and the failure to create an "independent economy" there has meant, first, the influx of cheap but skilled Arab labor into the Israeli economy and, then, the adverse pressure of that absorption as "austerity" affected this lowest segment more harshly. The familiar story in Latin America repeats itself: An anti-inflation austerity program is unfurled, the middle sectors applaud it, the hardest-hit class rebels, and, if the uprising is not crushed, the accord must be renegotiated.

Conclusion

The present dependence on U.S. aid increases, not lessens, the overall need for future loans. The military situation in the Middle East, fomented by donor and recipient alike, adds greater urgency to the economic aid and pressure to ignore the needed structural changes.

Economic independence and self-sufficiency requires deliberate movement toward lessening reliance on foreign capital and imports, strengthening internal linkages, equalizing incomes, and consolidating the labor force. It means seeking and following a program that will lead to increased *self-reliance* and the creation of a larger home market.

The true goal of "economy," (*cal-ca-lah*, a doubling of the Hebrew root *cli*) is to provide a reinforced *vessel* to hold a nation's spirit, the collective and individual souls of a people. A strong, correct economy does this. The goal of a "self-sufficient economy" (*cal-ca-lah atz-ma-it* in Hebrew) is to allow the *essence* of a people—their inner character—to emerge and realize itself. In the case of Israel, this is done by a threefold union of a people following a particular path on its own land. The Talmud carries clear behavioral and spiritual guidelines on correct economy.[36]

The interrelatedness of the economic world has been demonstrated by the impact of the "oil shock" following the 1973 Yom Kippur War, which triggered worldwide inflation. There are also clear global dangers to maintaining the present state of armed readiness in the Middle East.

Attempts to link material and spiritual phenomena—to specify the relationships between the laws of economy and the laws of the spirit—make modern economists, not to mention bankers and managers, uneasy. It was the contribution of the Jewish tradition to later religions to recognize explicitly the moral quality of every concrete action. This freed society from the narrow constraints of earlier religion and placed all material action on a spiritual footing. Public policy as well as individual conduct took on a spiritual standard derived from the Mosaic Code of Law.[37]

This, then, is the notion of a people designated to carry out scriptural pathways. Only in this context does the land become "promised." Israel is, in fact, a land of promise, the place to carry out a specified program just as the post-70 AD exile from the land of Israel to other lands has been the transitory setting for the past two millennia.

The modern Israeli economy must cope with contradictory mandates. The first is modern economic practice and theory. The second is the Jewish ethical tradition, which not only legitimizes Jewish presence in the land, but places even greater spiritual and ethical demands on the Jewish population. The practice of economics itself becomes a sacred science and requires that an economic program in Israel be formulated in terms of its own ethical system, for example, the compliance with adequate living standards for *all* citizens, the modification of conspicuous consumption, the emphasis on land-based as well as materials-based activity, the reliance on foreign capital and on imported wage goods, the use of an extensive non-Jewish labor force, and the export of military equipment. Nor can any political agreement regarding the West Bank and Gaza be viable without a change in the underlying economic arrangement. Two separate states, with the work force of one dependent on the already-dependent economy of the other, may not be sustainable or beneficial in the long run for either people.

The Israeli experience stands as a lesson for other nations only when the policies for reconstructing its economy grapple with *both* the material and ethical directives involved in having slowed inflation.

By restructuring along these guidelines Israel may also be able to provide opportunities for the new waves of Soviet migrants and liberalize its own closed, bureaucratic economy. Israel still faces the challenge that its founders confronted forty years ago—to create a unique state against all odds in a physically inhospitable part of the world, and at the same time, achieve the goals of social justice and an honorable livelihood for all its people.

Notes

1. Foreword to Luiz Bresser Pereira and Yoshiaki Nakano, *The Theory of Inertial Inflation* (Boulder, Colo.: Lynne Rienner Publishers, 1987), p. viii.

2. See Inter-American Development Bank, *Social and Economic Outlook 1989*, p. 54–58; *Economist* (London), "Dither Dither," December 16, 1989, and "Cut Again," January 6, 1990; *New York Times*, "Argentina's Unlikely Disciplinarian," January 30, 1990.

3. See *Conjuntura Econômica* (Rio de Janeiro), May 31, 1989, "Não chores por ti, Argentina," pp. 9–12.

4. See IDB, *Outlook 1989*; Banco de Boston, *Newsletters*, July-August 1989; *Economist*, November 11, 1989; Jeffrey D. Sachs, "Social Conflict and Populist Policies in Latin America," National Bureau of Economic Research, Working Paper No. 2897 (October 1988), p. 21; *World Monitor*, "Reinventing Brazil," November 1989.

5. See Luis Felipe Lagos and Alexander Galetovic, "Los planes austral y cruzado. ¿Por qué no detuvieron la inflación?," *Cuadernos de Economía* 26, no. 78 (August 1989), p. 241.

6. John Sheahan, *Patterns of Development in Latin America: Poverty, Repression, and Economic Strategy* (Princeton: Princeton University Press, 1987), p. 190.

7. Sheahan, *Patterns*, p. 201.

8. Bresser Pereira, *Theory*, p. 119.

9. Sachs, "Social Conflict," p. 3.

10. UNICEF, *The State of the World's Children* (New York: Oxford University Press, 1989), Statistical Table 1.

11. UNICEF, *Children*, Statistical Table 4. See Israel, *Statistical Abstract 1989*, p. 600.

12. Banco de Boston, *Newsletter Brazil*, No. 11 (São Paulo, July 17, 1989), pp. 1–2, also No. 13 (August 7, 1989), p. 4.

13. Banco de Boston, *Newsletter Brazil*, No. 13 (August 7, 1989), p. 2.

14. See Richard Weisskoff, *The Economy of the Land of Israel* (forthcoming) for tracking of these pieces.

15. See Israel Katz, "Social Service Expenditure in 1986/87: Where Do We Go from Here?" in Yaakov Kop, ed., *Israel's Social Services 1986–87* (Jerusalem: Center for Social Policy Studies in Israel, June 1987), p. 4.

16. See Sheahan, *Patterns*, pp. 190–192, 196–199.

17. For other comparisons, see Richard Weisskoff, "Income Distribution and Economic Growth in Puerto Rico, Argentina, and Mexico," *Review of Income and Wealth* (December 1970), pp. 303–332, and R. Weisskoff and Adolfo Figueroa, "Income Distribution in Latin America," *Latin American Research Review* (1976), pp. 71–112.

18. Not revealed in the Israeli statistics are the incomes of the populations of Gaza and the West Bank, which, if properly included, render the income distribution much less equal and more comparable to the Latin American profiles. See Weisskoff, *The Economy of the Land of Israel* (forthcoming) for this calculation.

19. See Israel, *Statistical Abstract 1989*, pp. 179, 710. Wages are more difficult to compare between these groups because Israeli salaries are quoted by the month and are supplemented by benefits, while wages of registered West Bank and Gaza workers in Israel are quoted by the day.

20. Sheahan, *Patterns*, 180ff. See also U.S. State Department, *Country Reports on Human Rights Practices for 1988* (Washington: GPO, February 1989) and *Amnesty International Report 1989* (London) for case chronologies. The U.S. State Department Report is more comprehensive in the political, economic, and legal background material.

21. Robert R. Nathan, O. Glass, and D. Creamer, *Palestine, Problem and Promise: An Economic Survey*. (Washington, D.C.: American Affairs Press, 1946), p. 3.

22. See Richard Weisskoff, "The Economy of Israel," *Collier's Encyclopedia*, (New York: MacMillan, 1987), vol. 13, pp. 333–36. Also David Horowitz and staff, "Economic Development," in *Economy of Israel* (Jerusalem: Keter, 1973), reprinted from *Encyclopedia Judaica*.

23. The territories include the Gaza Strip and also Judea and Samaria, the official Israeli name for the West Bank. I use the names interchangeably.

24. One study of noncitizen Arabs suggests that the integration of a segregated work force at the bottom end of the scale may have pushed Israeli workers further up the ladder. But by competing with Israelis who traditionally held these low-paying jobs, the new recruits pulled down the income of Israeli workers still employed in these lower-paying occupations. See Moshe Semyonov and Noah Lewin-Epstein, *Hewers of Wood and Drawers of Water*, "Noncitizen Arabs in the Israeli Labor Market," (Ithaca, N.Y.: Industrial Labor Relations Press, 1987), p. 114.

25. See Eitan Berglas, "Defense and the Economy," in Ben-Porath, ed., *Israeli Economy* (Cambridge: Harvard University Press, 1986), Ch. 8, for spending through 1980. See also Aaron Dehter, *How Expensive Are West Bank Settlements?* (Jerusalem: West Bank Data Project, 1987).

26. Falling revenues from income and value-added taxes made additional sources of revenue critical. Compare Israel, *Statistical Abstract 1987*, p. 531, for 1984–1986, and *1989*, p. 559, for 1986–1988. Note also the higher

shekel-cost of dollars, purchase taxes, and duties collected from imports of vehicles for the years 1985 and 1986, the latter a "depression" year. See *Abstract 1987*, pp. 236–37, and compare to *1989*, pp. 252–53.

27. Israel, *Statistical Abstract 1988*, p. 146.

28. Sharon sees the prospect of the emergency aid package as peripheral to the settlement, acknowledging that it might have served as an inducement. He thus differs from Mario Blejer and Nissan Leviatan who write that "external support for the program seems to have played an important role." See "Fighting Inflation, Stabilization Strategies in Argentina and Israel, 1985–86," *IMF Staff Papers*, No. 34, p. 422. Sharon has also pointed out that the halting of the hyperinflation slowed the velocity of the circulation of money and reduced the need for foreign exchange. The emergency aid proved not to have been needed at all, he maintains, as flight capital returned to the stabilized economy and dollars no longer were held for speculation. Hyperinflation, on the other hand, necessitated foreign exchange, additional loans, and continual bailouts. However "unneeded," the emergency aid was never returned to the United States but probably has served to "ransom" the package deal from those who would gain from sabotaging it.

29. See Howard F. Rosen, "The U.S.-Israel Free Trade Area Agreement: How Well Is It Working and What Have We Learned?" in Jeffrey J. Schott, ed., *Free Trade Areas and U.S. Trade Policy* (Washington, D.C.: Institute for International Economics, 1989), pp. 97–119.

30. These workers have been called more appropriately noncitizen Arab "commuters," since many hold regular posts and travel daily to their homes. See Semyonov and Lewin-Epstein, *Hewers of Wood*, p. 14. At first glance, these 100,000 Arab workers seem but a minor fraction of Israel's 1.5 million civilian labor force. But since the household size in the territories averages more than six persons per family, a considerable share of the West Bank and Gaza population was directly affected by any change in Arab employment or wages in Israel. See Israel, *Statistical Abstract 1988*, pp. 328 and 718, for labor force statistics.

31. "Non-resident workers, mostly Palestinians from the West Bank and Gaza, may not organize and bargain collectively on their own, but they are entitled to the protection of collective bargaining agreements. . . . However, a sizeable minority work in the unorganized sector, without this protection, mostly in seasonal agricultural and small construction sites, restaurants, and garages." See U.S. State Department, *Country Reports on Human Rights Practices for 1988* (Washington, D.C.: GPO, 1989), p. 1371.

32. On documentation on the changes in village economy, see especially the appendix tables drawn from Israel Central Bureau of Statistics publications, as well as the text of David Kahan, *Agriculture and Water Resources in the West Bank and Gaza (1967–1987)* (Jerusalem: West Bank Data Project, 1987), and Sara Roy, *The Gaza Strip Survey* (Jerusalem: West Bank Data Project, 1986). The index of the average daily wage in Judea and Samaria and in Gaza fell precipitously in 1985 but then bounced back by 1986. Total employment rose by 8 percent in 1986 for territory residents working in both Israel and in the territories. See Israel, *Statistical Abstract 1988*, p. 732, and Meron Benvenisti, *1987 Report* (Jerusalem: West Bank Data Project, 1987), p. 10. The ratio of average consumption per capita in Israel remained at 4.5 times the Gaza levels and 3 times the levels in Judea and Samaria. Compare Israel, *Statistical Abstract 1989*, pp. 187, 704. The olive crop in 1985/86 also proved a significant boom, yielding 148,000 tons and NIS 225 million,

compared to the 19,100 tons and NIS 20 million harvest in 1984/85. See Israel, *Statistical Abstract 1989* p. 731, and *1988*, p. 735.

33. Benvenisti, *1987 Report*, pp. 40–41.

34. See Zachary Lockman and Joel Beinin, eds., *Intifada* (Boston: MERIP, South End Press, 1989), esp. pp. 127–30, and "The Uprising and the Economy," pp. 225–29.

35. Compare, for example, Yoram Ben-Porath, *The Israeli Economy, Maturing Through Crisis* (Cambridge: Harvard University Press, 1986), and Richard Weisskoff, "All Wrong Economics" *Jerusalem Post*, December 31, 1986, op. ed. page.

36. See Meir Tamari, *With All Your Possessions: Jewish Ethics and Economic Life* (New York: Free Press, 1987).

37. Max Weber pointed out sixty years ago Judaism's twofold contribution to the modern order: first, its direct historical influence on the formation of Christianity and Islamism; and second, its significance in the development of the "modern economic ethic," which is the permission that a society assumes in pursuing its economic impulses within the specified practical and psychological boundaries of divine law. See Max Weber, "The Social Psychology of the World Religions," in H. H. Gerth and C. Wright Mills, *From Max Weber* (New York: Oxford, 1946). The original essay was published in 1923 under the title, "The Economic Ethic of the World Religions." See also Max Weber, *Ancient Judaism* (New York: Free Press, 1952) for his analysis of Jewish Law and ritual.

Bibliography

Argentina

Arranz, Juan Miguel. "Indexación y pensamiento económico." *16th Annual Meeting of the Argentine Association of Economy*, Bahia Blanca, Argentina.

Canavese, Alfredo J. "Structural Inflation, Price Fixing and Argentina, August 1982." *Annals of the 17th Annual Meeting of the Argentine Association of Political Economy*, La Plata, Argentina.

Gaba, Ernesto. "Indexación y sistema financiero," *Revista Argentina de Finanzas 2*, (1977).

Krieger Vasena, Adalbert, and Enrique Szewach. "Inflation and Argentina." In John Williamson, ed. *Inflation and Indexation—Argentina, Brazil, and Israel*. Institute for International Economics, Cambridge, Mass.: MIT Press, 1985.

Olivera, Julio H. "Causas no monetarias de inflación en Argentina," *Journal of Economic Research*, Faculty of Economic Science, University of Buenos Aires, 1968.

Szewach, Enrique. "Inflación estructural, concertación d política salarial." (Coment on Canavese, Structural Inflation." *Annals of the 17th Annual Meeting of the Argentine Association of Political Economy*, La Plata, Argentina, 1982.

Teixeira, Ib. "O setor público no calcanhar do austral." *Econômic* (January 1986):135–38.

Wynia, Gary W. "Readjusting to Democracy in Argentina." *Conjuntura* (January 1987):5.

Brazil

Almonacid, Ruben D. "Os rumos do Plano Cruzado." *Conjuntura* (October 1986):91–96.

Almonacide, Ruben D., and Maria Cristina Pinotti. "O contrôle de preços." *Informaçóes FIPE* (May 1986):13.

———. "A política monetária do Plano Cruzaso." *Econômica* (June 1986):95–99.

153

Arida, Pérsio. "Reajuste salarial e inflação." *Pesquisa e Planejamento Econômico* 12 (April 1982).

―――., "Neutralizar a inflação: uma idéia promissora." *E? Perspectiva* (September 1984).

―――. "A ORTN serve apenas para zerar a inflação inercial," *Gazeta Mercantil*, October 19, 1984.

―――. "Economic Stabilization in Brazil." Working Paper, Woodrow Wilson International Center, Washington, D.C. (November 1984).

―――. "Entrevista." *Senhor*, March 25, 1986.

Arida, Pérsio, and André Lara Resende. "Inertial Inflation and Monetary Reform: Brazil" in John Williamson, ed. *Inflation and Indexation— Argentina, Brazil and Israel*. Institute for International Economics. Cambridge: MIT Press, 1985.

―――. "Recessão e taxa economia brasileira no inico dos anos 80." *Revista Política* (forthcoming).

Bacha, Edmar, and Francisco Lopes. "Inflation, Growth and Wages: In Search of a Brazilian Paradigm." *Journal of Development Economics* (1984).

Bresser Pereira, Luiz, and Y. Nakano. "Política administrativa do da inflação." *Revista de Economia Política* (July–September 1984).

Chacel, Julian, Pamela S. Falk, and David Fleischer, eds. *Brazil's Economic and Political Future*. Boulder, Colo. Westview Press, forthcoming.

Cohen, Roger. "Brazilian Effort to Moderate Economy, Improve Trade Surplus Draws Criticism." *Wall Street Journal*, November 24, 1986.

Deserções no cruzado." *Veja*, November 26, 1986.

"O gigante volta às compras." *Conjuntura* (July 1986).

Lara Resende, André. "Incompatibilidade distributiva e estrutural." *Estudos Econômicos* (1980).

―――. "O programa brasileiro de estabilização: 1964–1968 e *Planejamento Econômico* 12 (1982).

―――. "A moeda indexada: uma proposta para eliminar a inflação inercial." Texto para discussão no. 75, Departamento de Economia, Pontifícia Universidade Católica do Rio de Janeiro, September 1984.

―――. "A moeda indexada: nem mágica, nem panacéia." Texto para discussão no. 81, Departamento de Economia, Pontifícia Universidade Católica do Rio de Janeiro, December 1984.

Lara-Resende, André, and Francisco L. Lopes. "Sobre as causas da recente aceleração inflacionária." *Pesquisa e Planejamento Econômico* 11 (December 1981).

Lopes, Francisco. "Inflação e nivel de atividade no Brasil: um estudo econométrico." *Pesquisa e Planejamento Econômico* 12 (December 1982).

―――. "Política salarial e dinamica do salário nominal." *Pesquisa e Planejamento Econômico* 13 (November 1983).

―――. "Só um choque heterodoxo pode derrubar a inflaçã." *Economia em Perspectiva* (August 1984).

―――. "Inflação inercial, hiperinflação e desinflaçã: notas e conjecturas." Texto para discussão no. 77, Departamento de Economia, Pontifícia Universidade Católica do Rio de Janeiro, November 1984.

Lopes, Francisco, and Eduardo Modiano. "Indexação, choque externo e nivel de atividade: notas sobre o caso brasileiro." *Pesquisa e Planejamento Econômicos* (1980).

Martone, C. L. "A reforma monetária." *Informações FIPE* (March 1986):3.
Modiano, Eduardo. "A dinamica de salários e preços na economia brasileira: 1966–1981." *Pesquisa e Planejamento Econômico* 13 (April 1983).
————. "Salarios, preços e cambio: os multiplicadores de choques em uma economia indexada." *Texto para discussão* no. 70, Departamento de Economia, Pontifícia Universidade Católica do Rio de Janeiro, 1984.
Nassar, José R. "Crescimento complusório." *Senhor*, June 29, 1986, p. 24.
Pang, Eul-Soo, and Laura Jarnagin. "Brazil's Cruzado Plan." *Current History* (January 1987):13.
Riding, Alan. "Brazil Economy: Faith Turns to Fear." *New York Times*, February 9, 1987, p. D1.
Rocca, C. A. "Os preços desalinhados." *Informações FIPE* (March 1986):5.
Simonsen, Mario Henrique. *Inflação: gradualismo versus tratamento de choque.* Rio de Janeiro: Editora APEC, 1970.
————. "Indexation: Current Theory and the Brazilian Experience. In Rudiger Dornbusch and Mario H. Simonsen, eds. *Inflation, Debt and Indexation.* Cambridge, Mass." MIT Press, 1983.
————. "Desindexação e reforma monetária." *Conjuntura Economica* (November 1984).
Soares, Paulo de T. P. Leite. "Avaliação e desafio." *Informações FIPE* (February 1986):6.
————. "A inflação vai cair, mas. . . ." *Informações FIPE* (May 1986).
————. "Algumas reflexões sobre o Plano Cruzado." Draft manuscript. Universidade de São Paulo, June 1986.
Stepan, Alfred C. *Patterns of Civil-Military Relations: The Brazilian Political System.* Princeton: Princeton University Press, 1971.
Toledo, Joaquim E. C. de. "Uma reforma incompleta." *Informações FIPE* (March 1986):8.
————. "Em debate o Plano Cruzado." *Informações FIPE* (June 1986):4.
————. "A mágica da inflação." *Veja*, December 17, 1986, p. 118.

Israel

Ben Porath, Yoram, ed. *The Economy of Israel: Maturing Through Crises.* Jerusalem: Falk Institute, forthcoming.
Brenner, Reuven, and Don Patinkin. "Indexation in Israel." In Erik ed. *Inflation Theory and Anti-Inflation Policy.* London: 1977.
Bruno, Michael. "Sharp Disinflation Strategy: Israel 1985." *Economic Policy* (April 1986).
Bruno, Michael, and Stanley Fischer. "The Inflationary Process in Israel: Shock and Accommodation." In Yoram Ben Porath, ed. *The Economy of Israel: Maturing Through Crises.* Jerusalem: Falk Institute, forthcoming. (Also available as National Bureau of Economic Research. Paper No. 1483.)
Fischer, Stanley. "The Economy of Israel." *Carnegie-Rochester Conference Series on Public Policy 20,* 1984.
————. "Inflation and Indexation: Israel." In John Williamson, ed., *Inflation and Indexation—Argentina, Brazil, and Israel.* Institute for International Economics, Cambridge: Mass.: MIT Press, 1985.

Fischer, Stanley, and Jacob Frenkel. "Research Issues Arising from Current Inflation in Israel." 1981.

Halevi, Nadav. "Perspectives on the Balance of Payments." In Yoram Ben Porath, ed. *The Economy of Israel: Maturing Through Crises.* Jerusalem: Falk Institute, forthcoming.

Kidron, Peretz. "Israel: If This Doesn't Work—Disaster." *Midola International,* July 12, 1985.

————. "Guns Galore but Little Butter." *Middle East International,* July 26, 1985.

Kleiman, Ephraim. "Indexation in the Labor Market." In Yoram Ben Porath, *The Economy of Israel: Maturing Through Crises.* Jerusalem: Falk Institute, forthcoming.

Lebow, David. "The Inflation Tax in Israel." B.S. thesis, Cambridge, Massachussetts Institute of Technology, 1983.

Leiderman, Leo, and Aryeh Marom. "The Estimates of the Demand for Money in Israel," Bank of Israel Research Department Discussion Report, pp. 83–89, 1983.

Lewis, Samuel W. "Israel" The Peres Era." *Foreign Affairs* no. 3.

Liviatan, Nissan, and Sylvia Piterman. "Accelerating Inflation and Balance of Payments Crises: Israel, 1973–1984." In Yoram Ben Porath, ed. *The Economy of Israel: Maturing Through Crises.* Jerusalem: Falk Institute, forthcoming.

Melnick, Rafi. "Two Issues in the Demand for Money in Israel, 1970–1981." Bank of Israel Research Department, pp. 83–86, 1983.

Parkin, Michael. "The Economy of Israel: A Comment on Fischer." In *Carnegie-Rochester Conference Series on Public Policy 20,* pp. 53–56, 1984.

Rowen, Hobart. "And Now, Shamir." *Washington Post,* November 3, 1986, p. 5.

Sharansky, Ira. "Israeli Inflation: The Politics of an Economic Concept." *Jerusalem Quarterly,* no. 36 (Summer 1985).

Shiffer, Zalman. "Adjusting to High Inflation: The Israeli Experience." Federal Reserve Bank of St. Louis, May 1986.

Comparative

Arida, Pérsio. *Inflação zero: Brasil, Argentina e Israel.* Rio de Janerio: Paz e Terra, 1986.

Frankel, Roberto. "Inflação zero, só na suíça. *Veja* (February 18, 1987).

Hyperinflation—Taming the Beast." *The Economist,* November 15, 1986, pp. 55–64.

Kleiman, Ephraim. "Monetary Correction and Indexation: The Brazilian and Israeli Experience." *NBER Explorations in Economic Research* 4, no. 1 (Winter 1977).

Knight, Peter, F. Desmond McCarthy, and Sweder van Wijnbergen. "Escaping Hyperinflation." *Finance & Development* (December 1986):14.

Williamson, John, ed. *Inflation and Indexation—Argentina, Brazil, and Israel.* Institute for International Economics. Cambridge: Mass: MIT Press, 1985.

General/Background

Arida, Pérsio. "A hipótese estrutural na teoria da inflação: um comentário." *Estudos Econômicos* (January–March 1981).

Canavese, Alfredo J. "Structural Inflation and Indexation in Industrialized Economies and Those in the Process of Industrialization." *Revista Argentina de Finanzas* 4 (1979):45–57.

Chichilnisky, Graciela. *Trade and Development in the Eighties*. New York: Columbia University Business School, 1983.

———. *The Evolving International Economy*. Cambridge: Cambridge University Press, 1986.

Fischer, Stanley, "Wage Indexation and Macroeconomic Stability." *Carnegie-Rochester Conference Series on Public Policy*, 1977, pp. 107–48.

———. "Real Balances, the Exchange Rate, and Indexation: Real Variables in Disinflation." National Bureau of Economic Research Working Paper, 1984.

Frenkel, Roberto. *Inflación y salario real*. Buenos Aires: CEDES, 1984.

Friedman, Milton. "Monetary Correction." *Essays on Inflation Indexation*. Washington, D.C. American Enterprise Institute, 1974.

———. "Using Escalators to Help Fight Inflation." *Fortune*, July 1979, pp. 94–176.

Gray, A. J. "Wage Indexation: A Macroeconomic Approach. *Journal of Monetary Economics*, no. 2 (1976):221–35.

McKinnon, Ronald I. *An International Standard for Monetary Stablization*. Institute for International Economics. Cambridge: Mass.: MIT Press, March 1984.

Olivera, Julio H. "On Structural Inflation and Latin American Structuralism." *Oxford Economic Papers* (November 1964).

Patinkin, D. "What Advanced Countries Can Learn from the Experience with Indexation: Some Concluding Observations." *Explorations in Economic Research*, no. 4 (1977):177–87.

Current Trends

Alexander, Charles P. "Talking Tough to the IMF." *Time*, June 25, 1984, p. 55.

"Alfonsín Calls for 'Social Pact' to Defend Democracy." *Wall Street Journal*, May 2, 1987.

Alfonsín, Raúl. "Mensaje presidencial del Dr. Raúl Alfonsín a la Argentina, Assamblea Legeslative, 1 de mayo de 1984." Buenos Aires del Congreso de la Nación, 1984.

"Argentina and the Bankers." *Washington Post*, April 26, 1987.

"Argentina Gets Harsh Economic Therapy." *Miami Herald*, July 22, 1986.

"Argentina's New Hope." *Business Week*, February 6, 1984, pp. 60–61.

"Argentina's Unemployment Goes Up." *Southern Cone Report*, August 2, 1985, p. 2.

Asman, David. "Liberation Argentine Style." *Wall Street Journal*, May 4, 1987.

"At Long Last Reform Is On." *Southern Cone Report,* December 20, 1985, p. 6.

Banks, Howard. "Write Down Loans? Perish the Thought." *Forbes,* May 9, 1983, pp. 57–60.

Babetta, Carlos. "Argentina Seeks New Route Out of the Debt Treadmill. *El Periodista de Buenos Aires,* April 26, 1987.

Bonacina, César Augusto. *El ahorro en la Argentina.* Buenos Aires: Editorial Sudamericana, 1982.

"Consumer Squeeze Bodes Ill for All." *Southern Cone Report,* August 2, 1985, p. 2.

Coone, Tim. "Alfonsín Calls for Coalition to Bring in Reforms." *Christian Science Monitor,* April 15, 1987.

————. "Argentina Pins Fiscal Hope on Tax Amnesty." *Foreign Times,* February 16, 1987.

"Deeper and Deeper in Debt." *Maclean's,* October 17, 1983, p. 49.

DeMott, John S. "A Plan, At Long Last a Plan." *Time,* October 8, 1984, p. 58.

Dentzer, Susan. "Argentina's Game of Chicken." *Newsweek,* June 25, 1984, pp. 57–58.

————. "Argentina Fashions a Miracle." *Newsweek,* August 26, 1985, p. 46.

Díaz Redondo, Regino. "A Talk with Argentina's Alfonsín." *World Press Review,* October 1986, p. 47.

"Do Not Pay $40 Billion, Go Directly to Jail." *Newsweek,* October 17, 1983, p. 38.

Dreizzen, Julio. *Fragilidad financiera e inflación.* Buenos Aires: Centro de Estudios y Sociedad, 1985.

Ferrer, Aldo. *Puede pagar Argentina su deuda externa?* Fundación pára la Democracia en Argentina. Buenos Aires: El Cid Editor, 1983.

Fierman, Jaclyn. "John Reed's Bold Stroke." *Fortune,* June 22, 1987, pp. 26–30.

Galbraith, John Kenneth. "A Journey to Argentina." *New Yorker,* April 21, 1986, p. 70.

Gall, Norman."Paying the Piper." *Forbes,* July 28, 1986, p. 102.

Gelman, Eric. "Betting the Democracy." *Newsweek,* June 24, 1985, p. 105.

Graham, Bradly. "Argentina Declares Bank Holiday." *Washington Post,* February 25, 1987.

————. "Argentina Freezes Wages and Prices." *Washington Post,* February 26, 1987.

"A Growing Threat." *New York Times,* March 7, 1987.

Helguera, Eduardo. "A Prisoner of the Past." *Forbes,* November 3, 1986, p. 132.

Henry, James S. "Three Cheers for Citicorp's Initiative." *U.S. News & World Report,* June 1, 1987, p. 48.

Instituto de Estudios Latinoamericanos. "Argentina 1984: el acuerdo con el FMI y la deuda externa." Buenos Aires: Instituto de Estudios Latinoamericanos, 1984.

Kessler, Richard A. "A Purge at the Top May Not Prevent Economic Anarchy." *Business Week,* March, 4, 1985, p. 46.

Kessler, Richard A., Sarach Bartlett, and Frederic A. Miller. "Alfonsín's Shock Treatment Could Cure—or Kill." *Business Week,* July 1, 1985, pp. 34–35.

Lavergne, Nestor. "El debate sobre el programa económico del gobierno constitucional." Buenos Aires: Centro de Investigaciones Sociales sobre el Estado y la Administración, 1984.

Magneir, Mark. "Argentina Plan Could Save Nation Millions." *Journal of Commerce*, June 29, 1987.

Main, Jeremy. "The Argentinian Web Trapping U.S. Lenders." *Fortune*, August 20, 1984, pp. 122–126.

Morais, Richard. "Insurers to the Rescue." *Forbes*, October 8, 1984, p. 232.

Morgan, Jeremy. "Argentina Confronts Cash Crunch." *Journal of Commerce*, November 21, 1987.

Oppenheimer, Andrés. "Needed: Therapy of a Different Sort for Argentina's Stagnated Economy." *Miami Herald*, February 15, 1987.

Pearson, John, Bruce Nussbaum, and Sarah Bartlett. "Interview with Raúl Alfonsín: The Big Problem Is Inflation, Not Debt." *Business Week*, February 6, 1984, p. 62.

Perdia, Roberto Cirilo. *Esiste otra Argentina posible*. Buenos Aires: González Olguin Editor, 1986.

Pine, Art. "Argentina to Get $2 Billion in Loans Over Two Years from the World Bank." *Wall Street Journal*, January 13, 1987.

Riding, Alan. "Alfonsín's New Drive on Debt." *New York Times*, March 1987.

Riemer, Blanca. "Baker's New Debt Plan: Really Sick Countries Need Not Apply." *Business Week*, November 18, 1985, p. 59.

Roberts, Paul Craig. "Argentina Sold the IMF a Prescription." *Business Week*, December 24, 1984, p. 12.

Rowe, James L., Jr. "U.S. Joins in $500 Million Emergency Aid to Argentina." *Washington Post*, February 27, 1987.

Ryser, Jeffrey, and Richard A. Kessler. "A Talk with Alfonsín the Debt Cannot Be Paid." *Business Week*, June 22, 1987, p. 66.

Scherschel, Patricia M. "How to Take a $1 Billion Loss and Look Good." *U.S. News & World Report*, June 1, 1987, pp. 46–47.

Shapiro, Arthur M. "Alfonsín's Experiment." *The New Leader*, March 11, 1985, pp. 10–12.

Smith, Kenneth S. "World Bank, IMF—Do They Help or Hurt Third World?" *U.S. News & World Report*, April 29, 1985, p. 43.

"Sourrouille's List of Worries." *Southern Cone Report*, April 19, 1985.

"Sourroville's 'Quietist' Option." *Southern Cone Report*, March 8, 1985, p. 2.

"The Real Kiel Plan for Argentina." *Southern Cone Report*, August 2, 1985.

"They Came to Protest." *The Herald*, March 26, 1987.

Thurow, Lester C. "Who Said Military Dictatorships Are Good for the Economy?" *Technology Review* November–December, 1986:22–23.

Truell, "Argentine Pact Threatens Other Debt Accords." *Wall Street Journal*, April, 16, 1987.

"Trying with Less Success." *U.S. News & World Report*, June 16, 1986, p. 37.

Tweedale, Douglas. "The Taming of Inflation." *Maclean's*, January 6, 1986, p. 68.

"What Could Make the Powder Keg Explode." *Business Week*, January 17, 1983, pp. 46–47.

Winograd, Carols. *Economía abierta y tipo de cambio prefijado: que aprendemos del caso argentino?* Buenos Aires: Centro de Estudios de Estado y Sociedad, 1984.

About the Contributors

Pamela S. Falk is a senior research scholar at Columbia University's School of Public Affairs, where she is on the faculty and teaches foreign policy. She is also project director of *International Security Studies*, a research project of the Pew Charitable Trusts.

Hugo Presgrave de A. Faria is with Citibank, W.A., in Buenos Aires. His publications include "The Role of External Constraints in Macroeconomic Policy Making: A Case Study of the Brazilian *Plano Cruzado*."

David D. Hale is a first vice president and chief economist of Kemper Financial Services, Inc. and vice president and director of Kemper-Murray Johnstone International, Inc. He is a member of the National Association of Business Economists and the New York Society of Security Analysts.

Miguel A. Kiguel, an Argentine economist, is currently assistant professor of economics at the University of Maryland. He has been an economist with the World Bank in the Developing Countries division.

Luiz Bresser Pereira has been finance minister of Brazil since 1987 and has served as chief of staff (secretário do governo) for the state of São Paulo. He is also professor of economics at the Getúlio Vargas Foundation.

Santiago O. del Puerto, an Argentine economist and an expert on finance and monetary issues, is regional general manager of the Banco Rio de la Plata in New York City. He is a former Argentine finance representative to the United States and Canada.

Emanuel Sharon is a senior industrial specialist with the World Bank. He is former director general of the Ministry of Finance of Israel (1984–1987) and was professor of operations research at Hebrew University, Jerusalem (1968–1972).

Herbert M. Singer is a partner in the law firm of Singer, Netter, and Dowd. Internationally he has served as special representative to Ecuador from the U.S. Department of State, consultant to the World Health Organization, and memeber of the Council Against Poverty.

Richard Weisskoff is an associate professor at the Graduate School of International Studies, University of Miami. He has taught at Yale, Iowa State, and Bar Ilan University in Israel. He served as consultant to the Department of International Economic and Social Affairs of the United Nations and the InterAmerican Development Bank.

Index

Abreu, Hugo, 84
Alderete, Carlos, 50
Aliança Democrática, 88, 99
Aliança Renovadora Nacional, 79
Arabs in Israel, 127, 137, 144–145, 147, 150 (notes), 151 (notes)
Argentina; austral currency, 40, 43; Austral Plan (*see* Austral Plan); and Brazil, 131–139, 134 (table), 136 (tables); budget deficits, 48 (table), 54; debt/equity programs, 36–38; disinflation efforts, 128–130; exchange rate freeze, 43; fiscal policy, 54 (note); forced savings scheme, 42; indebtedness, 35; inflation, 39–40, 41 (fig.), 46 (table), 53 (note); and Israel, 128, 131–139, 134 (table), 136 (tables); Ministry of Economy, 37; monetary policy, 54 (note); money supply, 54 (note); negotiations with Citibank, 35–36; 1987 Financing Plan, 36; past programs against inflation, 39; peso, 43; Plan Primavera (*see* Plan Primavera); public sector, 48 (table); public sector debt, 53–54 (note); public sector price increase, 42; tax collection, 42; trade tax increase, 42
Arida, Pérsio, 61, 62
Arraes, Miguel, 110
Austral Plan, 62, 72, 128; desagio (financial conversion mechanism), 44; disinflation under, 45; failure of, 47–50; fiscal policy, 41–42; initial results, 45; and Israeli plan, 40; monetary policy, 43–44, 45;

monetary reform, 43; nominal anchors, 42–43; policy lessons, 52–53; purpose, 40; reasons for failure of, 51–52

Bacha, Edmar, 62
Bailey, M., 122
Bank of Israel, 122, 143
Bank of Japan, 28
Batista de Figueiredo, João, 79, 83, 84, 85, 87, 88
Berglass, E., 122
Bracher, Fernao, 62, 94; resignation of, 109
Brady, Nicholas, 31
Branco, Castelo, 77
Brasília, 76
Brazil; *abertura* period, 82–87; and Argentina, 72, 98, 131–139, 134 (table), 136 (tables); bankruptcies and insolvencies, 68 (table); Bresser Plan (*see* Bresser Plan); Costa e Silva administration, 78–79; coup of 1964, 76–79, 111 (note); Cruzado Plan (*see* Cruzado Plan); deindexation, 99; disinflation efforts, 130–131; economic growth, 77 (table); financial disequilibrium, 70; foreign debt, 80, 81 (tables), 82 (table), 100 (table); Geisel administration, 83–87; government debt, 11; income distribution, 82 (table), 112 (note); indexation, 104; inertial inflation theory, 58–60; inflation, 2, 57, 59 (table), 64 (table), 73 (note), 80 (table); and Israel, 72, 98, 128, 131–139, 134 (table),